Published by:
Women Winning Against Breast Cancer

Just Peachey, Cooking Up A Cure is the realization of our need to join together to make a difference for all women, past and present, who have been touched by Breast Cancer, and for those who will be touched tomorrow. Women Winning Against Breast Cancer is our support group in the Warsaw, Indiana area. Many women and men from across the country have joined us in our project to support Breast Cancer Research at the Indiana University Cancer Center. We also want to recognize Cathy Peachey who teaches all of us the importance of fighting for what is right.

We are supported in our endeavors from beginning to end and without limitation by Carole Cross and Dr. Richard W. Cross to whom we will always be grateful.

Illustration by Robin M. Brown

Who knew when Mom put a crayon in my hand, I might actually be able to draw something. But I have been drawing since I can remember, on any scrap of paper that I could find. Not long ago, a friend of mine reminded me how much drawing and painting meant to me. So, thanks to Mom for the crayon, my friend for the kick in the pants and thanks to the wonderful women who have allowed me to participate in the production of our cookbook.

Valued Advisors

Marcia Adams
Chuck Harpel
Allan Rucka
We wish to acknowledge Biomet, Inc. for their generous support of this project.

While the recipes in this book may not all be original, they were donated as favorites by the contributors.

Date and number of first publication: July, 1995 - 15,000 copies.
Date and number of second publication: August, 1995 - 10,000 copies.
Date and number of third publication: October, 1995 - 10,000 copies.
ISBN 0-9646719-0-5

The recipes in this book are not to be considered in compliance with any dietary guidelines. Please alter to fit your own needs.

Printed by:
R.R. Donnelley & Sons Company

Just Peachey: Cooking Up a Cure

Connie Rufenbarger, Editor

Members of our Steering Committee

Deb Allen
Robin Brown
Carol Clay
Carole Cross
Pam Kolter
Betty LeCount
Mary Louise Miller
Julie Walsh Seiler
Deb Wiggins

Our Committee Members

Lynn Allegret	Lynda Moryl
Mary Armstrong	Lois Neimier
Donna Arnett	Nita Oppenheim
Jason Cross	Carolyn Peachey
Shelly Gilliland	Jim and Sara Peachey
Angel Hall	Karol Piecuch
Paula Harris	Pam Plesher
Joyce Hohman	Kim Reiff
Shannon Jenks	Christy Schmidt
Roberta King	Jim Seiler
Laura Kipker	Ilene Snider
Carla Kiser	Linda VanOsdol
Chelsea LeCount	Murray Welch
Jo Lemon	Jana Williamson
Norman Metzger	Joan Younce

Contributions or endowments to the
Catherine Peachey Fund, Inc. may be sent in care of:

The Catherine Peachey Fund, Inc.
P.O. Box 1823
Warsaw, IN 46581-1823
Voice 219-268-9015
Fax 219-267-8268

Our Underwriters

Five Star Chefs ($1000 and Up)

Mrs. Patricia Lenke
Eli Lilly and Company
Johnson, Smith, Pence, Densborn, Wright and Heath
Mrs. Nancy Boaz
Dr. Richard W. Cross
Arthur DeWispelaere
Nancy Lenke Johnson
James and Lavon Kelley
Mary Louise and Dane Miller
Jackie and Allan Rucka
Sherry and Bill Winn - Warsaw Pill Box Pharmacy
Peter Wilson, Pyromation, Inc.
Creighton Brothers, L.P.
Campbell, Peachey & Associates
Mossberg & Company, Inc.

Four Star Chefs ($500 and Up)

ABC Industries, Inc.
Debbie and Tom Allen
June B. Bertsch
Galliher Photography
Indiana University Foundation
Dr. Thomas and Lynda Moryl
Connie and Steve Rufenbarger
University Plastic Surgery Associates, I.U. Medical Center

Three Star Chefs ($250 and Up)

Carol and John Clay
Mrs. Carole Cross
Dr. Lawrence and Claudette Einhorn
Pam and Bill Kolter
Michele Kuntz Wood and Gary Wood
Dr. S. Chace Lottich
Memorial Hospital of South Bend
Gary R. Moore
Clyde Powers, Indianapolis Colts

Master Chefs ($100 and Up)

Carolyn Andretti, Stacy and Howard Cox
Avon Products, Inc.
Blue Heron Art Works
Michael Conroy
Barbara Cook
Deborah and Ralph Farmer
Diane and Jef Farmer
1st Source Bank
Susyn and Mark Giaquinta
Delores Glaser
A.J. and Christine Hackl
Judith and Thomas Hayhurst
Mrs. Betty Lawson
Marilyn Lemon

Joanne L. Mazurki
Sandra and Joseph Morrow
Ann Biddinger Murphy
NBD Indiana, Inc.
Nita Oppenheim
Pamela Sue Perry
Breast Care Center, Indianapolis, Indiana
Julie and Jim Seiler
Mrs. Dorothy Snyder
Mary and Bob Steele
Roberta and Larry Tucker
Mrs. Mildred Willhoff
Dr. Stephen and Kay Williams
Joan Younce

Friends of the Cookbook ($25 and Up)

William and Beth Ambriole
Joyce Boggs
Barkley Twilight Club
Harriet Chalfant
Barbara and Bruce Creek
Culver Extension Homemakers
Early Birds Extension Homemakers Club
Friends and Neighbors Club
Jean and Thomas Glaser
Greene Township Extension Homemakers
Shari and Randy Hansen
Judith and Thomas Hayhurst
Brandon Hepler
Nathan Hepler
Susan Jaskulski
The Family of Phil and Shannon Jenks
Junior League of Indiana
Kappa, Kappa, Kappa, Inc.
Fernande Kolter
Ann Lankford
Betty and Charles LeCount

Jo and Tom Lemon
Rita and Michael Lewis
Mary Maxwell
Nite-Timer Extension Homemakers
Printing Plus
Dr. Marcus and Brabham Randall
Ruth and Larry Reese
Joan E. Rhodes
Patricia A. Rideout Family
Rockport Home Managers
Karen and Fred Rowland
Chad Rufenbarger
Stephanie Rufenbarger
Saint Joseph's Medical Center
Dr. Douglas and Peggy Sawyer
Sue and Charles Scholer
Irene Stavropulos
Margaret Trausch
The Union Thrifty Club
George and Lee Walsh
Senator Katie Wolf
Ann Zerr, M.D., F.A.C.O.G.

Cookbook Committee left to right (seated) Pam Plesher, Connie Rufenbarger, Robin Brown, Kim Reiff; (standing) Pam Kolter, Jana Williamson, Betty LeCount, Lynda Moryl, Mary Louise Miller, Deb Allen, Carol Clay and Carole Cross.

*We started with a handful of women and an idea to
raise money and awareness for Breast Cancer.
Every step of the way doors opened and people wanted to help.
We are not unique . . .all you have to do is ask . . .
pick a project, have fun, raise money.*

FIND A CURE.

Table of Contents

Each page of our book represents untold hours of volunteer efforts and freely given professional services. Expertise and loving guidance have made our year-long project one that will raise awareness and research dollars. The greatest gift is the gift of achievement crowned with new friendships.

Connie Rupenbarger

I do believe there are angels among us.

"It is not uncommon for organizations to call me for advice on creating and publishing a cookbook, for in the beginning, the hows and whys of such a project are a real puzzle to the uninitiated. Some of it is still a puzzle to me!

When I first met with the steering committee for *Just Peachey, Cooking Up A Cure*, I found it a profound experience. The women, and unabashedly, this is a women's project, were filled with enthusiasm and ideas; they were well-organized and positive about what they were setting out to do. And all of them were breast cancer survivors or dedicated to the issue. They were and are, special.

I was touched by their determination to work on a book whose proceeds would further develop research and treatment for this insidious disease that strikes so many women.

This book is a testament to their will. And happily, the recipes are really wonderful!"

Essen Gut! Eat Good!

Marcia Adams

INTRODUCTION

I am not fond of sweet punches, but this is an exception. It is more like an elegant milk shake and quite irresistible. The coffee base gives it richness of flavor which adults will appreciate, but children are apt to pass this up. Serve it in punch cups or squat old-fashioned glasses; little dollops of ice cream should be included in each serving.

Dr. Campbell's Ice Cream Punch

1 1/3 cups water
1 2/3 cups sugar
2 cups instant decaffeinated
   coffee granules
2 quarts whole milk
1 quart chocolate ice cream
1 quart French vanilla ice cream

In a deep saucepan (and it must be deep for the instant coffee foams up in a most surprising manner), bring the water to a full boil. Add the sugar and continue boiling for 2 minutes. Gradually whisk in the coffee granules. Whisk until coffee is dissolved; this takes awhile. Set aside and cool. Pour into a glass jar, cover and refrigerate until needed.

Approximately 1 hour before serving, remove the ice cream from the freezer and allow it to soften. Transfer the coffee mixture to a punch bowl. Add the milk and combine. With a cookie dough scoop or small ice cream scoop, dip out small dollops of ice cream and drop into the punch. Mix gently.

To serve: With a ladle, fill each punch cup or glass with both punch and a scoop of the ice cream. Serves 30.

To serve 90 to 100, here are the proportions: 4 cups water, 3 1/2 cups sugar, 1 (20 ounce) jar instant decaffeinated coffee, 1 1/2 gallons milk, 3 quarts vanilla ice cream, 3 quarts chocolate ice cream. The original handwritten recipe given to me (and it was an old one) added—"This will serve 90 little old ladies who drink one dainty little cupful. Double for all others."

Marcia Adams

If you like the Reuben sandwich, you'll adore this soup version!

Creamy Reuben Soup

1/2 cup onion, finely chopped
1/4 cup celery, finely chopped
3 tablespoons butter
3 cups chicken stock
1/4 cup Minute Tapioca
1 cup sauerkraut, well drained
1/2 pound deli-sliced
    corned beef, shredded
1 1/2 cups whole milk
1 1/2 cups skimmed milk
12 ounces Swiss cheese,
    shredded
salt and pepper to taste
6-8 slices rye bread, toasted
    and quartered

In a stockpot over medium heat, saute the onion and celery in the butter until tender, about 5 minutes. Add the chicken stock and tapioca, then remove from the heat; let stand for 5 minutes. Put the mixture back on over medium heat and bring to a boil, stirring frequently. Reduce the heat and simmer 5 minutes longer. Stir in the sauerkraut, corned beef, milks and 1 cup of the shredded cheese. Cook and stir frequently for 30 minutes until slightly thickened. Salt and pepper to taste. To serve, ladle into 8 ovenproof bowls, top each with toasted bread and sprinkle with cheese and then broil until the cheese is melted. Serve immediately.

Marcia Adams

Photo by E. Anthony Valainis, *Indianapolis Monthly Magazine*

"She didn't let

cancer get in the

way of living."

Cindy Baldauf

"Although there is no cure now, I believe that can change with enough research support. I have a hunch that we can unlock doors and solve more than one problem at a time."

Cathy Peachey

JUST
PEACHEY

David

Ariel

Urana

Nathan

Jesse

Dino

Norman

Ingredients For An Activist

Cathy Peachey, for whom this book is named, was voted one of the "12 Most Intriguing Individuals in Indianapolis" for 1994. She was well-known in the world of Breast Cancer activists and was one of the founders of the Indiana Breast Cancer Coalition. Cathy was one of the leaders in lobbying for passage of the Off-Label Drug Bill (which guarantees access to non-FDA approved anti-cancer drugs for cancer patients). This law subsequently was passed in Indiana.

Washington D.C. 1993—Representative Andy Jacobs (Indiana) and Cathy.

Politics and breast cancer have become intertwined as women and their loved ones look for solutions to a sadness which has gone unchecked in our country. Money and legislation are not the answer to every problem, but they are proving to be one of the most powerful weapons in the War Against Breast Cancer.

Every once in a while a star shines so brightly that many people notice the glow and wonder at its beauty. Cathy Peachey was that star for so many people in Indianapolis, Breast Cancer patients across Indiana and the wonderful staff at the Indiana University Cancer Center.

Cathy has left us with a loving ache in our hearts and the pressing urgency and responsibility to make a difference. She also left us with a wealth of potential

White House 1993—Cathy and President Clinton.

and possibilities created by her energy and her relationships. Cathy loved Indiana University Cancer Center and the richness she found in the people there.

The Catherine Peachey Fund, Inc. was established in memory of Cathy Peachey. All of the proceeds from *Just Peachey, Cooking Up a Cure* will go directly to Breast Cancer research at the Indiana University Cancer Center. This fund is a 501 (c)(3) for tax purposes. Donors may deduct contributions to the Catherine Peachey Fund, Inc. as provided in section 170 of the Internal Revenue Code.

Many people have asked: "What made Cathy so special to so many people?" The question has been partially answered as we on the committee have spoken with many people who consider themselves "one of Cathy's best friends." No one was just an acquaintance. Cathy came from a family of "best friends," and she shared her heritage with each of us.

White House 1993—Michele Kuntz Wood, Cathy and Connie Rufenbarger.

To know Cathy was to love her . . . is to love her. She lives in many hearts.

Catherine Marie was born to Sarah Nell during a chilly Indiana March of 1951. It was much colder in Korea. While mother and daughter crossed trimesters, father crossed the 38th parallel. News of birth and joy came over phone wires he had strung through battle. Cathy was his ticket home; the U.S. Marines thought a father of four was more useful at home than at war. Cathy joined Carolyn, Jimmy and Lannie to welcome their father. The Chinese lured two wire teams into ambush the week he left. They cut the wires and waited.

So began the combat that was the American 50's and 60's. Harry's birth, when Cathy was four, moved the family from Carolina Avenue to the roomier Carrollton. If Cathy lost privileges, a youngest son Harry was paid back doubly by the arrival of twins and new recruits Steven and John in '58. Sgt. Peachey, by now just Peachey, conceded command to General Sarah. It was a life of roll call, surprise inspection, K.P. and meals.

Meals and more meals. Nine mouths three times a day. Nine thousand eight hundred and fifty meals a year. Plus guests. It was a rare day without a guest at the table. Bad aim? Follow the aroma, the clatter, the laughter. It was a contest. Invite everyone to the kitchen. Points for new faces and old favorites. Thanksgiving was big. It was a rule: food extended the family.

The kitchen was a royal court, a courtroom, for courting. It was a stage and Cathy a main character. Out, out brief candle. She was younger and older. Defender, prosecutor, princess. Her entrance or exit could break a heart. She was the Allied Forces. In a certain mood she was a Cold War Russian. To Cathy, food meant détente. She was sergeant at arms. She was Harriet Tubman. She could tell a joke like no one else. We'd howl. There was a yardstick with a red rubber ball and two feet of elastic stapled to it. A reminder to any child who forgot the rules. Cathy was an expert. Bop on the forehead. It was the greatest joke of all; the perfect bomb. Cathy should have been President. Have a State Dinner. Invite everyone. Bop on the head. Have coffee. Have Peace.

John Peachey

"Everyone is Invited to Dinner"
Hammond Times - 9/15/78

CICERO, Ind. (AP) —Everyone is invited to dinner here Sunday. That's right—James Peachey has personally invited 1,300 families to share his weekend repast in Cicero Town Park.

A newcomer in town, Peachey decided the best way for him to get acquainted was to serve dinner

The Peach did not fall far from the tree.

for the entire community. The menu is awesome. It includes 1,200 chickens, deep-fried homemade biscuits with apple butter, potato salad, green beans, corn on the cob and "whatever comes to mind at the last minute," Peachey explained.

"I found that all Cicero is divided into two parts," Peachey said. "There's pretty much old Cicero made up of the people who have lived in the town many years, and new Cicero, the families who have moved here since the Morse Reservoir Development. I thought it might be a good way for the new residents to meet the old residents if everyone got together for Sunday dinner."

The long-time Indianapolis resident moved to this Hamilton County community about 25 miles north of the capital city last year. He says he "loves to cook" and isn't intimidated by the large dinner party because he owns a commercial catering company. The chickens will be cut up to serve between 8,000 and 10,000 pieces "for as long as the food holds out." His invitations have been met with some skepticism by those who either don't believe the affair is free or are looking for a gimmick, Peachey said.

Peachey's Catering began in 1974 as an extension of a love for good food and large crowds. It evolved from many things: a history, a diner in Camby, a dairy products/sandwich stand in the old City Market. The concept was simple: cook at the party to make the food fresh and hot. The trucks had fryers, stoves, ovens, and cold storage on board. No party was too big or too small. There were hors d'oeuvres for 8 or 800.

There were Bar B Ques for eight thousand. It was a family business and famous for two things: the annual "Y'all come" free dinner for up to four thousand residents of Cicero and Arcadia, and fried biscuits with homemade apple butter.

Jim Peachey, Cathy's father, said that during the family's years in the catering business there were two most frequently asked questions, 1) How did we make the fried biscuits? and 2) Where could they buy the apple butter? His responses were ready.

Number 1 is easy. Go to your favorite supermarket and buy a package of refrigerated biscuits, any brand. I have found little difference in any of them, regardless of price. You will need a deep fat fryer, preferably one that will heat to 375 degrees. Simply drop the biscuits into the hot fat one at a time, no more than six at one time. As the biscuits cook, you can watch them puff up. When the biscuits are brown on the bottom, turn them over with a cooking spoon. Total cooking time is about five minutes.

Number 2 Question - Where do we buy our Apple Butter? We didn't, we made our own. This is reduced to a suitable size for a family.

Grandma Peachey's Apple Butter

3/4 #10 can applesauce
1/4 #10 can apple butter
3/4 cup sugar
3/4 ounce cinnamon
1/2 ounce allspice
1/4 ounce ground cloves
2 tablespoons redhots

Pour applesauce and apple butter in large pan. In separate pan blend all remaining ingredients thoroughly. Add blended spices to apple mixture. Mix well until smooth. Bake at 350 degrees for 4 hours stirring occasionally. Let stand until cool. After cool, pour into desired containers and refrigerate until needed. May be reheated at anytime. Serve hot or cold.

The Peachey Family

Vegetable Tray with Crab-Avocado Dip

4 avocados softened
8 teaspoons lemon juice
2 teaspoons Worcestershire sauce
16 ounces cream cheese softened
1 cup sour cream
1 teaspoon salt
1/4 teaspoon pepper
6 tablespoons minced
     green onions
1 pound flaked crab meat

Place mashed avocados, lemon juice, and Worcestershire sauce in bowl, mix well. Add cream cheese, sour cream, salt and pepper, blend well. Stir in green onions, celery and crab meat. Cover and chill. Makes approximately 4 cups. Serve with a complete selection of your favorite fresh vegetables.

James H. Peachey, Cathy's Father
Cicero, Indiana

Creamy Spinach Dip

8 ounces of sour cream
1 cup mayonnaise
1/2 teaspoon celery salt
1/2 teaspoon dill weed
1/4 cup chopped green onion
3 cups Green Giant Cut Spinach
    (frozen) chopped well, drain
1 can water chestnuts chopped
3 teaspoons chopped red peppers

Combine sour cream, mayonnaise and seasonings. Stir in onion, spinach, water chestnuts and red peppers. Cover and refrigerate.

Serve with fresh vegetables or bread cubes.

The Peachey Family

Peachey Fruit Dip

1/2 cup butter
1 cup brown sugar firmly packed
1 cup sour cream
3 teaspoons vanilla extract

Melt butter over medium heat. Add brown sugar and stir until smooth. Remove from heat and cool well. Add sour cream and vanilla extract to cooled mixture. Makes 2 1/2 cups. Serve as a dip with your favorite cut fresh fruits. Try green apple wedges, strawberries or peaches.

The Peachey Family

Easy Seafood Dip

1 large carton sour cream
1 package Ranch Dressing Mix
1 can drained minced clams
1 pound flaked crab meat
    (imitation is fine)
Fresh ground black pepper
    to taste

Mix all ingredients together and chill overnight. Serve with crackers, chips, or vegetables.

Beth Bartchy Smith, Cathy's Cousin
Piney Flats, Tennessee

Smoked Salmon Ball

1 regular size can of salmon
    (deboned)
3 ounces cream cheese
4-5 drops of liquid smoke
chopped pecans and/or parsley

Mix salmon, cream cheese and liquid smoke together and chill overnight. Roll in a ball and cover with chopped pecans and parsley. Serve with crackers or bread.

Beth Bartchy Smith, Cathy's Cousin,
Piney Flats, Tennessee

Broccoli Cheese Soup

4 chicken bouillon cubes
1 cup diced onion
2 1/2 cups diced raw potatoes
2 cans cream of chicken soup
1 quart of water
20 ounces frozen broccoli
1 pound Velveeta cheese, cubed

Combine bouillon cubes, onion and water and cook 20 minutes. Add potatoes and frozen vegetables and cook 30 minutes. Add soup and stir to blend. Add cheese and stir to melt. Heat to taste.

Ralph and Debbie Farmer, Cathy's Cousins
Martinsville, Indiana

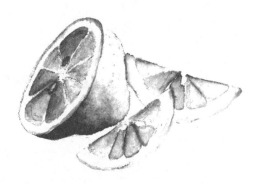

60 Minute Presto French Bread

Step 1
1/4 cup plus 1 tablespoon butter
    or margarine melted
1/3 cup grated Parmesan cheese
2 tablespoons sweet basil
2 tablespoons parsley
2 tablespoon snipped chives
1 teaspoon powdered garlic or
    1 clove fresh garlic, minced
Mix well and set aside.

Step 2—Combine:
2 cups bread flour
1 package Rapid Rise yeast
1 teaspoon salt

Step 3—Stir in:
1 cup very warm water
    (125 to 130 degrees) with
1 tablespoon butter or margarine
Mix well.

Step 4—Add: 1 cup flour or enough to make a soft dough. Knead until smooth, about 6 minutes. Roll dough on floured board to 15 X 12 inches. Spread herb mixture to within 1/2 inch of edges. Roll up tightly from long end as for jelly roll; pinch seam and ends to seal. Taper ends. Place loaf, seam side down, on greased baking sheet. With sharp knife, make one lengthwise cut, 1/8 inch deep, to within 1 inch of ends. Cover. Place large shallow pan on counter; half fill with boiling water. Place baking sheet over pan; let rise 10-20 minutes.

Bake at 400 degrees for 25 minutes or until golden. Remove from sheet; cool on wire rack. Makes one loaf—great with spaghetti.

Hylda Smith, Cathy's Aunt
Piney Flats, Tennessee

Hot Chicken Salad

1 can cream of chicken soup
3/4 cup salad dressing
3 teaspoons lemon juice
1/2 teaspoon salt
1/4 teaspoon pepper
3 cups diced cooked chicken
    (1/4 inch cubes)
1 cup finely chopped celery
1 medium onion finely chopped
    blanched almonds
1 can sliced water chestnuts
3 hard boiled eggs, sliced
2 cups crushed potato chips

Make a sauce by blending together the chicken soup, salad dressing, lemon juice, salt and pepper. Add to the diced chicken, celery, onion, almonds and water chestnuts. Place half of the mixture in a buttered 7 x 11 x 2 baking dish. Cover with boiled eggs. Add remaining mixture. Top with potato chips. Bake at 450 degrees for 20 minutes, or until sauce is bubbly. Serve at once. Serves 8.

NOTE: Use boiled whole fryer and pull meat. May make up to 24 hours ahead of time before baking.

The Peachey Family

Honeyed Chicken

1 3 - pound fryer, cut up
1 egg yolk
2 tablespoons butter, melted
2 tablespoons soy sauce
2 tablespoons lemon juice
1/2 cup honey
salt and pepper to taste
paprika to taste

Place chicken in shallow pan. Mix remaining ingredients and pour over chicken. Bake at 325 degrees for 1 hour or until chicken is done. Turn several times while baking.

Dianne Farmer, Cathy's Cousin
Camby, Indiana

Enchilada Casserole

1 2-3 pound chicken
1 1/2 cups chicken broth
1 can cream of mushroom soup
1 can cream of chicken soup
1 15 ounce can mild enchilada
    sauce (or 15 ounce
    tomato sauce)
1 big bag taco flavored corn chips
1-2 cups grated cheese

Boil and bone chicken. Heat broth, soups, and sauce. Layer ingredients in a 9 x 13 baking dish in this order:
    1/2 of slightly crushed chips
    1/2 of chicken
    1/2 of cheese
    1/2 of sauce/soup mixture
    other half of chips
    other half of chicken
    other half of sauce/soup mixture

Bake 20 minutes at 350 degrees. Add rest of cheese. Return to oven for additional 10 minutes.

Nancy Smith Ross, Cathy's Cousin
Johnson City, Tennessee

Potatoes Romanoff

4 potatoes quartered
2 tablespoons butter
1 cup sour cream
4 whole green onions sliced
1 1/4 cups cheddar cheese
    shredded
1 teaspoon salt
1/8 teaspoon black pepper
paprika to taste

Boil potatoes until tender. Mash with butter, sour cream, onions, 3/4 cups cheese, salt and pepper. Turn mixture into buttered 1 1/2 quart casserole. Sprinkle with remaining cheese and paprika. Bake uncovered at 350 degrees for 40 minutes. Makes 6 servings.

Steven Peachey, Cathy's Brother
Noblesville, Indiana

Red Cake

1/2 cup vegetable shortening
1 1/2 cups sugar
2 eggs
1 teaspoon vanilla
2 ounces red food coloring
2 1/2 cups flour
1/2 teaspoon salt
1 tablespoon cocoa
1 cup buttermilk
1 teaspoon baking soda
1 teaspoon vinegar

Frosting:
1/4 cup flour
1 cup milk
1 cup sugar
1 cup Crisco

Cream shortening and sugar until light and fluffy. Add eggs and mix well. Add vanilla. Slowly add coloring. Sift together the flour, salt and cocoa. Add dry ingredients alternately with the buttermilk. In a small bowl, mix together the baking soda and vinegar. Gently fold into batter. Put in two well-greased 9 inch cake pans. Bake at 350 degrees for 25 to 30 minutes, or until cake tests done. Cool and frost with frosting.

Frosting: In a small sauce pan mix together flour and milk. Cook until thickened. Cool completely. In a mixer bowl, beat sugar and Crisco until fluffy. Then add cooled flour mixture and beat until very fluffy. Frost the red cake with this frosting. This makes a very pretty cake for Christmas, Valentine's Day or birthdays. Cathy loved it, too!

Marilyn Metzger Lemon, Cathy's Sister-in-law
Columbia City, Indiana

Michele Kuntz Wood, R.N.
Indiana Breast Cancer Coalition
Indianapolis, Indiana

Old Fashioned Cream Pie

1 cup plus 3 tablespoon sugar
1/3 cup plus 2 tablespoons flour
salt
1 cup water
1/4 cup butter
1 cup evaporated milk
1 teaspoon vanilla
5 drops lemon juice

Mix sugar, flour and salt together well and set aside. In a sauce pan, bring to a boil the water and butter. To this add dry ingredients, milk, vanilla and lemon juice. Pour into unbaked 9 inch pie shell. Sprinkle cinnamon and pieces of butter on top. Bake 15 minutes at 450 degrees. Reduce temperature to 400 degrees and bake an additional 10 minutes.

Fran Peachey Amos, Cathy's Aunt
Camby, Indiana

Never Fail Pie Crust

4 cups all purpose flour
1 3/4 cups vegetable shortening
1 tablespoon sugar
2 teaspoons salt
1 tablespoon vinegar
1 egg
1/2 cup water

Mix together flour, shortening, sugar and salt with fingers or fork. Set aside. Shake together vinegar, egg and water. Combine the two mixtures until all are moistened. Shape into a ball. Chill 15 minutes before rolling into desired shapes. Can be left in the refrigerator up to 3 days or frozen. No matter how much you handle the dough, it is always flaky and tender. Makes two 9 inch double crust pies and one 9 inch shell.

Fran Peachey Amos, Cathy's Aunt
Camby, Indiana

Best Fudge Nut Brownies

1 pound butter
8 ounces unsweetened
    baking chocolate
4 cups sugar
6 large eggs beaten
2 teaspoons vanilla
2 cups flour sifted
1 1/2 cups walnuts chopped
6 ounces chocolate chips
1 teaspoon baking powder

Toppings:
6 ounces chocolate chips
1 1/2 cups walnuts

Melt butter and chocolate over low heat until all chocolate is melted. Stir frequently so as not to scorch chocolate. Combine all ingredients in a large mixer bowl. Mix the ingredients one at a time as listed above (except for toppings). Before spreading out on baking tray, put a piece of parchment paper on the tray and spray with cooking spray, coating the sides and ends thoroughly. Level mixture evenly. Over the top, spread remaining chocolate chips and walnuts. Using the palm of your hand, lightly pat the chips and nuts into the batter. Bake at 350 degrees for 25 minutes; then rotate tray from top to bottom and turn tray from front to back. Bake an additional 25 minutes. Remove tray from oven and cool on rack. After cooling, use knife around edges to loosen brownies from sides of pan. Turn tray over carefully and gently remove parchment paper from bottom of baked brownies. Turn brownies right side up and cut into 2 x 2 squares.

Note: Use one 18 x 13 x 1 baking sheet pan or two 9 x 13 cake pans. Prepare pans with parchment paper and cooking spray.

James H. Peachey, Cathy's Father
Cicero, Indiana

Easy Strawberry Rhubarb Jam

6 cups rhubarb, cut in
    1 inch pieces
4 1/2 cups sugar
6 packages strawberry jello

Pour sugar over rhubarb. Let stand overnight. Next day put in blender for a few seconds. Boil for 10 minutes. Immediately add strawberry jello. Stir until dissolved.

Pour into sterilized glass jars and seal. When cool, store in refrigerator until used. 1 1/2 recipe makes 10 junior baby food jars.

Wally Smith, Cathy's Cousin
Aurora, Illinois

Perfect Cappuccino (a Cath, Inc. specialty)

dark roast coffee,
    ground for espresso
fresh cold milk
measuring cup
10 ounce coffee mug
thermometer
12 or 20 ounce stainless
    steel pitcher
(optional - 1 rounded teaspoon
    ground chocolate (we think
    Ghirardelli is the best!),
    cinnamon, or 3/4 ounce
    flavored syrup)

Pour cold water into machine according to manufacturer's instructions. Fill espresso group filter with ground espresso and pack firmly with flat bottom espresso measure. Insert group into espresso machine. Pour cold milk into pitcher, taking care not to fill the pitcher more than half way. Insert thermometer and set aside. Turn on machine. When espresso begins to brew, insert steamer nozzle just under the surface of the milk and turn on steamer. When steaming properly, it should make a noise similar to the air being let out of a tire. The idea is to double the size of the milk, so you will move the pitcher closer to the counter as the milk is steaming. When milk reaches 140-160 degrees, turn steamer off. Allow espresso to finish brewing. Grasp top of pitcher and drop it on the counter 4-5 times. This will help to separate the foam from the steamed milk. Pour 2 1/2 ounces brewed espresso into coffee mug. Add 2 1/2 ounces steamed milk, and spoon foam to top. Garnish with cinnamon, nutmeg, ground shaved chocolate. Sip slowly and enjoy! P.S. Practice makes perfect.

Marissa Honey - Manager of Cath, Inc., City Market,
Indianapolis, Indiana

See's Toffee (One of Cathy's Christmas favorites)

1 pound butter (no substitutes)
4 cups white sugar
1 - 1 1/2 pounds finely
    chopped pecans
26 plain Hershey milk
    chocolate bars
12 x 17 inch cookie sheet
    (with 1 inch edge) or
    jelly roll pan (jelly roll pan
    will use fewer chocolate bars
    and toffee will be thicker)

Unwrap chocolate bars then cover the bottom of the pan with chopped pecans. Place a layer evenly over the pecans. Save the other half of the unwrapped bars and pecans for the top. Melt butter in 3 - 4 quart pan over medium heat. When the butter is melted, add sugar and increase heat to medium-high. Stir constantly, mixture will boil. Continue stirring boiling mixture (it will change several times) until butter and sugar caramelize and turn a toffee color (think of the center of a Heath Bar). Toffee will be bitter if burned. From this point work quickly. Immediately pour hot toffee mixture evenly over chocolate bars in pan. Carefully place remaining chocolate bars writing side down on top of hot toffee. Be careful not to touch the toffee mixture to avoid burns. Cover top of melting chocolate with chopped pecans and lightly press with back of spatula. Set on rack to cool for several hours. Break into pieces and enjoy.

Katherine Heikes
Indianapolis, Indiana

27

Yeast Coffee Cake

3 1/2 cups all purpose flour
2 packages active dry yeast
1 1/2 cups milk
1/4 cup sugar
1/2 cup margarine
1 teaspoon salt
1 egg

Filling:
margarine
dark brown sugar
white sugar
ground cinnamon
nuts and/or raisins are optional

In mixing bowl combine 1 1/2 cups of the flour and yeast. Heat milk, sugar, margarine and salt until warm, stirring constantly until margarine melts. Cool milk mixture slightly, stir into flour yeast mixture. Gradually stir in remaining flour. When the mixture becomes too thick to stir, turn onto a floured surface and knead. Dough will be sticky, but knead in enough to make dough manageable by hand. Knead dough for about 5-8 minutes, form into a ball, place into greased bowl, turn once with greased surface on top. Cover with a warm damp towel until doubled (45 - 60 minutes). Punch down and let rise again (about 30 minutes). Turn onto lightly floured surface and cut in half.

Filling: On lightly floured surface roll 1/2 of dough into a 16 x 8 rectangle. Spread generously with margarine, cover with dark brown sugar, sprinkle with white sugar, sprinkle with ground cinnamon and/or nuts or raisins.

Roll dough as for jelly roll starting on 16 inch edge. Seal edge. Turn roll to smooth edge and pull slightly. Cut roll evenly down the center and carefully shape 1/2 into a snail shape (sugar/cinnamon should be on top). Carefully place into an 8 inch pie pan (disposable are best). Take remaining half and carefully place around the dough in the pan. Prepare second half in the same manner. Cover and let rise until almost double in size. Bake in a 375 degree oven for about 20 minutes (bread will be golden brown and when tapped with fingernail will sound hollow), sugar mixture will be bubbly. Remove from oven to cool on rack.

*Marissa Honey - Manager of Cath, Inc., City Market,
Indianapolis, Indiana*

28

Catering Tips from Jim and Sarah Peachey

Serve 100 people

Coffee	3 pounds
Milk	6 gallons
Fruit Cocktail	2 1/2 gallons
Fruit Juice	4 #10 cans
Soup	5 gallons
Wieners	25 pounds
Meatloaf	24 pounds
Ham	40 pounds
Beef	40 pounds
Roast Pork	40 pounds
Hamburger	30-36 pounds
Potatoes	35 pounds
Scalloped Potatoes	5 gallons
Vegetables	4 #10 cans
Baked Beans	5 gallons
Cauliflower	18 pounds
Cabbage for Slaw	20 pounds
Bread	10 loaves
Rolls	200
Butter	3 pounds
Potato Salad	12 quarts
Fruit Salad	20 quarts
Lettuce	20 heads
Salad Dressing	3 quarts
Pies	18
Cakes	8
Ice Cream	4 gallons
Cheese	3 pounds
Pickles	2 quarts
Nuts	3 pounds

To serve 50 people, divide by 2
To serve 25 people, divide by 4

State House Rotunda—Indianapolis, Indiana, 1992

Indiana Breast Cancer Coalition Begins

Washington D.C. 1993

"The National Breast Cancer Coalition teaches women how to fight for their lives—in the hearing rooms and hallways of government where such battles are waged.

We have learned that a citizen's campaign can be successful if it is sufficiently widespread and vocal. We have learned from our own losses that nothing less than a dynamic national movement will claim the resources and attention necessary to change the nation's agenda on breast cancer."

*National Breast
Cancer Coalition
Annual Report
1991—1993*

JUST
POLITICIANS

President Bill Clinton's Favorite Recipe: Chicken Enchiladas

Cooking oil
2 4-ounce cans chopped green
   chilies
1 large clove garlic, minced

1 28-ounce can tomatoes
2 cups chopped onion
2 teaspoons salt
1/2 teaspoon oregano

3 cups shredded, cooked chicken
2 cups dairy sour cream
2 cups grated cheddar cheese
15 corn or flour tortillas

Preheat oil in skillet. Saute chopped chilies with minced garlic in oil. Drain and break up tomatoes; reserve 1/2 cup liquid. To chilies and garlic, add tomatoes, onion, 1 teaspoon salt, oregano and reserved tomato liquid. Simmer uncovered until thick, about 30 minutes. Remove from skillet and set aside. Combine chicken with sour cream, grated cheese and other teaspoon salt. Heat 1/3 cup oil; dip tortillas in oil until they become limp. Drain well on paper towels. Fill tortillas with chicken mixture; roll up and arrange side by side, seam down, in 9" x 13" x 2" baking dish. Pour tomato mixture over enchiladas and bake at 350 degrees until heated through, about 20 minutes. Yields 15 enchiladas.

Bill Clinton

THE WHITE HOUSE

Hillary Clinton's Chocolate Chip Cookies

1 1/2 cups unsifted all-purpose flour
1 teaspoon salt
1 teaspoon baking soda
1 cup solid vegetable shortening
1 cup firmly packed light brown sugar

1/2 cup granulated sugar
1 teaspoon vanilla
2 eggs
2 cups old-fashioned rolled oats
1 (12-ounce) package semi-sweet chocolate chips

Preheat oven to 350 degrees. Grease baking sheets. Combine flour, salt and baking soda. Beat together shortening, sugars and vanilla in a large bowl until creamy. Add eggs, beating until light and fluffy. Gradually beat in flour mixture and rolled oats. Stir in chocolate chips. Drop batter by well-rounded teaspoonful on to greased baking sheets. Bake 8 to 10 minutes or until golden. Cool cookies on sheets on wire rack for 2 minutes. Remove cookies to wire rack to cool completely.

Hillary Rodham Clinton

Chicken Enchiladas

Cooking oil
2 4-ounce cans chopped
    green chilies
1 large clove garlic, minced
1 28 ounce can tomatoes
2 cups chopped onion
2 teaspoons salt
1/2 teaspoon oregano
3 cups shredded, cooked chicken
2 cups dairy sour cream
2 cups grated Cheddar cheese
15 corn tortillas

Preheat oil in skillet. Saute chopped chilies with minced garlic in oil. Drain and break up tomatoes; reserve 1/2 cup liquid. To chilies and garlic, add tomatoes, onion, 1 teaspoon salt, oregano and reserved tomato liquid. Simmer uncovered until thick, about 30 minutes. Remove from skillet and set aside. Combine chicken with sour cream, grated cheese and other teaspoon salt. Heat 1/3 cup oil; dip tortillas in oil until they become limp. Drain well on paper towels. Fill tortillas with chicken mixture; roll up and arrange side by side, seam down, in 9 x 13 x 2 inch baking dish. Pour tomato mixture over enchiladas and bake at 350 degrees until heated through, about 20 minutes. Yields 15 enchiladas.

Bill Clinton,
President of the United States

Hillary Clinton's Chocolate Chip Cookies

1 1/2 cups unsifted
    all-purpose flour
1 teaspoon salt
1 teaspoon baking soda
1 cup solid vegetable shortening
1 cup firmly packed light
    brown sugar
1/2 cup granulated sugar
1 teaspoon vanilla
2 eggs
2 cups old-fashioned rolled oats
1 (12-ounce) package semi-sweet
    chocolate chips

Preheat oven to 350 degrees. Grease baking sheets. Combine flour, salt and baking soda. Beat together shortening, sugars and vanilla in a large bowl until creamy. Add eggs, beating until light and fluffy. Gradually beat in flour mixture and rolled oats. Stir in chocolate chips. Drop batter by well-rounded teaspoonful on to greased baking sheets. Bake 8 to 10 minutes or until golden. Cool cookies on sheets on wire rack for 2 minutes. Remove cookies to wire rack to cool completely.

Hillary Clinton,
First Lady of the United States

State Dinner Created Especially for Indiana
The White House Executive Chef
Walter Scheib

Herb-Roasted Pheasant Breast
with Wild Mushroom Risotto
and Tomato Basil Coulis

Pan Seared Salmon Loin
with Key Lime and Ginger
Vegetable Confetti and Crisp Rice Noodles
Marinated Goat's Cheese and Vegetable Terrine
with Young Greens and Balsamic Dressing

Fresh Fruit Salad Surprise
White House Pastry Chef
Roland Mesnier

Herb-Roasted Pheasant Breast

Ingredients for Pheasant:
3 medium (1 1/2 pound) pheasant
1 ounce chopped garlic
1 ounce chopped basil
1 ounce chopped tarragon
1/2 ounce chopped chives

Method for Pheasant:
Remove legs from pheasant and roast separately. Reserve meat for risotto. Loosen skin on pheasant breasts by working fingers between the skin and the meat. Insert chopped garlic and herb mixture under skin and spread evenly. Place breasts on roasting rack in oven at 350 degrees. Roast until just done (about 20 minutes). Let cool slightly before removing meat from rib cage. Hold warm until service.
6 Portions

Wild Mushroom Risotto

Ingredients for Risotto:
10 ounces Arborio rice
1 ounce butter
2 ounces chopped shallots
1 ounce grated Asiago cheese
2 ounces stock or water
4 ounces leg meat from
    pheasant, diced
2 ounces small diced tomatoes
1 ounce julienne of basil
3 ounces sauteed
    wild mushrooms

Method for Risotto:
Saute shallots in butter until tender. Add rice. Stir to coat until tender. Add stock bit by bit while stirring rice. Only add a little stock at a time and then more when the stock is absorbed. When rice is finished, this will take about 20 minutes, stir in grated cheese. At service, fold in the diced leg meat, tomatoes, basil and wild mushrooms.

Tomato Basil Coulis

**Ingredients for Tomato
Basil Coulis:**
1/2 ounce olive oil
1 pound ripe tomatoes
1 1/2 ounces fresh basil leaves
1/2 ounce garlic
1 ounce shallots
stock, as needed, to
    adjust consistency
salt and pepper
aged sherry vinegar, to taste

Method for Tomato Basil Coulis:
Blanch, peel and seed tomatoes. Rough chop. Saute shallots and garlic in olive oil. Add tomatoes and basil. Let simmer 30 minutes. Add some stock if mixture is too dry. Simmer 20 minutes more. Puree mixture in blender (not too smooth). Adjust seasoning and finish with a dash or two of aged sherry vinegar.

Basil Leaf Garnish

6 each large green basil leaves
2 ounces oil

Method for Garnish:
Heat oil. Drop basil leaves, one by one, in oil. (Take caution as the leaves will pop.) Fry until crisp. Remove and hold until service.

To Assemble Dish
In heated soup plates, place one portion of risotto in center. Ladle about 2 ounces of tomato coulis around risotto. Slice pheasant breast on the bias and arrange around the risotto. Sprinkle dish with grated Asiago cheese. Place basil leaf on top of risotto and serve.

Pan-Seared Salmon Loin

Ingredients for Salmon:
3 pound side of salmon
1 ounce chopped ginger
1 tablespoon lemon zest
1/2 ounce garlic, chopped
2 ounces chopped parsley
1 ounce olive oil
salt and pepper
string or butcher twine

Ingredients for Sauce:
3 ounces fish stock
1 ounce white wine
1/2 ounce key lime juice
1 teaspoon key lime zest
1/2 ounce grated ginger
1 ounce parsley puree
arrowroot starch

Method for Salmon:
Skin and bone salmon fillet. Cut in 12 equal slices by cutting straight down through the fillet, forming slices that are about 3/4 inch thick. Combine remaining ingredients to form a paste. Place one ounce of the parsley mixture between two pieces of salmon flat faced side-by-side. Form salmon into a disk, shaped by overlapping the thin end and the thick end in a circle. Tie one piece of string around the outside edge of the disk and pull tight to hold shape. At time of service, sear the salmon in a hot pan to form a crust on the outside. Finish cooking in a medium hot oven. Hold for service. 6 Portions

Method for Sauce:
Simmer stock, wine, lime juice and lime zest for about 20 minutes until flavors blend. Thicken to consistency desired with arrowroot. Adjust seasoning. Blanch and puree parsley and hold for addition at time of service.

Key Lime and Ginger Vegetable Confetti

Ingredients for Vegetables:
2 ounces daikon, cut in 1/4 inch
    wide strips
2 ounces carrots, cut in 1/4 inch
    wide strips, blanched
2 ounces snow peas, cut in
    1/4 inch wide strips
2 ounces shiitake mushrooms,
    cut in 1/4 inch wide strips
2 ounce bok choy

Method for Vegetables:
Quickly stir-fry all the vegetables in sesame oil. Do not overcook. They should remain crisp and very bright.

Dressing ingredients:

1 ounce rice vinegar

1 tablespoon garlic, chopped

1 tablespoon cilantro, chopped

1 ounce peanuts, chopped

1 tablespoon ginger, grated

1 teaspoon sugar

1 teaspoon (or to taste)
    chili paste

2 tablespoons sesame oil

Combine all dressing ingredients and toss cooked vegetables in mix.

Crisp Rice Noodles

Method for Rice Noodles:

Soak 2 ounces of oriental rice noodles in water until soft. Drain well and deep fry until light and crispy. Form into small "haystacks" and reserve for service.

To Assemble Dish:

Place one portion of the stir-fried and dressed vegetables at center of a heated dinner plate. Remove string from salmon dish and lean it on the side of the vegetable portion. Add parsley puree to sauce base. Do not do this until just before service. (If the parsley puree is added too soon, it will lose its color.) Ladle sauce around salmon. Sprinkle black and white sesame seeds into sauce. Place noodle "haystacks" at back of plate near salmon as garnish.

Marinated Goat's Cheese and Vegetable Terrine with Young Greens and Balsamic Dressing

Goat's Cheese

6 ounces of high quality
    fresh goat's cheese
1/2 ounce rosemary
1 ounce garlic
1/2 ounce thyme

Method for Goat's Cheese:

Cut cheese into 1 ounce portions and marinate them with other ingredients for about three days. When ready to make terrine, mix cheese and some of the marination liquid until smooth and the consistency of room-temperature cream cheese.
6 Portions

Vegetables
Ingredients for Vegetables:

3 each Roma tomatoes
1 each zucchini
1 each yellow squash
1 small eggplant
1 each yellow and red
    bell peppers
1/2 ounce rosemary, chopped
1/2 ounce garlic, chopped
1 ounce balsamic vinegar
salt and pepper

Method for Vegetables:

Slice tomatoes 1/4 inch thick. Dice zucchini, yellow squash, eggplant and peppers into 1/4 inch slices. Toss vegetables with other ingredients. Drain and place on a sheet pan. Broil vegetables until tender. (Some coloring will take place.) Let cool. Season with salt and pepper.

Young Greens
Ingredients for Greens:

Variety of young leaves and lettuce, which may include: frissa, spinach, red oak lettuce, arugula, trevise, romaine, best greens and or mache.

Method for Greens:

Wash and clean greens well, being sure any stems or ribs are removed. Be sure all excess water is drained.

Phyllo Crisps
Ingredients for Phyllo Crisps:

3 sheets phyllo dough
1 tablespoon olive oil
1 tablespoon chopped herbs

Method for Crisps:

Layer phyllo with olive oil and herbs three times. Cut into long thick triangles and bake at 375 degrees until golden brown and crisp. Hold for service.

Balsamic Dressing
Ingredients for Balsamic Dressing:
2 ounces balsamic vinegar
5 ounces olive oil
1 tablespoon dry mustard
1/2 ounce garlic, chopped
1/2 ounce shallots, chopped
2 tablespoons fresh herbs,
    chopped
salt and pepper

Method for Dressing:
Whisk ingredients until blended. Rewhisk at service.

To Assemble Terrine:
In a small, 2-inch wide by 3-inch tall, cylinder form, layer alternating layers of soft cheese mixture and broiled vegetables. Remove layered terrine from form and place in center of chilled plate. Toss greens with dressing and arrange around layered terrine.
Garnish with two phyllo triangles.

Fresh Fruit Salad Surprise

2-3 medium size oranges,
    in segments
1/3 of fresh pineapple, peeled
grapes, seeded
strawberries
bananas
ripe pears
plums
sugar to sweeten
Cointreau liqueur
1/3 jar apricot jam
vanilla ice cream
1 teaspoon vanilla extract
4 tablespoons granulated sugar
3 egg yolks
4 egg whites
pinch of salt
powdered sugar

Prepare fresh fruit salad using fruit, sugar to taste and Cointreau liqueur. Add a half jar of apricot jam diluted with a little liquor of your choice.

Place the fruit salad in a 1 1/2 quart souffle dish. Cover with vanilla ice cream and put in freezer.

In mixing bowl, beat 3 egg yolks with 1 teaspoon vanilla extract and 1 1/2 tablespoons granulated sugar until stiff. Put stiff egg yolks in a small bowl for later use. Beat 4 egg whites and a pinch of salt with 2 1/2 tablespoons of granulated sugar until stiff. Fold egg yolks into meringue mixture. Pipe meringue on top of ice cream. Sprinkle generously with powdered sugar. Bake in 425 degree oven until golden brown, 2 to 3 minutes. Serve immediately.

Artichoke Dip

1 cup mayonnaise
1 cup Parmesan cheese
1 cup drained artichoke hearts

Chop artichokes. Mix all and bake 15-20 minutes at 350 degrees. Serve with crackers.

Sue Anne Gilroy, Indiana Secretary of State
Indianapolis, Indiana

Spiced Nuts

1 pound pecan halves
1 egg white, slightly beaten
1/2 teaspoon salt
1/2 cup sugar
2 tablespoons cinnamon

Place egg white and nuts in bowl. Stir well to coat. Mix sugar, salt, and cinnamon together. Add to nuts and mix to coat well. Place on cookie sheet and bake at 300 degrees for 30 minutes.

Sue W. Scholer, State Representative
West Lafayette, Indiana

Multibean Soup

1 1-pound 4-ounce dried
    15-bean soup package
1 smoked turkey thigh, leg,
    wing, or breast
3 quarts water
3 large cloves garlic, minced
1/2 teaspoon dried thyme
1/4 teaspoon crushed
    red pepper
1 large onion, chopped
1 medium carrot, sliced
2 stalks celery, chopped
1/2 green pepper, chopped
salt and pepper—
    season to taste

Tenderizing Bean Options:
1. Wash beans thoroughly and place in large bowl covered with water. Cover and soak overnight; drain.
2. Or, use the quicker method of tenderizing beans by covering beans with cold water, bring to a boil and simmer for 2 minutes. Remove from heat and let stand, tightly covered, for one hour.
3. Or, finally, blanching beans for 2 minutes is equivalent to 8 hours of soaking.

Place smoked turkey in dutch oven, add water, garlic, thyme and red pepper. Bring to a boil; cover and reduce heat. Simmer smoked turkey part for one hour; then remove meat from bones. Place meat back into dutch oven. Add beans and continue cooking for another hour. Add remaining ingredients and cook for 30 minutes or until beans and vegetables are done. Yields 10 servings.

Honorable Pamela Carter, Attorney General of Indiana

The Famous Senate Restaurant Bean Soup Recipe

Take two pounds of small Michigan Navy Beans, wash, and run through hot water until the beans are white again. Put on the fire with four quarts of hot water. Then take one and one-half pounds of smoked ham hocks, boil slowly approximately three hours in a covered pot. Braise one onion chopped in a little butter, and, when light brown, put in the Bean Soup. Season with salt and pepper, then serve. Do not add salt until ready to serve. Serves 8 persons.

Whatever uncertainties may exist in the Senate of the United States, one thing is sure: Bean Soup is on the menu of the Senate Restaurant every day.

Carl Levin, United States Senator
Michigan

Giant Apple Popover (For Brunch)

6 eggs
1 1/2 cups flour
1/2 teaspoon salt
1 tablespoon sugar
1 1/2 cups milk
3/4 cup butter
3 large apples, peeled, cored,
    thinly sliced
lemon juice
3/4 cup sugar
2 tablespoons cinnamon

Heat oven to 425 degrees. Beat eggs, stir in flour, salt and 1 tablespoon sugar until smooth; gradually stir in milk (batter may be made ahead). Divide butter between two 9-inch skillets. If handle is not ovenproof, wrap it with foil to protect from heat. Sprinkle apple slices with lemon juice and divide between the two pans. Divide sugar and cinnamon over apples and saute until glazed and golden (may be made ahead). Put pans in oven and divide batter into pans. Bake 20-25 minutes until puffed and golden brown. Serve at once. Makes 8-10 servings.

Arlen Specter, United States Senator
Pennsylvania

Apple Streusel Muffins

2 cups flour
1/2 cup sugar
2 teaspoons double-action
    baking powder
1/2 teaspoon salt
1/2 cup (one stick) butter,
    room temperature
1 large tart apple, pared, cored
    and diced (about 1 cup)
1/2 teaspoon freshly grated
    lemon zest
1 egg, well beaten
2/3 cup milk
1/2 teaspoon freshly grated
    lemon zest
1/4 cup chopped walnuts
2 tablespoons sugar

Preheat oven to 425 degrees. Sift together flour, 1/2 cup sugar, baking powder and salt. Cut in butter. Reserve 1/2 cup of this mixture for crumb topping. Stir together apple and 1/2 teaspoon lemon zest. Add egg and milk; blend this with flour mixture, stirring lightly until evenly moist. Spoon into 12 greased medium-size muffin cups.

Blend reserved crumb mixture with 1/2 teaspoon lemon zest, 1/4 cup walnuts and 2 tablespoons sugar. Sprinkle over batter and bake until toothpick or wire tester comes out clean, about 20 minutes. Makes 12 muffins.

Evan and Susan Bayh
Governor and First Lady of Indiana
Indianapolis, Indiana

Non-fat Banana Bread

2 cups all-purpose flour
1/2 cup + 1 tablespoon sugar
1 teaspoon baking powder
1 teaspoon salt
1/2 teaspoon baking soda
1 teaspoon cinnamon
1/2 (heaping) cup applesauce
2 1/2 medium (or 2 large) finely
    chopped ripe bananas
4 egg whites

Preheat oven to 350 degrees. Prepare 9 x 5 inch loaf pan (spray with PAM, etc.); Combine ingredients and blend well at medium speed with mixer. Pour into loaf pan. Bake 1 hour (may take 65 minutes in some ovens). Store sliced loaf in Ziploc bags in refrigerator. Reheat single slices about 12 seconds on HIGH in microwave. (Serve warm either plain or with non-fat butter/spread.)

Barb Garton, Wife of
Indiana Senate President Pro Tem, Robert Garton
Columbus, Indiana

Cranberry Fluff

1 package cranberries
    (cleaned and frozen)
3/4 cup sugar
1/2 package miniature
    marshmallows
1 big bunch of seeded,
    red grapes (cut in halves)
1 small can Dole pineapple
    tidbits (drained)
whipping cream

Grind frozen cranberries and add sugar. Let stand until sugar is well dissolved. Add marshmallows and let set for a few hours or overnight. Then add grapes and pineapple. Mix all together and just before serving, fold in real whipped cream. This is a family favorite and makes a beautiful holiday dish.

Jeff Plank, Mayor of Warsaw, Indiana

Italian Spaghetti Sauce with Meatballs

1 pound neck bones pork or beef
Italian oil
1 onion, finely chopped
1 clove garlic minced
2 stalks celery, finely chopped
1 green pepper, finely chopped
salt, pepper, and oregano to taste
1 large can tomato puree
1 small can tomato paste
3 small cans water
1 1/2 tablespoons sugar

Meatballs
2 pounds ground meat
2 eggs
salt and pepper to taste
3 slices hard white bread
1 clove garlic, minced
1 teaspoon parsley flakes
1/2 cup Romano cheese, grated
1/2 cup Parmesan cheese, grated
bread crumbs
Italian oil

Brown neck bones in oil. Brown onions celery, and green peppers with garlic, salt, pepper and oregano in oil.

Bring tomato puree, paste, and water to boil in a large pot. Turn heat down very low and add bones and vegetables, including seasonings to sauce. Simmer at low heat for 2-3 hours. If sauce gets too thick, thin with small amounts of water.
When done, remove bones.

Combine meat with eggs. Mix in salt and pepper. Run bread under cold water; squeeze it out and crumble into meat. Mix. Add parsley and garlic. Mix cheeses. Mix in enough bread crumbs to make mixture firm enough to form meatballs.

Brown meatballs in oil. Add to sauce 1 hour before serving.

Sue Landske, Indiana State Senate
Cedar Lake, Indiana

Sicilian Pasta with Meat Sauce

2 teaspoons olive oil
1 cup finely chopped onions
2 teaspoons minced garlic
1 teaspoon cumin
1/2 teaspoon cinnamon
1 pound extra lean ground beef
1 teaspoon salt
1/2 teaspoon freshly
    ground pepper
2 tablespoons tomato paste
1 can (28 ounce) tomatoes
1/3 cup raisins
1 pound tubetti, anelletti
    (ring-shaped) or corkscrew
    pasta, cooked
1/4 cup chopped flat-leafy parsley
1/4 cup pine nuts (pignolt) or
    almonds, toasted

1. Heat oil in large skillet over medium-high heat. Add onions and cook, stirring, until translucent, 5 minutes. Stir in garlic, cumin and cinnamon and cook 30 seconds. Add beef, salt and pepper; cook, crumbling beef with spoon, until browned, 5 minutes.
2. Stir in tomato paste, tomatoes with their liquid and raisins. Bring to boil, breaking up tomatoes with spoon. Reduce heat and simmer 10 minutes.
3. Toss sauce with pasta and parsley. Sprinkle with pine nuts. Makes 4 servings.

Margaret Goldsmith, Juvenile Division
Marion County Superior Court
Indianapolis, Indiana

Stuffed Cabbage

Combine:
1 pound ground beef
1/4 cup uncooked rice
1 egg
grated onion or onion powder
    to taste
1/4 teaspoon salt

Roll in steamed cabbage leaves. Cook in 1/4 cup lemon juice and/or vinegar, 1/4 to 1/2 cup brown sugar, 1 cup tomato sauce, water or tomato juice to cover. Simmer at least one hour, but as long as possible (as long as several hours). Can be frozen.

Carl Levin, United States Senator
Michigan

Prime Rib

Get 4-5 pounds bone-in rib roast. Line large roasting pan with tin foil, extending foil about 12 inches on each end for folding over later. Put about 1 inch of rock salt in pan over entire bottom. Place roast in pan, pour Worcestershire sauce over entire roast. Cover (encase) entire roast in rock salt, so that there is at least 1 inch of rock salt over entire roast. Fold over tin foil to cover completely. Put in hot oven (500 degrees) for 22 minutes per pound. (4 pounds-88 minutes; 5 pounds-110 minutes; medium rare). Remove and scrape off salt. If too rare, slice and use broiler for about 1 minute.

David A. Wolkins, Indiana State Representative
Winona Lake, Indiana

Swedish Meatballs

3/4 pound lean ground beef
1/2 pound ground veal
1/4 pound ground pork
1 1/2 cups soft bread crumbs
1 cup light cream
1/2 cup chopped onion
1 egg
1/4 cup finely chopped parsley
1 1/2 teaspoons salt
1/4 teaspoon ginger
1/8 teaspoon pepper
1/8 teaspoon nutmeg
2 tablespoons all-purpose flour
1 cup light cream
1/2 teaspoon instant coffee

Have meat ground together twice. Soak bread in cream for 5 minutes. Cook onion in 1 tablespoon butter till tender. Mix meats, crumb mixture, onion, egg, parsley and seasonings. Beat vigorously till fluffy (5 minutes on medium speed or 8 minutes by hand). Form in 1 1/2 inch balls (easier to do with wet hands and chilled mixture). Brown lightly in 2 tablespoons butter, shaking skillet to keep balls round (don't try to do too many at once). Remove balls. Reserve dripping. Make gravy: Stir flour into drippings in skillet; add light cream and coffee. Heat and stir till gravy thickens.

Return balls to gravy, cover, cook *slowly* about 30 minutes, basting occasionally. Makes 3 dozen 1 1/2 inch balls.

This is a family recipe. Vera Swanland Coats was born in Sweden.
Swedish meatballs is a Coats' family tradition.

Dan Coats, United States Senator
Indiana

Veal Stuffed Manicotti

1 cup chopped onions
1 clove garlic, minced
2 tablespoons olive oil
1 can (16 ounce) diced tomatoes
    (puree)
1 can (16 ounce) tomatoes (cut-up)
1/2 teaspoon dried basil, crushed
1/2 teaspoon thyme
1/2 teaspoon oregano
1 teaspoon Worcestershire sauce
1 pound ground veal
1/4 cup milk
1 egg, slightly beaten
1 teaspoon salt
1/4 teaspoon black pepper
6 ounces manicotti

Saute 1/2 cup onion and the garlic in oil. Add the diced tomatoes, cut-up tomatoes, thyme, basil, oregano and Worcestershire sauce. Bring to a boil. Reduce heat and simmer for 30 minutes. Preheat oven to 375 degrees. Combine the veal, milk, egg and remaining onion along with salt and pepper. Mix well. Stuff the uncooked manicotti shells with the veal mixture. Pour half the tomato sauce into an oblong baking dish. Arrange the shells in the dish. Pour remaining sauce over top. Cover and bake for 60 minutes.

Tom Alevizos, Indiana State Representative
Michigan City, Indiana

Pork Chops with Orange Rice

4 pork chops (1-inch thick)
2 tablespoons butter or margarine
1/2 cup water
2 tablespoons flour
1/4 teaspoon seasoned salt
dash of black pepper

Orange Rice:

2/3 cup rice
1/2 cup orange juice
1 cup chicken bouillon
1/4 teaspoon ginger
1/4 teaspoon dry mustard

Combine flour and seasonings. Dust on pork chops. Brown chops on both sides in butter or drippings. Add water and cover. Cook slowly for 20 minutes.

Preheat oven to 350 degrees. Combine all ingredients. Place in shallow (2-quart) casserole. Cover with foil and bake 20 minutes. Put chops on rice. Cover again and bake 40 minutes.

Note: An excellent recipe for entertaining. Do the browning and steaming early in the day and let them bake while you enjoy your guests.

Katie Wolf, Indiana State Senator
Monticello, Indiana

Easy Breakfast Casserole

2 pounds pork sausage
16 ounces sour cream
12 eggs, beaten
8 ounces Cheddar cheese, grated

Preparation: Cook, crumble and drain sausage. Layer ingredients in order listed in a 9 x 13 inch baking dish. Bake at 350 degrees for 30-40 minutes until firm. Serves at least 12.

Paul S. Mannweiler, Speaker, Indiana General Assembly
Indianapolis, Indiana

Lemon Flip Cake

1 tablespoon butter
2 tablespoons flour
3/4 cup sugar, scant
2 eggs, separated
1/4 cup fresh lemon juice
1 cup milk

Cream butter, flour and sugar. Add beaten egg yolks, lemon juice and milk. Fold in stiffly-beaten egg whites. Bake in 8 inch ungreased dish set in a pan of water at 350 degrees for 35 minutes. When cool, flip cake over onto a plate. Sauce (custard consistency) is now on the top.

Richard Lugar, United States Senator
Indiana

Chicken Cacciatore

2 1/2 - 3 pounds cut-up chicken
2 medium onions sliced
2 cloves garlic minced
1 16-ounce can crushed tomatoes
1 8-ounce can seasoned
    tomato sauce
1 teaspoon salt
1/2 teaspoon celery seed
2 bay leaves
1 teaspoon oregano
1/4 teaspoon pepper
1/4 cup Sauterne wine

Brown chicken in oil. Remove. Add onion and garlic until tender. Combine remaining ingredients except wine. Add chicken; pour sauce over. Simmer 45 minutes. Pour in wine. Cook 20 minutes or until thickened. Remove bay leaves. Mix in 8 ounces cooked shell macaroni if desired.

Betty Lawson, Retired Indiana State Senator
South Bend, Indiana

Lime and Cilantro Grilled Turkey Breast in Pita Pockets

1 1/2 pounds turkey
    breast tenderloins
2 limes, juiced
1 tablespoon paprika
1/2 teaspoon onion salt
1/2 teaspoon garlic salt
1/2 teaspoon cayenne pepper
1/4 teaspoon white pepper
1/2 teaspoon fennel seeds
1/2 teaspoon thyme
10 Pitas, cut in half
1 1/2 cups lettuce, shredded
1 1/2 cups avocado salsa
    (recipe follows)
1 1/2 cups sour cream sauce
    (recipe follows-optional)

Rub turkey with juice of limes. In small bowl, combine paprika, onion salt, garlic salt, cayenne pepper, white pepper, fennel seeds and thyme. Sprinkle mixture over filets. Cover and refrigerate for at least one hour.

Preheat charcoal grill for direct heat cooking. Grill turkey 15-20 minutes until meat thermometer reaches 170 degrees and turkey is no longer pink in the center. Turn turkey tenderloins over halfway through grilling time. Allow turkey to stand 10 minutes. Slice in 1/4 inch strips. Fill each pita half with turkey, lettuce, avocado salsa and, if desired, the sour cream sauce. Serves 10.

Richard Lugar, United States Senator
Indiana

Avocado Salsa

1 avocado, diced
1 lime, juiced
2 tomatoes, seeded and diced
1/2 cup green onion, minced
1/2 cup green pepper, minced
1/2 cup fresh cilantro

In small bowl, combine avocado and lime juice. Stir in tomatoes, green onion, green pepper and cilantro. Cover and refrigerate until ready to use.

Richard Lugar, United States Senator
Indiana

Sour Cream Sauce

1 cup sour cream
1 teaspoon salt
1/4 cup green onion, minced
1/4 cup green chilies, minced
1/4 teaspoon cayenne pepper
1/2 teaspoon black pepper

In small bowl, combine sour cream, salt, onion, chilies, cayenne pepper and black pepper. Cover and refrigerate until ready to use.

Richard Lugar, United States Senator
Indiana

Chicken Fajitas

1 tablespoon chili powder
2 teaspoons vegetable oil
1 pound boneless, skinless
    chicken breasts
4 corn or flour tortillas
    (8 inch), heated
2 cups shredded iceberg lettuce
1 tomato, diced
4 tablespoons prepared salsa
1/2 cup avocado dip or
    prepared guacamole
1/4 cup sour cream

Prepare stovetop grill pan or broiler. Combine chili powder and oil in small bowl. Rub evenly over chicken breasts. Grill or broil 4 inches from heat source for 4 minutes per side.

Slice chicken crosswise into strips. Divide evenly among warm tortillas and top with lettuce, tomato, salsa, avocado dip and sour cream. Makes 4 servings.

Steven Goldsmith, Mayor of Indianapolis, Indiana

Mushroom Chicken Breasts

3 boneless chicken breasts
    split and skinned
1/4 pound butter
1/3 cup white wine
1 can cream of mushroom soup
1 can cream of chicken soup
1 4-ounce can mushroom pieces

Brown chicken in butter; place in flat 2 quart baking dish. Mix wine and soups and pour over chicken. Top with mushrooms and cover with foil. Bake at 350 degrees for 1 hour and 45 minutes. Serve over rice or noodles. Serves 4.

Vaneta Becker, Indiana State Representative
Evansville, Indiana

Chicken Casserole

6-8 boneless chicken breasts
    (cut in half)
1 can cream of mushroom soup
1 can cream of chicken soup
1 cup sour cream
2 boxes Chicken Stove Top
    dressing

Line a pyrex dish with chicken breasts. Bake at 350 degrees for 1/2 hour. Mix soups and sour cream, pour mixture over chicken. Spread dressing (mixed as directed on box) on top of chicken. Cover with foil. Bake at 350 for 45 minutes.

Note: You may wish to NOT pre-bake the chicken. If you don't, then bake for 90 minutes at end.

Sally Rideout Lambert, Indiana State Representative
Booneville, Indiana

Tuna Casserole

Mix together:
1 6-ounce can tuna
1 can cream of mushroom soup
1 cup drained peas
Crushed potato chips

Place a heavy covering of crushed potato chips in a 1 1/2 quart casserole dish, lightly greased. Cover with tuna mixture. Lightly cover tuna mixture with more crushed chips. Bake at 375-400 degrees about 25 minutes; until heated through and lightly browned. Serves 2.

Lawrence L. Buell, Indiana State Representative
Indianapolis, Indiana

Cioppino California

1 - 2 dozen cherrystone clams
1 - 2 pounds filleted fish
1/2 pound shrimp, shelled
    and deveined
1 - 2 pounds mussels
1/4 cup olive oil
1 clove garlic
1 onion, minced
2 16-ounce cans tomatoes
1/2 cup water
1 large can tomato sauce
1 tablespoon basil
1 cup white wine
Tabasco and salt to taste

Heat oil in very large pot. Add garlic and onion and saute. Add tomatoes, water, tomato sauce, basil and wine and stir. Add Tabasco and salt to taste. Simmer for one hour. (Sauce should be thick enough to cling to the fish). Add clams and mussels. Cover and simmer 10 minutes. Add fillets and simmer 10 minutes. Add shrimp. Cioppino is ready to serve when fillets flake easily and clams and mussels open.

Teresa Lubbers, Indiana State Senate
Indianapolis, Indiana

Gnocchi (Italian Potato Dumplings)

2 1/4 pounds mealy
 (Idaho or baking) potatoes
1 3/4 cups flour (divided use)
2 egg yolks
1 teaspoon salt or to taste

In a large saucepan, cook potatoes in their skins in boiling water until very tender. Drain, peel and mash. In a bowl, combine the mashed potatoes with half the flour and the egg yolks. Add salt and season to taste. Knead mixture until a firm, smooth dough is formed.

Divide the dough into pieces. Coat hands well with flour and roll each piece into a narrow sausage shape on a surface sprinkled with most of the remaining flour. Cut these into sections about 1 1/4 inches long. Roll each section on the prongs of a fork while pressing lightly with your thumb to form a shape similar to seashell pasta.

Drop the shaped dumplings onto a well-floured board. At this point, they can be kept for a couple of hours at room temperature.

Bring a large pot of lightly salted water to a boil. Add the dumplings a few at a time and remove them with a slotted spoon as they rise to the surface. Place in a warm serving bowl. You may serve the Gnocchi with a tomato or meat sauce of your choice. Serves about 6.

Jack Cottey, Sheriff of Marion County
Indianapolis, Indiana

Summer Squash Casserole

9 small yellow squash
4 eggs
1 cup sugar
3/4 cup butter or margarine
1/3 medium onion
salt and pepper to taste

Clean and cut squash into small squares. Boil until tender. Drain and mash with potato masher. Add the rest of the ingredients. Bake in an 8 x 8 inch casserole (use non-stick spray) for 1 1/2 hours uncovered until golden brown.

Steven Buyer, United States House of Representatives
Kokomo, Indiana

Portabella su Excclancia (for two)

6 ounces Portabella mushrooms
(sliced)
1 large clove of garlic
5 tablespoons Spanish olive oil
1 teaspoon salt
cracked pepper
1 1/2 tablespoons red wine

Finely grate garlic and reserve in a bowl; save husk for frying pan. Wash mushrooms and dry on paper towels-liberally sprinkle with salt and pepper. Pour olive oil into heavy frying pan and heat over medium-low heat. Throw garlic husk into oil and saute until brown (then remove husk). Add mushrooms and reduce heat to low-medium. Saute 3 minutes on each side. Add garlic gratings. Add wine and raise heat to High. When at a boil, reduce to medium and saute until 1/2 wine evaporates. Serve hot immediately; serves 2.

David McIntosh, United States House of Representatives
Muncie, Indiana

Mississippi Mud Cake

2 cups sugar
4 eggs
1/3 cup cocoa
3 teaspoons vanilla
5 ounces miniature marshmallows
1 cup butter
1 1/2 cups flour
1/4 teaspoon salt
1 cup nuts

Cake: Cream sugar and butter and add eggs. Sift flour, cocoa and salt together and add to creamed mixture. Add vanilla and nuts. Pour into greased and floured 9 x 13 inch pan and bake 35 minutes at 300 degrees. Remove from oven and put marshmallows over the top and return to 350 degree oven about 5 minutes or until marshmallows melt. Cool cake one hour before frosting.

Frosting:
1/2 cup cocoa
1 1-pound box powdered sugar
2 sticks butter or margarine-melted
1/3 cup milk
1 teaspoon vanilla
1 cup nuts

Frosting: To make frosting, sift sugar and cocoa together; mix with melted butter. Add milk, vanilla and nuts. Frosting is soft but will firm up.

Irene Heffley, Indiana State Representative
Indianapolis, Indiana

Cheese Cake with Sour Cream Topping

27 ounces of cream cheese
3 eggs
juice of 1 lemon
1 package of Zwieback
    teething crackers
scant teaspoon cinnamon
1 stick of butter
1/2 pint of sour cream
1 3/4 cups sugar

Crust: Roll Zwieback very fine and mix in 3/4 cup of sugar, adding a scant teaspoon of cinnamon. Melt butter in top of double boiler and add 3/4 of the butter to the crumb mixture. Take springform pan and butter all around sides and bottom. Pat the Zwieback crumbs into it, starting on sides and then cover the bottom. Set aside.

Filling: Place cheese in bowl, add 1 cup of sugar, let mixer turn and add whole eggs one at a time until all are in, then add lemon juice. Pour mixture onto crust and place in preheated oven at 375 degrees, baking for 20 minutes.

Topping: Beat sour cream with 2 tablespoons of sugar. Pull cake out of the oven (leave on rack) and spoon the sour cream on top of it. Sprinkle it with a few of the crust crumbs (which you have saved for this). Push back into oven, let bake about 10-15 minutes until solid.

Remove from oven. Let cool in pan. When cooled, put into refrigerator until ready to serve. This can be cut into twelve to sixteen thin slices. In preparation for doing so, take off side of springform, leave cake on the bottom of the pan and place on platter.

Tim Roemer, United States House of Representatives
South Bend, Indiana

Perfect Chocolate Cake

1 cup cocoa
2 cups boiling water
1 cup butter, softened
2 1/2 cups sugar
4 eggs
2 3/4 cups flour
2 teaspoons baking soda
1/2 teaspoon baking powder
1/2 teaspoon salt
1 1/2 teaspoons vanilla extract

Perfect Chocolate Frosting:
6 ounces semi-sweet
   chocolate chips
1/2 cup half & half
3/4 cup butter
2 1/2 cups sifted powdered sugar

Cake: Combine cocoa and boiling water, stirring until smooth; set aside. Cream butter; gradually add sugar, beating well. Add eggs, one at a time, beating well after each addition. Combine flour and next 3 ingredients; add to creamed mixture alternately with cocoa mixture, beating at low speed, beginning and ending with flour mixture. Stir in vanilla. DO NOT OVERBEAT. Pour batter into 3 greased and floured 9 inch round cake pans. Bake at 350 degrees for 20 minutes (or until toothpick inserted in center comes out clean). Cool in pans 10 minutes. Remove from pans and cool completely. Spread whipped cream filling between layers; spread Perfect Chocolate Frosting on top and sides. Chill until serving time. Yield: One 3-layer cake.

Whipped Cream Filling: 1 cup whipping cream and 1 teaspoon vanilla extract beaten until foamy; gradually add powdered sugar (1/4 cup, sifted) until soft peaks form. Chill.

Frosting: Combine first 3 ingredients in a heavy saucepan; cook over medium heat, stirring until chocolate melts. Remove from heat, add powdered sugar, mixing well. Set saucepan in ice, and beat at low speed until frosting holds its shape and loses its gloss. Add more drops half & half, if needed, to make spreading consistency.

Note: This is our daughter, Lisa's, favorite birthday cake.

Marcia Coats, Wife of United States Senator Dan Coats,
Indiana

Light (but Luscious) Devil's Food Cake

1 3/4 cups sifted cake flour
3/4 cup sugar
1/2 cup unsweetened cocoa
1 teaspoon baking soda
1/4 teaspoon baking powder
1/4 teaspoon salt
1 cup water
1 cup non-fat mayonnaise
2 tablespoons vegetable oil
    (may substitute natural
    applesauce)
1 teaspoon vanilla extract
2 1-ounce squares semi-sweet
    chocolate, melted
1 egg
vegetable cooking spray
1 tablespoon powdered sugar
1 tablespoon unsweetened cocoa

Combine first 6 ingredients in a bowl; stir well. Combine water and next 5 ingredients; add to dry ingredients, stirring just until dry ingredients are moistened (batter will not be smooth). Pour into 9 inch round cake pan coated with cooking spray. Bake at 350 degrees for 45 minutes or until a wooden pick inserted in center comes out clean. Cool in pan 10 minutes on a wire rack; remove from pan. Cool completely on a wire rack.

To garnish, fold 2 (10-inch) pieces of aluminum foil in half lengthwise; lay 1 piece over cake leaving a 1 1/2-inch strip of cake exposed. Sift powdered sugar over exposed area. Lift and move foil to expose another 1 1/2-inch of cake. Shield sugared area with the second piece of foil. Sift cocoa over exposed area. Repeat procedure alternating sugar and cocoa. Top with 3 strawberry halves in center of cake.

Scott Newman, Marion County Prosecutor
Natalie Newman, Health Care Fraud Investigator
Indianapolis, Indiana

Carrot Cake

1 cup flour
3/4 cup sugar
1 teaspoon baking powder
1/2 teaspoon cinnamon
1/2 teaspoon salt
5/8 cup oil (1/2 cup plus 1/8 cup)
2 eggs
1 cup grated carrots
small can crushed pineapple
  (drained)
1/2 cup roughly chopped walnuts

Put all dry ingredients in food processor and mix 5-10 seconds. Add eggs and oil and mix 30 seconds (will be very thick). Add carrots and pineapple and mix thoroughly. Add nuts and mix only to distribute. Bake in greased pan about one hour at 350 degrees.

Frosting: 3 ounces butter, 1/2 teaspoon vanilla, 3 ounces cream cheese, 6 ounce confectioner's sugar, (3 heaping tablespoons). Process butter, cheese and vanilla for about 20 seconds. Add sugar and continue mixing. When cake is cold, pat all over top. The recipe is geared for a food processor; however, it can be adapted to a mixer.

Carl Levin, United States Senator
Michigan

Cherry Dessert

2 cans Thank-you Cherry
    Pie filling
1 box white or yellow cake mix
1 cup melted butter or margarine
1 cup chopped nuts

Grease 9 x 13 inch pan with margarine. Put pie filling in pan and pour dry cake mix directly from box over pie filling. Pour melted margarine over cake mix and sprinkle nuts on top. Bake 45 minutes at 350 degrees.

Kathy Kreag Richardson, Indiana State Representative
Noblesville, Indiana

Cedar Hill Peach Cobbler

1 stick melted margarine
1 cup granulated sugar
1 cup self-rising flour
1 cup milk
1 large can sliced peaches (drained)

Combine first four ingredients, add peaches and mix. Put in a large baking dish. Bake at 350 degrees until golden brown; approximately 1 hour.

Patricia L. Miller, Indiana State Senator
Indianapolis, Indiana

Lemon Pie

1 cup sugar
1/3 cup flour
1/4 teaspoon salt
1 1/2 cups milk
2 eggs (separated)
1/3 cup lemon juice
1 teaspoon butter
1 8-inch graham cracker pie shell
1/4 cup sugar

Separate egg yolks from whites. Beat yolks with fork. Set aside. Blend sugar with flour and salt in a saucepan. Add milk. Stir until mixture is smooth. Place over a low flame. Stir constantly until mixture thickens to a paste. Place 2 tablespoons of the hot mixture into the well-beaten egg yolks. Mix and pour egg yolks into the balance of the hot mixture. Stir. Add butter. Stir. Add lemon juice. Stir. Allow to cool.

Beat egg whites. Add sugar and continue to beat until mixture has the consistency for meringue. Pour cooled mixture into graham cracker crust. Add top layer of egg whites (meringue). Place in oven. Bake until evenly brown at 350 degrees. Serves 6.

Vernon G. Smith, Ph.D., Indiana State Representative
Gary, Indiana

Pecan Pie

1/2 cup sugar
1/4 cup margarine
1 cup light corn syrup
3 eggs
1 cup pecans (whole)
1/4 teaspoon salt (if desired)

Cream sugar and butter; add syrup and salt; beat well; beat in eggs, one at a time; add pecans. Pour into a 9 inch pastry-lined pie pan. Bake at 350 degrees for 1 hour and 10 minutes or until knife comes out clean.

Nancy and Lee Hamilton,
United States House of Representatives
Jeffersonville, Indiana

Rock Hermits

Step 1—Mix 1 teaspoon soda in 6 teaspoons boiling water. Pour over 2 pounds chopped dates. Set aside.

Step 2—Mix in mixing bowl:
3 cups sugar
2 cup shortening

Step 3—Add:
1 teaspoon cinnamon
1 teaspoon ground cloves
1 teaspoon allspice
6 beaten eggs
5 cups flour

Step—Stir in dates and 2 cups English walnuts. Drop by teaspoon on greased cookie sheet. Bake 10-12 minutes or until lightly browned.

Thomas J. Wyss, Indiana State Senate
Fort Wayne, Indiana

Oatmeal Cookies/Apple-Oatmeal Cookies

3 cups flour
1 teaspoon baking soda
1 1/2 teaspoon cinnamon
1/2 teaspoon nutmeg
1 cup butter
1/2 cup shortening
1 cup sugar
1 cup light brown sugar
1 cup sour cream
2 eggs
1 teaspoon vanilla
1 cup raisins
3 cups oatmeal
1 cup chopped nuts

Sift flour and spices and soda together 3 times. Cream shortenings and sugars. Add sour cream, eggs, and vanilla. Stir in flour mixture, then oatmeal, raisins, and nuts. Preheat oven to 375 degrees. Drop onto greased cookie sheet. Bake about 10 minutes.

*Apple-Oatmeal Cookies Variation: Omit sour cream. Add 1/4 cup light brown sugar and 2 tablespoons milk or cream. Omit vanilla and add 1 cup chopped apples.

Mae Dickinson, Indiana State Representative
Indianapolis, Indiana

Caramels

4 cups granulated sugar
2 cups light Karo syrup
6 cups light cream
1/8 teaspoon salt

Mix Karo syrup, salt and sugar with 2 cups cream; heat to soft ball stage (234° to 240°F). Add 2 cups of cream slowly and continue to cook to soft ball stage. Add last 2 cups of cream and cook to hard ball stage (250° to 265°F). Pour immediately onto a greased cookie pan. One end of pan can be covered with walnuts which will help loosen caramels from pan. When cool, cut into squares.

This recipe is one my grandmother always made and is a tradition in our family.

Frank O'Bannon, Lieutenant Governor of Indiana
Indianapolis, Indiana

Peaches and Cream

3/4 cup flour
1 teaspoon baking powder
1 small package instant
   vanilla pudding, dry
4-5 medium peaches,
   sliced and sweetened
3 tablespoons soft margarine
1 egg
1/2 cup milk

Cream Topping:
8 ounces cream cheese
   (low-fat may be used)
1/2 cup sugar
3 tablespoons peach juice

Spray 9 inch pie pan with non-stick spray. Combine all ingredients except peaches to make thick dough or batter. Spread in pie pan to make "crust." Place drained peaches over batter, as if filling a pie. Mix the topping. Spread topping over peaches. Sprinkle with 1 tablespoon sugar and 1/2 teaspoon cinnamon. Bake at 350 degrees for 30-35 minutes or until crust is brown.

Bill Friend, Indiana State Representative
Macy, Indiana

Mark's Mom's Banana Ice Cream

4 bananas
1 teaspoon vanilla extract
fresh lemon juice
1/2 cup lowfat milk

Peel bananas, cut out tips and brown spots, remove strings. Squeeze lemon juice over bananas, wrap in plastic bag and freeze until solid. Chill 4 champagne glasses or bowls.

Near serving time, cut bananas into small pieces. Blend in food processor or blender with vanilla extract and milk until very smooth. If mixture becomes too thick, add more milk. Pour into chilled glasses or bowls. Return to freezer for no longer than two hours. Garnish with strawberries, kiwi slices, or other fresh fruit and serve. Serves 4.

NOTE: 12 large strawberries may be added to give this ice cream dessert a pink color. Great snack while watching election returns!!!

Mark R. Kruzan, Indiana State Senate
Bloomington, Indiana

Wassail

4 cups pineapple juice
4 cups cider
1 cup orange juice
1 1/2 cup apricot nectar
6 inch cinnamon stick
1 teaspoon whole cloves

Combine all ingredients. Bring to a boil and simmer 20 minutes. Strain before serving. Makes 9 cups.

This cold weather beverage is a Coats' family favorite.

Dan Coats, United States Senator
Indiana

Indian Green Chutney

2 bunches parsley, no stems
1 bunch scallions, some green
2-3 hot chili peppers,
    seeds removed
1 small piece fresh ginger, peeled
1/4 cup unsalted peanuts
3 tablespoons brown sugar
    (or Indian jaggery)
3 tablespoons coconut
2 tablespoons sesame seed
2 tablespoons lemon juice
    (or mango powder)
1 tablespoon coriander and
    cumin powder
1/2 teaspoon hing (asafoetide
    powder) (can be omitted)
1/2 tablespoon turmeric
2 teaspoons cumin seed

Place all the dry ingredients in a food processor or blender; blend very well. Add the greens and blend till very smooth. Add more lemon, brown sugar and green chilies as desired. Note: This works best in a food processor and with great difficulty in a blender.

Arlen Specter, United States Senator
Pennsylvania

Basic Nutburger Recipe

7 tablespoons butter
    or margarine
1/3 cup onions or shallots
1 teaspoon minced garlic
3/4 cup finely chopped pecans
1 1/2 cups fresh bread crumbs
1 1/2 cups grated Gruyere cheese
    (or brick or farmer's cheese)
salt and pepper to taste
3/4 teaspoon dried rosemary,
    crushed well
2 eggs
1/2 cup catsup

Melt the butter in a heavy skillet over medium heat. Add the chopped onions and saute, stirring 2 to 3 minutes. Add the garlic and pecans and stir 2 minutes more. Toss in the bread crumbs and cheese and stir until the cheese has almost melted, about 2 more minutes. Remove the mixture from heat and add salt, pepper and crushed rosemary. Stir to mix. Let cool to handle. Stir in eggs and catsup to meatloaf or burger consistency. The mix best resembles ground meat if the nuts are very finely ground in a food processor and Gruyere cheese gives the best taste. Bake meatloaf at 350 degrees for 30 minutes or pan fry burgers with a little oil.

Andy Jacobs, Jr., United States House of Representatives
Indianapolis, Indiana

Lobby, Lobby, Lobby

Our Indiana Breast Cancer Coalition traveled back to Washington and the Annual Meeting of the National Breast Cancer Coalition during April, 1995.

Our bus trip was underwritten by the Indiana Breast Cancer Coalition and the women of Delta Delta Delta Sorority and the men of Sigma Chi Fraternity, Lambda Chapter, both of Indiana University Bloomington Campus.

Pictured left to right: Carole Cross, Betty Green, Representative Tim Roemer, Connie Rufenbarger and Barbara Jones.

Pictured left to right: Carol Rogers, Claudia Kruggel, Claudia Lord, Representative Dan Burton, Michele Wood, Kathleen Maloney, Pam Kolter.

"We all want to find the cures for cancer. It is up to us to provide the resources to continue I.U.'s role in that search."

Marilyn Tucker Quayle

"Cancer is a crafty and treacherous foe. It must be attacked in a comprehensive and sophisticated fashion. We have new ideas that can cure this awful disease, but to do that, frankly we need more research support."

George W. Sledge, Jr., M.D.

I.U. CANCER CENTER

JUST

Marilyn Tucker Quayle

Chair, Cancer Leadership Committee,
Indiana University School of Medicine Capital Campaign
Carmel, Indiana

Persimmon Pudding

2 cups persimmon pulp
2 cups sugar
2 eggs beaten
1 3/4 cups flour - sifted
2 teaspoons baking powder
1 cup half & half
1 cup buttermilk
1 teaspoon baking soda
1/3 cup melted butter
dash of cinnamon

Combine pulp, sugar and eggs. Stir flour with baking powder. Add to pulp mix with combination of half & half, buttermilk, butter and baking soda. Mix well. Pour in 13 x 9 inch pan and bake at 325 degrees for one hour.

Dan Quayle

Former Vice President of the United States
Carmel, Indiana

Peach Cobbler

1 cup all-purpose flour
1/3 - 2/3 cup sugar
1 teaspoon baking powder
1/4 cup sugar
1 tablespoon cornstarch
1/2 teaspoon ground cinnamon
3 tablespoons margarine or butter
1 beaten egg
3 tablespoons milk
1/4 cup water
4 cups fresh or frozen peaches
   or unsweetened peach slices

Prepare filling: In a saucepan combine sugar and cornstarch. Add water. Stir peaches. Cook and stir until thickened and bubbly. Keep hot.

For topping: Mix flour, 1/4 cup sugar, baking powder and if desired, cinnnamon. Cut in margarine until mixture resembles coarse crumbs. Combine egg and milk. Add to flour mixture, stirring just to moisten.

Transfer filling to an 8 x 8 x 3 inch baking dish. Drop topping in 6 mounds atop hot filling. Bake in 400 degree oven 20-25 minutes or until a toothpick inserted into topping comes out clean.

INDIANA UNIVERSITY
CANCER CENTER

INDIANA
UNIVERSITY
MEDICAL
CENTER

Indiana University School of Medicine has earned international acclaim for our many contributions to the study, detection and treatment of cancer. While we are proud of these achievements, what drives our efforts is the desire to rid the world of cancer. In this pursuit, we are inspired by our patients—who are our partners in exploring new, potentially life-saving treatments—and by the medical students, residents, oncology fellows and visiting professors whose intellectual curiosity invigorates us.

The Indiana University Cancer Center's interdisciplinary research programs in breast, gastrointestinal, gynecologic, head and neck, melanoma, neurologic, pediatric, thoracic and urologic cancers unite experts from each appropriate medical specialty to confer regularly with each other—and with each patient— to design the treatment plan that best suits the needs of the patient.

Indiana University Cancer Care Building

With expected occupancy in late spring of 1996, new construction of this four-story clinical cancer building will unite the adult outpatient cancer clinics and treatment facilities in one building. The IU Cancer Care Building is being constructed on top of the existing Radiation Therapy Building at the corner of Barnhill Drive and Michigan Street at the IU Medical Center. This building will ad 89,000 gross square feet of teaching and clinical research space above the renovated radiation oncology clinic in the basement.

When completed, the first floor will provide space for the Radiation Oncology departmental offices, the Hoosier Oncology Group, a 90-seat auditorium, a patient library, education and outreach center, and meeting space available for community and cancer support meetings. Other multidisciplinary cancer clinics housed on the second floor of this building include: Breast and Gynecologic, both located in the Women's Center, Gastrointestinal, Head and Neck, Lung (Thoracic), Melanoma, Neurologic, and Urologic. The general Hematology/Oncology clinic and laboratory, chemotherapy suites and clinical research offices will occupy the third floor. IU Cancer Center administrative offices and cancer faculty offices will be situated on the fourth floor. Patient parking will be available in lots across Barnhill to the west and across Michigan to the south.

Basic Cancer Research Building

With expected completion anticipated in late 1997, new construction of a 100,00 square foot laboratory building will bring together in a single facility the adult and pediatric cancer investigators, along with shared equipment and core facilities. Located at the corner of Barnhill Drive and Walnut Street across from Riley Hospital for Children at the IU Medical Center, the Basic Cancer Research Building will have four floors and a basement, housing the adult Hematology/Oncology cancer laboratories, including the Elks Cancer Research Center, the Walther Oncology Center, and the pediatric cancer laboratories of the Wells ResearchCenter.

By uniting scientists from a variety of disciplines now scattered across campus, the new cancer research building will facilitate communication and collaboration among cancer researchers and enhance the IU Cancer Center's multidisciplinary approach.

Funding for these two new cancer buildings has been provided through the Cancer Initiative of the IU School of Medicine's capital campaign. Many generous friends have given of their time talents and financial resources to make these new buildings a reality. The IU Cancer Center and School of Medicine are deeply grateful for their contributions.

These new cancer facilities are more than building: rather, they are building blocks toward expanded research and eventual cures.

"Expanding our facilities will help expand our search for cures,"
Stephen D. Williams, M.D.,
Director of the Indiana University Cancer Center.

Baked Stuffed Mushrooms

1 pound mushrooms with
    1-2 inch caps
1/4 cup chopped onion
1/2 cup biscuit mix
3 tablespoons Parmesan cheese
1 tablespoon chopped parsley
1 pound ground sausage

Clean mushrooms; remove stems. Place caps open side up on baking tray. Set aside. Finely chop mushroom stems and onion. Brown sausage, mushroom stems and onion. Combine mixture with biscuit mix, Parmesan cheese and seasonings. Fill caps with stuffing mixture. Pack cups firmly. Sprinkle with paprika. Bake at 400 degrees for 15 minutes. Serve warm.

Vivian Murphy, R.N., Chemotherapy Nurse
Indiana University

Belgium Summer Sausage

5 pounds ground beef
5 rounded teaspoons tender
    quick salt
2 1/2 teaspoons coarse
    ground pepper
2 1/2 teaspoons garlic salt
2 1/2 teaspoons mustard seed
1 teaspoon hickory salt

Add together all above ingredients. Mix each day for 3 days. (Keep refrigerated in an air-tight container.) Make into rolls on 4th day and put on broiler pan, sides not touching. Bake 8 hours at 175 degrees or at 250 degrees for 6 hours. Remove from oven and cool, then wrap in freezer paper and place in freezer or refrigerator.

Linda Marquis, Secretary, Division of Hematology/Oncology
Indiana University

Cool Fruit Dip

Variety of fruits chunked: whole
    strawberries, banana, apple,
    melon, pineapple
1/2 cup sour cream
2/3 cup softened cream cheese
1/2 cup powdered sugar

Arrange fruit chunks on platter and set aside. Blend together remaining ingredients in small bowl. Put out toothpicks to serve. Kids love this simple dessert!

Pamela Perry, Medical Center Relations
Indiana University

Cape Cod Fish Chowder

1 large onion, chopped
4 tablespoons (1/2 stick) butter
    or margarine
3 (4 cups) large potatoes, pared
    and sliced very thin
1-2 teaspoons salt
1/2 teaspoon dried basil
1/4 teaspoon ground
    black pepper
2 8-ounce bottles clam juice
1 pound "white fish" fillets (cod,
    haddock, or orange roughy),
    cut into 1-inch cubes
2 6 1/2-ounce cans minced clams
    with liquid
1 can (12 or 16 ounces) whole
    kernel corn, drained
1 tall can evaporated milk

In a soup kettle, saute onion in butter or margarine until soft. Add potatoes, salt, basil, pepper and clam juice. Cover; simmer 15 minutes. Place cubed fish on top of potatoes. Cover. Simmer 15 minutes or until potatoes are done and fish flakes. Stir in clams, corn and evaporated milk. Cover. Heat just to boiling. Serves 4.

Patricia D. Bledsoe, C.C.S.W., Social Worker
Department of Hematology/Oncology
Indiana University

Potato Soup

2 cans undiluted chicken broth
2 cans water
1 cup chopped celery
1 cup chopped onion
3 cups cubed, peeled potatoes
1 tablespoon lemon juice
2 bay leaves
1 chicken bouillon cube
1 teaspoon sweet basil
1 teaspoon Nature's Seasoning
1/4 teaspoon rubbed sage
1/4 teaspoon rosemary
1/4 teaspoon thyme
1 tablespoon parsley
black pepper to taste

Combine all ingredients in large pot. Bring to a boil, reduce heat and simmer until potatoes are tender.

Rebecca Lawrence, Projects and Grants Coordinator
Indiana University Cancer Center

Cecilia's Gumbo

1 whole chicken
1 cup oil/bacon fat combination
1 cup flour
2 cups chopped onion
1 cup chopped celery
1 cup chopped bell pepper
1/4 cup minced garlic
1/2 -1 pound sliced smoked
    sausage
2-3 pounds raw shrimp
green onions, chopped
parsley, chopped
salt to taste
1 bay leaf
cayenne to taste
thyme to taste

Early in the day or the day before, boil chicken to make a good chicken stock using celery, carrots, onions, peppercorns, etc., but no salt. (Canned chicken soup may be substituted, but it is not as good). Pull chicken off the bones. Reserve the stock. Set all aside. Next, make a roux as follows: put oil in heavy pot over medium-high heat. Slowly whisk in flour, stir constantly until oil/flour mixture becomes caramel colored brown. Do not allow to scorch. Be patient about achieving proper color. Once the roux is brown, add chopped onions, celery, pepper and garlic. Saute 5-10 minutes. Add bay leaf, pinch of thyme, basil if desired. Slowly add ladles of hot chicken stock, stirring in. Amount of stock added depends on how thick you want the gumbo (about 8-10 cups). Mix thoroughly. Add sliced sausage and small chicken pieces. Cook over low heat about 30 minutes to one hour. Add chopped parsley and green onions. Add salt, cayenne pepper to taste. Add shrimp and cook about 5 more minutes. Adjust seasoning. Serve over cooked rice. Note: Best made ahead of time. Freezes well (remove bay leaf if freezing).

Michael Darling, Associate Director for Administration
Indiana University Cancer Center

Grandmother Ward's Poor Man's Loaf

1 1/2 cups hot water
2 tablespoons shortening
1 1/2 teaspoons salt
2 tablespoons sugar
1 package yeast
1/2 cup warm water
5 cups flour (more or less)

Melt together hot water, shortening, salt and sugar. Crumble yeast in 1/2 cup warm water, let stand 5 minutes. Add to above mixture. Mix enough flour into mixture to knead. Let raise in greased bowl covered with a warm moist towel. Raise until 3 times the size of the loaf, punch down and allow to rise (repeat twice). Put in loaf pans and allow to rise again. Bake at 350 degrees for about 25 minutes or until crust is brown.

Kim Wagler, R.N., Breast Cancer Survivor
Nurse Coordinator, Breast Care and Research Center
Indiana University

Nut or Poppy Seed Roll

Dough:
6 cups flour
2 pounds margarine
2 tablespoons sugar
1/2 cup sour cream
5 egg yolks
2 packages dry yeast

Filling:
1 1/2 pounds pecans, walnuts or
    freshly ground poppy seed
1 cup sugar
1 teaspoon vanilla
1 stick margarine, melted
1 egg

Mix flour, margarine and sugar like pie dough. Prepare 2 packages of dry yeast according to package. Make a well in the margarine, flour mixture; fill with prepared yeast, sour cream and egg yolks. Mix into a ball and cut into five pieces. Let rest for 10 minutes. Take one piece and roll it out on a floured board into a rectangle shape about 1/4 inch thick. Spread 1/5 of filling with 1 inch border. Roll from long side, seal ends and make 5 slits in top. Bake in 350 degree oven for 45 minutes until golden brown. Cool, slice and serve.

Filling: Mix together and add honey and coconut to taste. Add milk to moisten. Variation - Apple Strudel: In middle, spread bread crumbs, chopped apple, sugar and cinnamon. Apple strudel can be frozen before baking. If baked frozen, just bake a little longer.

Donna Mozdian, Community Outreach Coordinator
Cancer Information Service of Indiana and Michigan
National Cancer Institute

Sweet Potato Rolls

12 ounces sweet potatoes
  (scrubbed)
1 egg, slightly beaten
3 tablespoons honey
1 tablespoon butter, softened
2 teaspoons salt
1/4 teaspoon pepper
1 package dry yeast
3 1/2 cups flour
1 egg white, lightly beaten

Cook potatoes in boiling water until tender. Remove potatoes from water and reserve 1/2 cup of liquid. Peel potatoes and mash until smooth. Do not puree. Cool. Stir in egg, honey, butter, salt and pepper. Heat 1/2 cup reserved liquid to very warm (105-115 degrees). Dissolve yeast in liquid in large bowl. Stir in potato mixture and enough flour to make a soft dough. Knead until smooth, adding flour as needed. Place in greased bowl, cover with plastic wrap and refrigerate over night. Remove and let stand at room temperature for two hours. Punch down and knead 1 minute. Divide dough into 24 pieces and shape each piece into a ball. Place 2 balls per cup into a greased muffin tin. Let rise at room temperature for 1 hour. Brush top with egg white. Bake in 400 degree oven for 20 minutes or until golden brown.

Claudette Einhorn, wife of Lawrence H. Einhorn, M.D.
Distinguished Professor of Medicine
Division of Hematology/Oncology
Indiana University

Yeast Dough (for rolls or bread)

1 3/4 cups milk
1/3 cup water
1 package yeast
1 teaspoon sugar
1 1/2 teaspoons salt
1/3 cup sugar
1 heaping tablespoon
  shortening
1 egg
4 1/2 to 5 cups flour

Scald milk. Combine and let rise, water, 1 teaspoon sugar and yeast in a cup. Dissolve in scalded milk, salt, sugar and shortening. Add to milk mixture 1 cup flour and egg. Stir in yeast mixture. Add the rest of the flour until dough stiffens when spoon is removed. Cover with towel. Let rise 1 hour. Knead dough on floured surface; place in bowl. Cover with towel; let rise 1 hour. Knead dough on floured surface. Roll dough out. Shape into bread or your favorite shape rolls. Place on greased cookie sheet or loaf pan. Bake at 400 degrees; rolls 8 minutes, bread about 30 minutes.

Vickie Firkins, Program Director, Adult Ambulatory Services
University Hospital
Indiana University

Marinated Carrot Salad

2 pounds carrots,
    sliced lengthwise
1 medium size sweet onion,
    chopped
1 small green pepper, chopped
1 can tomato soup
1/2 cup vegetable oil
1/2 cup sugar
3/4 cup vinegar
1 teaspoon hot or spicy mustard
1 teaspoon Worcestershire sauce
1 teaspoon salt
1 teaspoon pepper

Cook carrots until just tender. Drain and cool. Add onions and mix remaining ingredients. Marinate overnight in refrigerator.

Karen McCracken, CTR
Medical Center Cancer Registry
Indiana University

Spinach Salad

1-pound package fresh spinach,
    rinsed and dried
2 cups bean sprouts, washed
    and drained
8 ounces water chestnuts, sliced
    and drained
4 hard boiled eggs, sliced
1/4 cup green onions
1/2 pound bacon, fried and
    crumbled
1 cup fresh mushrooms, sliced

Dressing:
3/4 cup sugar
1/4 cup vinegar
1/4 cup salad oil
1/3 cup catsup
1 teaspoon salt
1 teaspoon Worcestershire Sauce

Tear spinach into large bowl. Toss together remaining salad ingredients. Mix together all dressing ingredients. Pour over salad just before serving.

Christie M. Traycoff, Assistant Scientist
Division of Hematology/Oncology
Indiana University

Pasta Salad

1 pound spaghetti
1 medium green pepper
1 large tomato
5-6 large fresh sliced mushrooms
sliced black olives (optional)
sliced pepperoni (optional)
1 16-ounce jar Kraft Zesty
    Italian dressing
1 jar McCormick's Salad Supreme
    (spice)

Cook pasta and drain. Combine pasta and vegetables. Add salad dressing and Salad Supreme to taste (will require almost entire jar of both). Best to chill for 2 hours before serving. Serve cold.

Marci Pittman, Administrative Secretary
Breast Care and Research Center
Indiana University

Strawberry Pretzel Salad

1 1/2 cups crushed pretzels
3 tablespoons sugar
1 stick margarine, melted
1 8-ounce package cream cheese,
    softened
1 cup sugar
1 small carton Cool Whip
2 3-ounce packages strawberry
    gelatin
2 cups boiling water
1/2 cup cold water
2 10-ounce packages frozen
    strawberries

Mix together crushed pretzels, 3 tablespoons sugar and margarine. Reserve 1/2 cup of mixture and pat remaining mixture into a 9 by 13-inch pan. Bake at 350 degrees for 10 minutes. Combine cream cheese, 1 cup sugar and Cool Whip. Spread over cool pretzel crust. Dissolve gelatin in boiling water, add cold water and strawberries. Stir until strawberries are thawed. When gelatin starts to thicken, pour over cream cheese layer. Chill overnight. Top with Cool Whip and remaining pretzel mixture.

Janet L. Harlan, R.N., Oncology Nurse Clinician
Kathy Bryant, R.N., Clinical Nurse Coordinator,
Head & Neck/ Melanoma Oncology Programs
Indiana University

Sweet and Crunchy Sauerkraut Salad

1 2-pound bag sauerkraut, rinsed
    and drained
1 cup finely chopped celery
1 green pepper, finely chopped
    (1/2 cup)
1/4 cup chopped onion
1 cup sugar
1/2 cup cider vinegar
1/2 cup salad oil (good quality)

Combine vegetables and dressing. Cover and chill for 3-24 hours.

Charlotte L. Spring, Administrative Assistant
Department of Radiation Oncology
Indiana University

Cheese Grits

1 cup grits
3 1/2 cups water
1 1/2 teaspoons salt
1/2 cup butter
2 1/2 cups grated Cheddar
    cheese
1 teaspoon sugar
1 teaspoon baking powder
1/2 cup whole milk
4 eggs

Bring water to boil; add grits and salt. Cook for 5 minutes and remove from heat. Add butter and cheese immediately and stir to melt. Add sugar, baking powder, cheese and milk. Beat eggs until frothy and fold into grits. Fill casserole 2/3 full. Bake at 325 degrees for 45 minutes or more until center is firm and top is nicely browned. Great with barbecue chicken and pork or for brunch.

Julie Walsh Seiler, Senior Associate Director, Cancer Initiative
School of Medicine Capital Campaign
Indiana University

Wild Rice with Mushrooms and Almonds

1 cup uncooked wild rice
1/4 cup butter or margarine
1/2 cup slivered almonds
2 tablespoons snipped chives
    or green onions
1 8-ounce can mushroom slices
    or fresh sliced
3 cups chicken broth

Heat oven to 325 degrees. Wash and drain rice. Melt butter in large skillet. Add rice, almonds, chives and mushrooms. Cook and stir until almonds are golden brown—about 20 minutes. Pour rice mixture into ungreased 2 1/2-quart casserole. Heat chicken broth to boiling; stir into rice mixture. Cover tightly and bake about 1/2 hour or until all liquid is absorbed and rice is tender and fluffy.

Pamela Perry, Medical Center Relations
Indiana University

Chicken Tetrazzini

1 onion minced
garlic salt to taste
2 tablespoons margarine
4 cups milk
2 teaspoons steak sauce
4 cans cream of mushroom soup
4 cans cream of chicken soup
1 1/2 pounds shredded
    Cheddar cheese
2 1/2 quarts cooked chicken,
    diced
1 1/2 cups spaghetti

Cook onion in butter for 5 minutes; add steak sauce, milk, soups and 1/2 of the cheese. Cook until smooth. Add chicken, garlic salt (if desired) and mix well. Cook and drain spaghetti. Rinse in hot water and put in large, shallow baking pan. Pour chicken mixture over spaghetti. Sprinkle with remaining cheese. Bake at 375 degrees. Serves 25.

Linda Marquis, Secretary, Division of Hematology/Oncology
Indiana University

Linguini and Vegetables

8 ounces linguini or other pasta
2 tablespoons olive oil
1 clove garlic, crushed
1 small can diced tomatoes,
    with basil or hot peppers
3/4 cup sliced zucchini
1/2 cup fresh sliced mushrooms
1/3 cup diced onion
3 tablespoons diced
    green pepper
1 tablespoon parsley
1 teaspoon dried oregano
1 teaspoon dried basil
1/4 teaspoon salt
1/8 teaspoon pepper
1 cup shredded Provolone,
    or 3/4 cup Gorgonzola
    for more flavor
3 tablespoons Parmesan cheese

Cook pasta. Cook olive oil and garlic and onions until tender. Stir in remaining vegetables and seasonings. Saute until crisp–tender (4 minutes). Drain pasta and arrange on serving platter. Combine vegetable mix and cheese. Spoon over pasta. Toss before serving.

Beth and Hal Broxmeyer Ph.D.
Mary Margaret Walther Professor of Medicine,
Professor of Microbiology and Immunology
Scientific Director of the Walther Oncology Center
Indiana University

Manicotti

1 pound ground beef
1 clove garlic, crushed
1 cup creamed cottage cheese
    (8 ounces)
4 ounces shredded
    Mozzarella cheese
1/2 teaspoon salt
1/2 cup Hellmann's mayonnaise
10 manicotti noodles
1 16-ounce jar Ragu
    spaghetti sauce
Parmesan cheese
1/2 teaspoon oregano

Brown beef and garlic. Mix cheeses, salt and
mayonnaise. Stir in beef. Cook manicotti in boiling
salt water for 3 minutes. Drain and rinse in cold
water. Fill manicotti noodles with meat and cheese
filling. Place in 11 x 13 inch glass baking dish.
Cover with Ragu sauce. Sprinkle with oregano and
Parmesan cheese. Cover with foil and bake at
350 degrees for 30 minutes or until bubbling.
Remove foil and bake 5-10 minutes longer.

Julie Martin, Program Director
Bone Marrow Transplant
Indiana University

Shanghai Beef

1 1/2 - 2 pounds flank steak
2 cloves garlic, diced
3 tablespoons lemon juice
1 tablespoon soy sauce
1/2 teaspoon anise seed,
    crushed
1/4 teaspoon pepper
1/8 teaspoon salt
1 teaspoon ginger shavings

Prepare marinate by mixing 3 tablespoons lemon
juice with 1 tablespoon soy sauce and crushed
aniseed. Add pepper, salt, ginger and diced garlic.
Pour over meat. Puncture meat with fork several
times. Marinate meat 4-8 hours before barbecuing.
Cook meat to desired taste. Serve hot with a
cold beer!

Robert Goulet, Jr., M.D., Associate Professor of Surgery
Surgical Director, Breast Care and Research Center
Indiana University

Meatloaf

2 pounds ground beef
1/2 cup sour cream
1 tablespoon minced onion
1 4-ounce can mushrooms
    (drained)
1 cup dried bread crumbs
2 eggs
2 teaspoons salt
1/4 cup catsup

Mix ingredients. Put mixture in loaf pan. Bake at 350 degrees for 50 minutes. Pour off fat.

Michael Darling, Associate Director for Administration
Indiana University Cancer Center

Pork Surprises

pork tenderloin slices
    (1 per serving)
sliced onion
green pepper
tomato
2 slices bacon (per serving)

Cut tenderloin into slices, one inch in length. Flatten each slice. Cross two pieces of bacon. Place tenderloin slices on top. On top of this, put a slice of onion, green pepper and tomato. Wrap bacon over top and secure with toothpick. Cook slowly on gas or charcoal grill for about 20 minutes or until done.

Kay and Steve Williams, M.D., Professor of Medicine
Director, Indiana University Cancer Center

Creamed Chicken Paprikas

3 1/2 to 4 pound chicken
1 medium onion
3 tablespoons fat
1 teaspoon paprika
1 cup water
1 teaspoon salt
2 tablespoons flour
1 pint sour cream

Cut chicken into sections. Brown onion in fat in large pot; add washed chicken, salt, paprika and water; simmer until chicken is tender. Mix flour with sour cream until smooth in separate bowl. Add to chicken before serving. Serve with dumplings.

Frederick Stehman, M.D., Professor and Chairman
Department of Obstetrics and Gynecology
Indiana University

Chicken with Duck Sauce

2-3 pounds chicken
8 ounces Russian dressing
2 envelopes Lipton Onion
    Soup Mix
8 ounces apricot jam

Put chicken in open roasting pan. Mix all other ingredients together and spread over chicken. Bake 2 hours uncovered at 300 degrees.

Julie Martin, Program Director
Bone Marrow Transplant
Indiana University

Jeff's Enchiladas

6 chicken breasts (bones and
    skin included)
2 garlic cloves
4 tablespoons cilantro
1 teaspoon cumin
dash white pepper
chopped onion
2 15-ounce cans whole, peeled
    tomatoes
    (or equivalent fresh)
1 15-ounce can tomato sauce
celery
2 10-ounce packages frozen
    spinach, thawed
    (or one fresh bunch)
mushrooms, sliced
8-9 jalapenos (1 small can
    drained or broil fresh in the
    oven just until the skin
    puckers. Then submerge in
    cold water. Peel off skin and
    slice.)
1 green pepper, chopped
16 large soft-flour tortillas
large tub sour cream
grated Monterey Jack cheese

Place chicken, spices and onion in large pot; cover with water and boil for 45 minutes. Take chicken out, debone and set aside. Add chicken back to broth along with the tomatoes, tomato sauce, celery, spinach, mushrooms, jalapenos and green pepper. Bring to boil and simmer for 20-30 minutes. Using potato masher, pulverize the contents of the pot. Spread sour cream down the center of tortilla. Sprinkle with cheese. Strain and spoon the chicken mixture on top of the cheese. Wrap tortilla and place in a large, buttered glass baking dish (will hold 9-10 enchiladas). Fill 2 baking dishes. Spoon broth over the top and sprinkle each with the remainder of the cheese. Bake uncovered at 350 degrees until the cheese bubbles (approximately 1/2 hour). (Freeze one dish prior to adding broth, cheese, and baking.) The remaining broth will make a great vegetable soup base, but for this dinner use some of it to cook brown rice as a side dish. Serve with cold beer or hearty red wine.

Mary Maxwell, Media Manager, Medical Center Relations
Indiana University

Garlic Chicken (Roast Chicken with Garlic)

1 roasting chicken, 3 pounds
1 1/2 to 2 teaspoons salt
1/2 teaspoon oregano
1/2 teaspoon coarsely ground
    black pepper
1 head garlic
2 bunches scallions
1/2 cup olive oil (or corn oil)
1 to 2 cups water
6 to 8 red potatoes
1 small bunch fresh green parsley

Preheat oven to 450 degrees. Remove bag with giblets from cavity of chicken. Rinse chicken with cold water and pat dry. Combine salt, oregano and black pepper, and rub mixture on inside and outside of chicken, massaging into skin and cavity. Place chicken in roasting pan. Cut up garlic (peeled or unpeeled), splitting each clove into 2 or 3 pieces. Place some garlic in cavity and some on chicken and scatter remainder in roasting pan around chicken. Trim roots from scallions, then cut scallions into 2 or 3 parts, including greens. Place some in cavity and some on chicken, and scatter remainder in pan. Sprinkle oil over chicken, reserving 2 tablespoons for later use. Roast 15 minutes, then add enough water to cover bottom of pan. Tilt pan and baste chicken with pan liquid. Roast another 15 minutes, add water, and baste again; roast another 15 minutes and baste a third time. Cut red potatoes (peeled or unpeeled) in halves or quarters. Place in bottom of pan around chicken. Pour remaining oil over potatoes. Baste chicken and potatoes and roast another 15 minutes. Baste again and roast a final 15 minutes. (Total roasting time is 1 hour, 15 minutes for chicken and 30 minutes for potatoes.) To serve, remove chicken to serving platter, cut into serving pieces, and arrange potatoes around chicken. Discard oil. In a small bowl, offer roasting liquid that remains after pressing garlic and scallions through a sieve. Chop parsley coarsely and sprinkle over chicken and potatoes. Serve with Greek salad. Serves 3-4.

Peg Brand, Assistant Professor, Department of Philosophy
wife of Myles Brand, President, Indiana University

Layered Chicken Asparagus

3 cups medium noodles
3 tablespoons butter
1/2 pound sliced mushrooms
1/2 cup chopped celery
1 1-pound can tomatoes chopped
1-15 ounce can tomato sauce
1/2 cup light red wine
1/2 teaspoon sugar
1/2 teaspoon salt
1 teaspoon fresh garlic
1 8-ounce package cream cheese
1/2 cup sour cream
3 tablespoons milk
2 tablespoons chopped onion
dash of nutmeg
1 cup large chunks of cooked
    chicken
2 8-ounce packages frozen,
    cut-up asparagus, cooked
1/2 cup shredded Jack cheese

Cook noodles in boiling salted water until tender and set aside. Melt butter in large skillet, add mushrooms and celery. Cook over low heat until soft. Add tomatoes, tomato sauce, wine, sugar, salt and garlic. Simmer another 10 minutes. Spoon a little sauce into the bottom of a greased 12 x 8 x 2 baking dish. Arrange cooked noodles in sauce; add a little more sauce. Stir together cream cheese, sour cream, milk, chopped onion and nutmeg. Layer half of cream cheese mixture over the mixture in the baking dish, then all of the asparagus, then the chicken. Add remaining wine sauce. Cover and bake in 350 degree oven for 40 minutes or until bubbly. Uncover and spread remaining cream cheese mixture on top and sprinkle with jack cheese. Bake 10 minutes more or until cheese melts. Serves 6.

Betsy L. Fife, R.N., Ph.D., Associate Research Scientist
School of Nursing
Indiana University

Mandarin Cashew Chicken

2 whole chicken breasts
1 medium green pepper
4-5 scallions (bias cut)
1 green onion (bias cut)
1/2 teaspoon ginger root (grated)
1 medium red pepper
    (optional, but pretty)
1 tablespoon oil
4 ounces chicken stock
1 11-ounce can mandarin orange
    sections (reserve juice)
2 tablespoons packed brown sugar
2 tablespoons soy sauce
1 1/2 tablespoons vinegar
2 tablespoons cornstarch
1 ounce cashews
white rice (cooked)

Cut chicken and peppers in 1/2 inch strips. Bias-cut onions and scallions. Stir-fry ginger root; remove. Stir fry onions and scallions; remove. Stir-fry peppers; remove. Stir-fry chicken. Return onions and peppers. Add chicken stock; cover; cook 2-3 minutes. Add juice from mandarin orange can, brown sugar, soy sauce, vinegar and cornstarch. Stir until sauce is thick and bubbly. Add cashews and orange sections. Serve at once over white rice.

George W. Sledge, Jr., M.D., Professor of Medicine
Division of Hematology/Oncology
Indiana University

Low-Fat Chicken Fajita

1 1/2 cups diced (large) boneless,
    skinless chicken breasts
nonstick vegetable spray
1/2 teaspoon ground cumin
1/2 teaspoon curry powder
1/2 teaspoon dried basil, crushed
1/2 teaspoon garlic powder
1/2 teaspoon chili powder
1/4 cup water
1 15-ounce can tomatoes
    (chopped)
1/4 cup white vinegar
3 tablespoons lime juice
    (or concentrate)
flour tortillas
choice of toppings: lettuce,
    cheese, salsa, diced green
    peppers, ranch dressing.
    Great Northern beans or red
    kidney beans (rinsed and
    drained) work well also.

Spray nonstick vegetable cooking spray in large skillet. Saute until chicken is lightly browned and cooked through. Set aside. Combine liquids, tomatoes and spices; stir well. Add to chicken and mix well. Return to heat, stirring occasionally for an additional 5 minutes. Serve with choice of toppings.

Catherine C. Menke, R.N., Research Nurse
Bone Marrow Transplant
Indiana University

Shrimp Creole

1 1/2 pounds cooked shrimp
4 tablespoons bacon drippings
    (or butter)
1/2 tablespoon sugar
2-3 bay leaves
2 medium onions, chopped
1 tablespoon
    Worcestershire sauce
1 medium green pepper,
    chopped
1 28-ounce can tomatoes
1 15-ounce can tomato sauce
salt and pepper
hot sauce (optional)

Saute onion and green pepper in drippings (or butter). Add tomatoes, tomato sauce, sugar, bay leaves, Worcestershire sauce and salt and pepper to taste. Simmer slowly for approximately 45 minutes. Just before serving, bring to a boil and add shrimp. Boil for about 10 minutes. Serve over rice. Provide hot sauce for those who like a little spicier version.

Marcus E. Randall, M.D., Chairman and
William A. Mitchell Professor of Radiation Oncology
Indiana University

Pastore's Zucchini Casserole

1 large zucchini, thinly sliced
2-3 bell peppers, sliced in strips
2 cups Mozzarella cheese,
   shredded
1/4 cup Parmesan cheese, grated
1 teaspoon garlic powder
3 tablespoons margarine

Preheat oven to 350 degrees. Spray a 13 x 9 inch pan with vegetable cooking spray. Layer zucchini in pan 2-3 slices thick. Add 1/4 bell pepper strips over zucchini. Sprinkle with 1/3 of the Parmesan cheese, 1/4 teaspoon garlic powder and 1/4 cup Mozzarella cheese. Repeat layers, ending with fourth layer of zucchini and bell pepper, reserving 1/4 cup Mozzarella cheese. Dot with margarine. Bake for 1 hour, longer if still runny. During last 10-15 minutes of baking, sprinkle with 1/4 cup mozzarella cheese and continue baking until browned. Note: Fresh tomatoes may be added if desired.

Christy M. Traycoff, Assistant Scientist
Division of Hematology/Oncology
Indiana University

Rosemary Potatoes

4 pounds Russet potatoes
1/4 cup olive oil
2 cloves garlic, peeled and
   slivered
coarse kosher salt
2 tablespoons fresh rosemary

Combine olive oil, garlic, rosemary and salt. Cut potatoes into 8 full-length wedges each. Put in baking pan and toss with other ingredients. Let marinate for at least one hour, tossing occasionally. Preheat oven to 350 degrees. Spread potatoes evenly over roasting pan. Bake 45 minutes, stirring occasionally, or until cooked and a bit crispy.

Betsy L. Fife, R.N., Ph.D.; Associate Research Scientist
School of Nursing
Indiana University

Spinach with Coconut Milk and Peanut Sauce

2 pounds spinach, washed
salt (pinch)
2 tablespoons butter
1 cup onion, finely chopped
1 tablespoon fresh hot chilies
1 cup canned coconut milk*
1/2 cup unsalted roasted peanuts
   (crushed)

Cook spinach in water with pinch of salt over moderate heat for 8 minutes (until spinach is tender). Drain, squeeze dry and chop coarsely. Set aside. Melt butter in skillet and add onions and hot chilies; saute until brown (about 5 minutes). Add coconut milk and peanuts. Simmer over moderate heat. Add spinach and cook for 4-5 minutes. Serve in heated bowl immediately. (* To make your own coconut milk: Mix 1 cup of chopped chunks of coconut meat with 1 cup hot water. Place in blender on high for 1-2 minutes. Sieve contents through dampened cheesecloth. Press down with a wooden spoon to extract as much liquid as possible. Yields 1 cup of coconut milk.) NOTE: This lovely dish from East Africa is called Mchicha Wa Nazi.

Worta McCaskill-Stevens, M.D., Assistant Professor
Division of Hematology/Oncology;
Medical Director, Breast Care and Research Center
Indiana University

Almond Cake

1 cup butter, softened
1/2 cup margarine, softened
3 cups sugar
5 eggs
3 cups flour
1/2 teaspoon baking powder
1 cup milk
1 1/2 teaspoons almond extract
1/2 teaspoon vanilla extract
1/2 cup sliced almonds

Cream butter and margarine; gradually add sugar, beating well at medium speed. Add eggs one at a time, beating after each addition. Combine flour and baking powder. Add to creamed mixture, alternating with milk, beginning and ending with flour mixture. Mix after each addition. Stir in flavorings. Sprinkle almonds in bottom of a greased and floured 10-inch tube pan. Pour batter over almonds. Bake 1 hour or until a wooden pick inserted in center comes out clean. Let cool in pan 10 minutes. Remove from pan and cool completely on a wire rack.

Becky Qualitza, R.N., Oncology Nurse Clinician
Indiana University

Kahlua White Russian Cake

3 tablespoons Kahlua
   or coffee liqueur
2 tablespoons vodka
2 ounces (1/2 cup) white baking
   bar with cocoa butter,
   (chopped)
1 3/4 cups all-purpose flour
3/4 teaspoon baking soda
1/2 teaspoon baking powder
1 1/4 cups sugar
1/2 cup butter
2 tablespoons shortening
3 eggs
3/4 cup buttermilk
1/3 cup apricot jam

White Russian Cream:
2 cups whipping cream
1/2 cup sifted powdered sugar
1/4 cup kahlua
2 teaspoons vodka

In medium saucepan, combine Kahlua, vodka and baking bar. Cook over low heat until bar is melted. Cool slightly. Grease and flour three 8 inch round cake pans. In small mixing bowl, stir together baking soda, flour and baking powder and set aside. In large mixing bowl, combine sugar, butter and shortening; beat with electric mixer on medium speed until light and fluffy. Add eggs one at a time, beating until combined. Beat in the cooled liqueur mixture. Alternating, add flour mixture and buttermilk to egg mixture, beating low to medium speed after each addition until just combined. Spread batter evenly into prepared pans. Bake at 350 degrees for 20-25 minutes. Cool 10 minutes. Remove from pans and cool completely. To assemble, place one layer bottom-side-up on serving plate. Spread with 3 tablespoons jam and 1/3 cup White Russian cream. Place other layers, cover and cream. Chill.

Kahlua White Russian Cream: In chilled bowl, combine 2 cups whipping cream, 1/2 cup sifted powdered sugar. Beat on low until thickened. Gradually add 1/4 cup Kahlua and 2 teaspoons vodka. Beat until soft peaks form.

Robyn Leyden, R.N., Oncology Nurse Clinician
Indiana University

Poppy Seed Nut Cake (Makos-dios kalacs)

6 cups flour
3/4 pound butter
7 egg yolks
1 whole egg
1 1/4 teaspoons salt
2 tablespoons sugar
1 1/2 cups milk
1 1/2 cakes of yeast, dissolved in
    1/4 cup milk, warmed

Sift flour and salt. Cream butter and egg yolks, add sugar, mix well, add yeast mixture. Add flour alternating with milk, mix well by hand. Divide dough into seven parts; wrap each piece into waxed paper. Let stand in refrigerator for two hours. Roll out dough on lightly-floured board to 1/2 inch thickness. Spread with filling,* roll as jelly roll. Place in greased baking pan. Let rise for 1/2 hour. Brush top with beaten egg. Bake in 350 degree oven for 40 minutes. Cut in slices when cool. (* Fill with either nut or poppy seed filling—see page 72.)

Kathy Look, M.D., Associate Professor
Department of Obstetrics and Gynecology
Indiana University

Lemon Chess Pie

2 cups sugar
1 tablespoon flour
1 tablespoon cornmeal
1/8 teaspoon salt
4 eggs
1/4 cup melted butter
1/4 cup milk
2 tablespoons grated lemon rind
1/4 cup lemon juice

Mix dry ingredients together. Beat in eggs and add butter, milk, lemon rind, and juice. Pour into 9 inch unbaked pie shell. Bake at 350 degrees for 50-60 minutes or until set.

Tom and Jo Lemon, Cancer Leadership Committee
Indiana University School of Medicine Capital Campaign
Warsaw, Indiana

Raspberry Cream Cheese Coffee Cake

2 1/4 cups all-purpose
    or unbleached flour
3/4 cup sugar
3/4 cup butter or margarine
1/2 teaspoon baking powder
1/2 teaspoon baking soda
1/4 teaspoon salt
3/4 cup dairy sour cream
1 egg
1 teaspoon almond extract
1 8-ounce package cream cheese,
    softened
1/4 cup sugar
1 egg
1/2 cup seedless raspberry
    preserves
1/2 cup sliced almonds

Heat oven to 350 degrees. Grease and flour bottom and sides of a 9 or 10 inch springform pan. Lightly spoon flour into measuring cup; level off. In large bowl, combine flour and sugar. Using pastry blender or fork, cut in butter until mixture resembles coarse crumbs. Reserve 1 cup crumb mixture. To remaining mixture, add baking powder, baking soda, salt, sour cream, egg and almond extract; blend well. Spread batter over bottom and 1 inch up sides of prepared pan. In small bowl combine cream cheese, sugar and egg; blend well. Pour over batter in pan. Carefully spoon preserves evenly over cheese filling. (It's easier to evenly distribute the preserves over the cream cheese layer if you put the preserves in a plastic sandwich bag, clip a corner off and squeeze the preserves out like icing.) In small bowl, combine reserved crumb mixture and almonds. Sprinkle over top. Bake for 45-55 minutes or until cream cheese filling is set and crust is deep golden brown. Cool 15 minutes. Remove sides from pan. Serve warm or cool; cut into wedges. Refrigerate leftovers.

Patricia D. Bledsoe, C.C.S.W., Social Worker
Division of Hematology/Oncology
Indiana University

Rum Cake

1 cup chopped nuts (pecans)
1 package yellow cake mix
    (18.5 ounces)
1 package instant vanilla
    pudding mix (3.75 ounces)
4 eggs
1/2 cup Wesson oil
1/2 cup cold water
1/2 cup dark rum (80 proof)

Glaze:
1/4 pound butter
1 cup water
1/2 cup granulated sugar
1/2 cup dark rum (80 proof)

Pour nuts in a greased and floured 10-inch tube or bundt pan. Mix other ingredients well. Pour over nuts. Bake at 325 degrees for 1 hour. Cool on rack for 10 minutes; invert onto plate. To make glaze, melt butter, add water and sugar, boil 5 minutes. Remove from heat; add rum. After cake is completely cooled, poke holes in the top. Drizzle glaze over cake slowly. Wait a few minutes and repeat until glaze is used up. Note: I usually increase rum by 1/4 cup in both cake and glaze.

Jennifer McCloud, Administrative Secretary
Clinical Research Office
Indiana University

Saint Timothy's Coffee Cake

1 cup butter or margarine
2 cups sugar
1/2 teaspoon vanilla
2 eggs
2 cups unsifted flour
1 teaspoon baking powder
1/4 teaspoon salt
1 teaspoon cinnamon
1 cup chopped pecans
1/2 cup golden raisins
1 cup sour cream

Cream butter and sugar. Blend in vanilla. Add eggs one at a time. Sift together flour, baking powder, salt and cinnamon. Add nuts and raisins to flour mixture. Add dry ingredients to cream mixture alternating with sour cream. Put in bundt pan. Sprinkle with cinnamon/sugar. Bake at 350 degrees for 1 hour. Cool 1 hour. Turn out of pan and sprinkle with cinnamon/sugar.

Julie Martin, Program Director
Bone Marrow Transplant
Indiana University

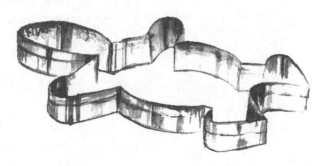

Strawberry Cake with Fluffy White Icing

1 package strawberry cake mix
2 10-ounce packages frozen
    strawberries, thawed

Fluffy Icing:
2 egg whites
1/4 teaspoon cream of tartar
pinch of salt
6 tablespoons cold water
1 1/2 cups sugar
1 teaspoon vanilla
2 teaspoons white corn syrup

Prepare cake according to package directions and bake in two round cake pans. Place ingredients for icing, except vanilla, in top of double boiler over boiling water. Beat with mixer for 4 minutes, or until icing is stiff enough to stand in peaks. Remove from heat and add vanilla. If any graininess appears, add a few drops of lemon juice and continue to beat until smooth. When cake is cool, slice each layer in half crosswise. To assemble, start with one layer, top with strawberries and juice, then layer of frosting. Continue with each layer, ending with icing on top and sides of cake. Must keep refrigerated or icing will slide off.

Betty Dearen, Medical Center Cancer Registry
Indiana University

Twelve Layer Chocolate - Cinnamon Torte

2 3/4 cups flour
2 tablespoons cinnamon
1 1/2 cups butter
2 cups sugar
2 eggs
1 square unsweetened chocolate
2 squares semi-sweet chocolate
4 cups heavy cream
2 tablespoons cocoa
12 maraschino cherries
12 walnut halves

Grease, line bottom with wax paper, grease again 9 inch layer cake pans. Cream butter with sugar; add eggs, beat until fluffy. Sift together flour and cinnamon. Slowly add to the butter mixture. Spread 1/3 cup mixture in each pan in a thin layer. Bake 8-10 minutes, or until golden brown, at 375 degrees. Immediately remove from pan to wire rack. Make at least 12 layers. Grate unsweetened chocolate, shred semi-sweet chocolate into curls using paring knife. Whip cream. Spread 1/3 whipped cream between layers. Fold cocoa, unsweetened chocolate into leftover cream. Heap on top. Decorate with semi-sweet curls, cherries and walnuts. Serves 12.

Patrick J. Loehrer, Sr., M.D.
Chairman, Hoosier Oncology Group
Professor of Medicine, Division of Hematology/Oncology
Indiana University

Strawberry Chocolate Pie

Prebaked 9 inch pie crust
1 1/2 pints strawberries, washed
and stemmed

Chocolate Filling:
1 cup semi sweet chocolate pieces
2 tablespoons melted butter
3 tablespoons Kirsh
(cherry liqueur)
1/4 cup sifted confectioners sugar
1 tablespoon water

Glaze:
3 tablespoons red currant jelly
1 tablespoon water

For chocolate filling: Melt chocolate in double boiler or microwave being careful not to overheat. When chocolate is 110 degrees, add melted butter and Kirsh. Whisk together until smooth. Add confectioners sugar and water, whisk until smooth. While chocolate is still warm, pour into baked pie shell. Place whole berries, tips up, on chocolate filling in a circle until chocolate is covered.

To prepare glaze: Mix currant jelly and Kirsh together over medium heat until smooth. Pour over strawberries. Refrigerate for 2 hours.

Ann D. Zerr, M.D.
Clinical Assistant Professor of Medicine
Indiana University

Bayou Brownies

1 box yellow cake mix
1 stick butter, melted
1 cup pecans
1 egg, beaten
1 8-ounce package cream cheese
1 box powdered sugar
2 eggs

Mix together by hand the cake mix, butter, pecans, one beaten egg and press into a 13 by 9-inch pan. Mix with electric mixer the cream cheese, powdered sugar and 2 eggs. Pour over mixture. Bake for 40-50 minutes at 325 degrees.

Linda Perdue, EDI Coordinator
Indianapolis, Indiana

Cream Cheese Brownies

12-ounce package cream cheese
3/4 stick margarine
1 teaspoon vanilla
3/4 cup sugar
3 eggs
1 1/2 cups unsifted flour
1 1/2 teaspoons baking powder
3/4 teaspoon salt
8 ounces (2 sticks)
    unsalted butter
6 ounces unsweetened chocolate
6 ounces semi-sweet chocolate
5 large eggs
1 1/4 cups sugar
1 1/2 cups brown sugar, packed
1 teaspoon vanilla
8 ounces (2 1/4 cups) pecans,
    in large pieces

Preheat oven to 350 degrees. Beat together cream cheese and butter until smooth. Add vanilla and 3/4 cup sugar, then 3 eggs, one at a time. Place mixture in refrigerator to stiffen. Thoroughly spray a 13 x 9 x 2 inch pan with nonstick spray. Adjust oven rack so brownies bake in middle of oven. Sift together flour, baking powder and salt. Set aside. Melt unsalted butter and both chocolates in a double boiler. Remove from heat. In a large bowl, beat together the 5 eggs, 1 1/4 cups sugar and 1 1/2 cups brown sugar and vanilla until well blended. On low speed, add still-warm chocolate mixture and then flour mixture. Put about 2 1/4 cups chocolate mixture in a small bowl and stir to mix. Spread the chocolate mixture evenly in the prepared pan. Pour the cream cheese mixture slowly in a wide ribbon over chocolate mixture in the pan. Stir the remaining chocolate mixture to soften a bit and then pour in a ribbon over cheese. Cut through with a knife to marbleize. Sprinkle remaining nuts on top. Bake for 1 hour, 15 minutes.

Angela Lee, CTR, Medical Center Cancer Registry
Indiana University

Double Chocolate Cookies

2 eggs, beaten
2 cups biscuit mix
1 6-ounce package
    chocolate chips
1/2 cup milk
2 4-ounce packages instant
    chocolate pudding mix
1/3 cup oil

Mix all ingredients. Drop by rounded spoonfuls onto cookie sheet. Bake for 10-12 minutes at 350 degrees.

Kari Blackley, Assistant Business Manager
Division of Hematology/Oncology
Indiana University

Oatmeal Raisin Cookies

1 cup packed brown sugar
1/2 cup melted Crisco
2 eggs
1 teaspoon vanilla
1 cup flour
1/2 teaspoon salt
1/2 teaspoon baking powder
1/4 teaspoon baking soda
2 cups minute oats
1/2 cup chopped nuts
1/2 cup raisins

Cream together the brown sugar and Crisco. Stir in remaining ingredients. Drop by teaspoonful onto ungreased cookie sheets. Bake at 350 degrees for 10 minutes.

Doris Sachs, Administrative Assistant
Division of Hematology/Oncology
Indiana University

Chocolate Fudge

2 cups sugar
2/3 cup evaporated milk
15 large marshmallows
1/2 cup butter
dash of salt
1 cup semi-sweet
    chocolate chips
1 teaspoon vanilla
1 cup chopped nuts (optional)

Mix sugar, milk, marshmallows, butter and salt in 2-quart sauce pan. Cook, stirring constantly, over medium heat to a boil. (Mixture will be bubbling all over top.) Boil and stir for 5 minutes. Remove from heat. Stir in chocolate chips until completely melted. Add vanilla and nuts. Spread in a buttered 8 inch square pan. Cool. Cut into pieces.

Vickie Firkins, Program Director
Adult Ambulatory Services, University Hospital
Indiana University

Sandy's Mustard Sauce

2 tablespoons flour
1/4 cup dry mustard
1 cup sugar
1 teaspoon salt
1 cup milk
3/4 cup cider vinegar
1/4 cup water
2 whole eggs, beaten

In 2-quart saucepan, combine all dry ingredients and eggs. Add milk a little at a time. Place over low heat until quite hot. Add vinegar mixed in the water, stirring constantly. Cook until thick. Simmer several minutes. Let cool. Serve hot or cold on ham, corned beef or sandwiches. Freezes well.

Sandy and Joe Morrow, Cancer Leadership Committee
Indiana University School of Medicine Capital Campaign
Schererville, Indiana

Chocolate Pound Cake

1 cup butter
1/2 cup shortening
3 cups sugar
5 eggs
3 cups sifted flour
1/2 teaspoon baking powder
1/2 teaspoon salt
4 tablespoons cocoa, heaping
1 cup milk
1 tablespoon vanilla

Cream together butter, shortening and sugar. Add eggs one at a time. Sift together flour, baking powder, salt and cocoa. Add alternately with milk. Add vanilla. Pour into a greased and floured bundt or tube pan. Bake at 325 for 1 hour and 20 minutes or until cake tests done. If you omit the cocoa, this recipe makes a delicious yellow pound cake. This cake also freezes well. This cake is our family birthday tradition served with my grandmother's homemade peppermint ice cream.

Julie Walsh Seiler, Senior Associate Director
School of Medicine Capital Campaign
Indiana University

Nellie's Peppermint Ice Cream

2 pounds King Leo
  peppermint stick candy
3 cups whole milk, additional
  as needed
2 pints whipping cream

Dissolve peppermint stick candy in whole milk overnight in the refrigerator. King Leo peppermint candy is very light and works better than other brands for this recipe; it can often be found in drug stores. When ready to freeze ice cream, pour candy and milk mixture into icecream maker container and put paddle into position. Add whipping cream and enough additional whole milk to fill container to 3/4 full; this recipe can be made in either a 4 or 6 quart ice cream maker, adding whole milk as needed. Freeze according to ice cream maker directions. Serve as soon as frozen or store in freezer until ready to serve. Great with chocolate pound cake!

Julie Walsh Seiler, Senior Associate Director
School of Medicine Capital Campaign
Indiana University

Plum Cake

2 cups self-rising flour
2 cups sugar
1 1/2 teaspoons ground cinnamon
1 1/2 teaspoons ground nutmeg
1 teaspoon ground cloves
2 jars baby food plums
    with tapioca
1 cup vegetable or canola oil
3 eggs, beaten
2 cups pecans, chopped

Mix together flour, sugar and spices. Add plums, oil and beaten eggs. Add nuts. Just mix these, do not beat. Bake at 350 degrees for about 1 hour in greased and floured bundt or tube pan. For a festive touch, dust with powdered sugar once the cake in cooled.

Julie Walsh Seiler, Senior Associate Director
School of Medicine Capital Campaign
Indiana University

The Indiana University Breast Care and Research Center was the first multidisciplinary program in the State of Indiana dedicated to the evaluation and care of women with breast disease. Since 1991, the breast center's mission has been threefold:

- to provide the women of Indiana with the highest quality, most advanced care available;

- to provide educational programs for professional and lay groups designed to promote informed decision making and treatment of women with Breast Cancer; and

- to encourage and support basic science and clinical investigations by center members and investigators from related disciplines.

Robert J. Goulet, Jr., M.D., Associate Professor of Surgery
Surgical Director, Breast Care and Research Center
Indiana University

New medical discoveries and initiatives have
increased demands on the national budget,
so the time has come for Hoosiers to bolster support of cancer research,
education, and patient care to assure that Indiana's
only medical school can remain on the cutting edge of cancer work.

Marilyn Tucker Quayle

Garfield—Jim Davis

© PAWS

"To be in the company of women of courage,
passion and great wit is lifegiving."
Michele Kuntz Wood

JUST CELEBRITIES

Hollis Sigler's Risotto with Morel Mushrooms

5 cups vegetable stock
   (recipe follows)
5 ounces butter
1 small onion, finely chopped
2 cups Aborio rice
1 cup dry white wine
1/2 cup (4g.) dry morel
   mushrooms or 8 ounces fresh
2 tablespoons cream
salt and pepper
Parmesan cheese

Vegetable Broth:
6 cups water
1 potato
1 stalk celery
1 carrot
1 onion with skin
2 or 3 mushrooms
2 bay leaves
10 peppercorns
2 tablespoons oil

Soak the dry mushrooms (if using) in hot water for 30 minutes. Heat vegetable stock and keep it at a simmer throughout recipe. In another sauce pan, heat 4 tablespoons of butter over moderate heat, add the chopped onion. Cook until the onion becomes transparent. Drain and chop mushrooms. Add to the onions and cook for 2 or 3 minutes. Then add the rice, stirring until the rice is coated with the butter. Add the white wine. Cook in this manner until the rice is cooked, approximately 25 minutes. Remove the pan from heat. Add the remaining butter, 2 tablespoons cream and Parmesan cheese. Serves 4.

Vegetable Broth: Heat oil in pan. The vegetables are roughly chopped. Cook them in the oil for 5 minutes. Add the water, bay leaves and peppercorns. Cook for 45 minutes. Strain and return to pan.

Hollis Sigler
Artist, Chicago, Illinois

Grilled Salami Appetizer

Slice and grill kosher salami. Eat on a little bread square with yellow mustard. Great!!

Dave Wolf

Dave Wolf, M.D. Astronaut
1982 School of Medicine, Indiana University
Houston, Texas

Soup Francine

Melt a large tablespoon of clarified butter (or margarine or corn oil) in a wide pan.
Add: 1 diced onion, 1 medium potato (diced), vegetables of your choice, cut up in small
pieces. If you use stalk vegetables, dice the stalk and all. Add: ground pepper and
seasonings of your choice. Parsley Patch All Purpose is very good. Sometimes a little
curry powder helps.

Leave all the ingredients in the melted butter on low heat and simmer until onions are
soft and a light golden color. Stir frequently, it takes about 15 minutes. Then add stock,
chicken or vegetable, a chicken cube with added boiling water for example. Bring to a
boil, then let simmer another 15 minutes. Let cool. Blend in blender. If too thick add a
little more stock, or if soup needs a little more zest, add V-8 juice. As it is stored in
the refrigerator, it may thicken, so add a V-8 juice as the week goes by. NOTE: amount
of stock used is optional. Cooking for a large family requires about a quart of stock.
For one or two people, a pint should do. Also if cooking for more than 2 people,
use 2 potatoes, and more vegetables. Carrot soup and broccoli soup turn out just
marvelously, but cauliflower, peas, tomatoes, celery, watercress, etc. can be used
equally as well. A leftover vegetable soup is good too.

JULIE ANDREWS

Julie Andrews, Actress

99

Vegetarian Chili

2 onions, chopped
4 cloves garlic, crushed
1 cup chopped celery
1 cup chopped carrots
1 cup chopped green peppers
1 can kidney beans
1/2 cup raw bulgur (optional)
1 cup tomato juice
1 large can tomatoes
juice of 1/2 lemon
1 can tomato paste
1 chili seasoning packet
    OR to taste: chili powder,
    cumin, basil, salt & pepper

If using bulgur, (it gives the chili a meat-like texture) heat tomato juice to boil and pour over bulghar. Cover and let stand at least 15 minutes. It will be crunchy so it can absorb more later. Saute onions and garlic in olive oil. Add carrots and celery. When vegetables are almost done, add peppers. Cook until tender. Combine all ingredients and heat together gently. Cook for at least 30 minutes. Serve with choice of onions (chopped), grated cheese, or low-fat sour cream.

Carol Krause

Carol Krause, Journalist
New York City, New York

Basic Bread

2 packages of dry yeast
    dissolved in 3/4 cups warm
    (not hot) water, with sugar as
    directed on the package
2 cups lukewarm milk
3 tablespoons sugar
1 tablespoon salt
2 tablespoons shortening
8 cups of flour, all purpose or
    bread flour
melted butter

Dissolve yeast. Add milk, sugar, salt, shortening, and half the flour; mix until smooth. Mix in rest of flour until dough is easy to handle. Knead on floured surface until smooth—10 minutes should do it. Put in greased bowl, cover with dish towel, and let rise about an hour, until double. Divide dough in half, shape into loaves, place in greased loaf pans, brush with butter, and let rise for another hour. Bake at 425 degrees about 25 to 30 minutes, until brown. To test for doneness, tap to see if they sound hollow. Brush with butter if you like. Makes 2 loaves.

"Baking bread is one of the ways I relax. I like kneading it, and I love the smell of it, the way it fills the house and makes your mouth water."—Stephen King

Stephen King, Author

Low-Fat Pumpkin Bread

3 1/2 cups flour
2 teaspoons baking soda
1 1/2 teaspoons salt
2 teaspoons cinnamon
1 teaspoon nutmeg
2 3/4 cups sugar
1 cup applesauce
16 ounces pumpkin (in can)
2/3 cup water
4 egg beaters
2 cups golden raisins

Mix all dry ingredients together. Add "wet" ingredients one at a time, mixing well. Place in pan and bake at 350 degrees for 50 to 60 minutes.

Tim and Christine Burke
Retired Professional Baseball Player
Columbia City, Indiana

Sour Cream Coffee Cake

1 3/4 stick real butter
2 cups sugar
2 eggs
1 cup sour cream
1/2 teaspoon vanilla
2 cups flour sifted
2 tablespoons flour
1 tablespoon baking powder
1/4 teaspoon salt
1/2 cup chopped nuts
1 teaspoon cinnamon
1/2 cup brown sugar,
    firmly packed

Blend butter and sugar in mixer until creamy. Add eggs, one at time, and beat well. Fold in sour cream and vanilla carefully. Set aside. Sift together all flour, baking powder and salt. Sift two more times. Fold dry ingredients a little at a time into "wet" mixture. Spoon half the batter into greased tube pan (springform pan, flat bottom), cover with a little more than half the topping of cinnamon, brown sugar and nuts. Then repeat. Bake at 350 degrees for 55 to 60 minutes. Cool completely before removing from pan. Sprinkle with powdered sugar.

Bob Knight, Men's Basketball Coach
Indiana University
Bloomington, Indiana

Great Mock Caesar Salad

1 large head of Romaine lettuce
1 large head of Boston lettuce
1 can artichoke hearts (cut up)
1 can hearts of palm (sliced)
pepper to taste

Dressing:
1/3 cup vegetable oil
1/4 cup red wine
1 to 1 1/2 cups Parmesan cheese

Combine ingredients in large salad bowl. Before serving, combine with dressing. Mix together so that dressing is thick . . . almost lumpy.

Anne Ryder, Evening Co-Anchor/Reporter
WTHR Eyewitness News 13
Indianapolis, Indiana

Joy's Pasta A La Passion for Regis

1 pound bow-tie pasta
2 tablespoons plus 1/4 cup
    olive oil
2 garlic cloves, minced
2 boneless, skinless chicken
    breasts, about 1/2 pound
    each, julienned
2 cups broccoli florets
1 cup oil-packed sun-dried
    tomatoes, drained and sliced
2 tablespoon chopped
    fresh basil
pinch red pepper flakes
1/2 cup dry white wine
3/4 cup chicken stock
salt
freshly ground pepper
1 tablespoon unsalted butter
freshly grated Parmesan cheese

Cook the pasta according to package directions. Drain well and place in a large mixing bowl. Pour 2 tablespoons of the olive oil over the pasta and stir to coat and separate. Set the pasta aside.

Pour the remaining olive oil into a large skillet or saucepan set over moderately high heat. Add the garlic and cook until slightly softened, about 1 minute. Add the chicken and cook thoroughly, about 5 minutes, turning occasionally. Remove the chicken to a plate, cover with foil to keep warm, and set aside. Reduce the heat to low and add the broccoli to the pan. Stir and toss until the broccoli is tender, about 10 minutes. Return the chicken to the pan and add the tomatoes, basil, red pepper flakes, wine, and chicken stock. Season to taste with salt and pepper. Add the butter, cover, and simmer over low heat for 5 minutes. Add the chicken and broccoli mixture to the bowl of cooked pasta. Stir to blend and serve at once with lots of Parmesan.

Joy and Regis Philbin, Talk Show Hosts

Clam Linguini

1 stick margarine
1/4 cup white wine
1 tablespoon lemon juice
1 teaspoon Spice Island Fine
　　Herbs (or similar)
salt
pepper
1 clove garlic chopped
1 can minced clams
　　(reserve juice)
2 to 4 ounces cream cheese
shrimp or scallops (optional)

Mix together ingredients in sauce pan and simmer. Blend juice from a can of minced clams in blender with 2 to 4 ounces of cream cheese. Add to margarine sauce along with clams. Spoon over the cooked pasta. You can also add some sautéd shrimp or scallops on top. For low-fat version: use 1 packet butter buds in place of margarine, 1 cup water and some chicken bouillon along with the other sauce ingredients, and substitute low-fat cream cheese.

Ara Parseghian

Ara Parseghian, former Football Coach
University of Notre Dame
South Bend, Indiana

Sour Cream Souffle

1/2 cup freshly grated
　　Parmesan cheese
1 1/2 cups commercial
　　sour cream
1/2 cup sifted flour
5 eggs separated
2 extra egg whites
1 generous teaspoon salt
1/4 teaspoon cayenne pepper
2 tablespoons chopped chives

Butter a 2 quart souffle dish. Coat with Parmesan cheese and refrigerate. Pour the sour cream into a large bowl and sift the flour into the sour cream, then thoroughly whip together with a wire whisk. Add yolks one at a time, whisking briskly after each addition. Then stir in the salt, pepper, chives and remaining cheese. Beat egg whites until they hold firm, shiny peaks when beater is held straight up. Fold into yolk mixture gently with a rubber spatula. Place in preheated 350 degrees oven and bake for 30-35 minutes.

Bill Blass, LTD.
New York, New York

Lunchtime Gloop

2 cans Franco American
   Spaghetti (without
   meatballs)
1 pound cheap, greasy
   hamburger

Brown hamburger in large skillet. Add Franco American Spaghetti and cook until heated through. Do not drain hamburger, or it won't be properly greasy. Burn on pan if you want —that will only improve the flavor. Serve with buttered Wonder bread.

"My kids love this. I only make it when my wife, Tabby, isn't home. She won't eat it, in fact doesn't even like to look at it." Stephen King

Stephen King, Author

Mostaciolli A La Karras

1/8 pound butter
4 tablespoons strained tomatoes
1 jigger vodka
1/2 cup cream
1 pound mostaciolli noodles
Parmesan or Romano cheese,
   grated

Cook noodles according to directions until they are al dente. In a large pan, melt butter over a medium heat. Add tomatoes and vodka. Slowly stir in cream. Add noodles to heated mixture. Sprinkle in cheese to taste and serve immediately.

Alex Karras, Actor/Retired Football Player

Cottage Cheese Meatloaf

1 pound lean ground beef or
   ground veal
1 cup (1/2 pint) cottage cheese
1 egg
1/2 cup quick rolled oats
1/4 cup ketchup
1 tablespoon prepared mustard
2 tablespoons chopped onion
3/4 teaspoon salt
1/8 teaspoon pepper
1/3 cup grated Parmesan cheese

Combine and mix all ingredients lightly until well blended (except Parmesan cheese). Press the mixture loosely into a shallow baking pan (about 8 inches square). Bake uncovered in a 350 degree oven for 20 minutes. Remove from oven and sprinkle Parmesan cheese evenly over the top. Return to oven and continue to bake for 10 more minutes. Let stand for 5 minutes before cutting into squares. Double the recipe and put one in the freezer for another time.

Julie Andrews, Actress

AlaNachos (Alan Henderson's Favorite Nachos)

2 pounds ground beef
2 packages chili seasoning
1/2 cup water
tortilla chips
Chihuahua cheese
lettuce
tomatoes

Brown ground beef. Drain. Add chili seasoning and water to beef. Simmer for 5 minutes. Line 9 x 13 inch pan with a layer of your favorite tortilla chips. Spoon the chili seasoned beef on top of the chips. Place 8 (or enough to cover beef) chihuahua cheese slices on top of beef. Bake at 325 degrees about 10 minutes or until cheese begins to melt. Cut into serving pieces. Top with shredded lettuce, diced tomatoes, and taco sauce. Serves 6. NOTE: Chihuahua cheese may be found at any fine cheese shop.

Alan Henderson, I.U. Basketball Star (#44, Forward)
Annette Henderson, Indiana Commission for Women
Carmel, Indiana

Mark Patrick's "No Fail" Roast

1 chuck or pot roast
1 can Campbell's Cream of
   Mushroom Soup
1 envelope Lipton Onion
   Soup (dry mix)
A-1 Steak Sauce
potatoes, cleaned and pared
carrots, cleaned and pared
onions, cleaned

Preheat oven to 350 degrees. Place roast in a covered roasting pan. (Spray pan with non-stick spray, if desired.) Pour A-1 Sauce over the top of the roast, covering the entire top. Then spoon on the Cream of Mushroom soup. Last, sprinkle the dry onion soup mix over the roast. **Cover tightly.** This is the secret. The roast must not get dry. No moisture should escape the pan. Cook for 2 1/2 hours. Then put the vegetables in with the roast, adding water if necessary. Cook an additional 1 1/2 hours. This roast is done after 4 hours and makes its own gravy.

Mark Patrick, Sports Director, WISH TV, Channel 8
Indianapolis, Indiana

Oven Stew

2 pound stew meat
   (raw, not browned)
6 - 8 carrots (cut into chunks)
3 medium onions (sliced)
4 - 5 potatoes (quartered)
1 tablespoon sugar
3 tablespoons tapioca
1 teaspoon salt
2 beef bouillon cubes
1 can Campbell's
   beef consommé
1 small can of V-8 spicy hot juice
   (or some V-8 and a few
   shakes of Tabasco sauce)

Mix all ingredients together in a small roaster.
Bake 5 hours (covered) at 250 degrees.

Hank Kuhlmann, Special Teams Coach, Indianapolis Colts
Indianapolis, Indiana

20 Minute Chicken Creole

4 medium chicken breast halves,
   skinned, boned, and cut
   into 1 inch strips
1 14 ounce can tomatoes (cut up)
1 cup low sodium chili sauce
1 1/2 cups chopped green pepper
   (1 large)
1/2 cup chopped celery
1/4 cup chopped onion
2 cloves garlic, minced
1 tablespoon fresh basil or
   1 teaspoon dried basil, crushed
1 tablespoon chopped fresh
   parsley or 1 teaspoon
   dried parsley
1/4 teaspoon crushed red pepper
1/4 teaspoon salt
non-stick spray coating

Spray deep skillet with non-stick spray coating.
Preheat pan over high heat. Cook chicken in hot
skillet, stirring for 3 to 5 minutes, or until no longer
pink. Reduce heat. Add tomatoes and their juice,
low sodium chili sauce, green pepper, celery, onion,
garlic, basil, parsley, crushed red pepper, and salt.
Bring to boiling; reduce heat and simmer, covered
for 10 minutes. Serve over hot cooked rice or whole
wheat pasta. Makes 4 servings.

Roosevelt Potts, Professional Football Player,
Indianapolis Colts
Indianapolis, Indiana

Baked Chicken Salad

4 large chicken breasts
2 cups chopped celery
3/4 cup slivered almonds
18 ounce can mushrooms, drained
1/4 cup grated Cheddar cheese
1 1/2 cups Hellman's Mayonnaise
2 tablespoons chopped onion
2 tablespoons lemon juice
3/4 teaspoon salt
3/4 teaspoon Accent
buttered bread crumbs for
    top (about 1 cup)

Cover chicken with water. Cook simmering below boiling point until tender when pierced with a fork. Drain, cool and remove skin. Cut meat into bite size pieces. In a large bowl: mix all ingredients except bread crumbs. Spread in a 9 x 13 x 2 buttered pan. Cover with bread crumbs, sprinkle with paprika. Cover with foil and refrigerate overnight. Bake uncovered at 350 degrees for 30 minutes.

Vince Tobin, Defensive Coordinator, Indianapolis Colts
Indianapolis, Indiana

Chicken Cacciatore in Marinara Sauce

2 broilers, quartered
    (or 8 pieces - legs, thighs,
    breasts)
2 cloves garlic, minced
2 medium onions, quartered
    or sliced thick
1 large can peeled tomatoes
    (or chopped tomatoes)
1 medium can tomato sauce
1 teaspoon oregano
2 green peppers, cut into
    1 1/2 inch chunks
2 celery ribs, cut into
    1 1/2 inch chunks
1/3 cup of Marsala wine
2 tablespoons minced parsley
salt and pepper to taste
1 pound pasta, cooked

Brown chicken pieces on all sides in a preheated kettle or dutch oven over medium to high heat. After the pieces are browned, remove to platter. Reduce heat, saute garlic and onion in chicken drippings until soft. Add tomatoes and tomato sauce (if using whole, peeled tomatoes, mash with fork first and potato masher). Add browned chicken pieces and oregano. Cover and simmer for 30 minutes. Stir once or twice and make sure sauce is not burning. If so, lower the heat. Add green peppers, celery, Marsala, parsley, salt and pepper. Cover and simmer for another 15 to 20 minutes or until chicken is done. To serve, arrange chicken pieces atop a bed of pasta and ladle vegetables and sauce over all. Rigatoni preferred, but any pasta is good. Offer grated Romano cheese on the side. Serves 4.

Jim Gerard, Broadcaster

Italian Chicken over Pasta

4 - 5 chicken breasts cut
    into pieces
1 15 ounce can tomato sauce
6 ounces can tomato paste
2 cups water
1 large onion chopped
3 - 4 cloves chopped garlic
1 teaspoon oregano
1 tablespoon parsley flakes
1 teaspoon thyme leaves
1/2 teaspoon salt
1/4 teaspoon pepper
1 teaspoon rosemary leaves
1 bay leaf
2 tablespoons oil

Saute onions over medium heat. Add meat and garlic, cook until browned. Add tomato sauce, paste and water. Add spices. Bring to a boil and simmer 1 1/2 hours. Serve over your favorite pasta. This dish has very low fat and is packed with flavor.

Trisha and Scott Haskin, Professional Basketball Player,
Indiana Pacers
Indianapolis, Indiana

Tandoori Chicken

2 tablespoons tandoori powder
    (purchase in specialty stores
    or combine the following
    ingredients:
    2 teaspoons garlic, minced
    2 teaspoons fresh ginger,
      minced
    1/2 teaspoon ground
      coriander
    1 teaspoon ground cumin
    1/4 teaspoon red chili
      powder
    1 teaspoon garam masala)
1 cup non-fat plain yogurt
1/4 cup fresh lemon juice
1 pound boneless, skinless
    chicken breasts

Combine tandoori powder or spices with the yogurt and lemon juice in medium bowl. Slice chicken into strips, add them to bowl and marinate covered in the refrigerator for at least 2 hours, preferably overnight. Drain off extra marinade. Broil chicken pieces for 7 minutes on each side, or until cooked through, but not dry. Serve with rice or vegetable curry.

Diane Sawyer, Journalist
New York City, New York

Gratin Doupbinois

2 pounds boiling potatoes
   (5 - 6 cups sliced)
1 large clove garlic
   (or 2 small cloves) peeled,
   crushed and chopped
   very fine
2 cups milk
1 1/2 cups heavy cream
3/4 teaspoon salt
1/2 teaspoon freshly ground
   white pepper
1 tablespoon butter
1/2 cup grated Swiss cheese
   (2 ounces)

Peel the potatoes. Wash and dry thoroughly. Slice fairly thin. Do not soak in water. Combine potato slices with garlic, milk, cream, butter, salt and pepper in a large sauce pan. Bring to a boil on medium heat, stirring with wooden spoon to prevent scorching. As liquid reaches a higher temperature, mixture should begin to thicken slightly. When mixture has thickened a bit, butter shallow baking dish 1 1/2 inches deep and pour in potato mixture. Sprinkle with cheese and place on a cookie sheet. Bake in a preheated 400 degree oven for about 1 hour until potatoes are nicely browned and tender when pierced with the tip of a paring knife. Allow the dish to rest 15 to 20 minutes before serving. MODIFICATIONS—I find 400 degrees too hot, the cheese browns too quickly, try 350 degrees. Also I use less salt and less cream, 3/4 to 1 cup and add extra milk so potatoes don't dry out. Also, use more cheese.

Julie Andrews, Actress

Potato Casserole

2 pounds frozen Southern Style
   hashbrowns
1/2 stick melted butter or
   margarine
1 teaspoon salt
1/4 teaspoon pepper
1/2 cup chopped onions
1 can cream of chicken soup or
   cream of mushroom soup
1 pint sour cream
10 ounces grated sharp
   Cheddar cheese

Mix above ingredients together and put in a 9 x 13 pan or dish. Mix together 2 cups crushed corn flakes and 1/4 stick melted butter or margarine. Sprinkle this mixture on top of potato mixture and bake uncovered at 350 degrees for 45 to 60 minutes.

Hank Kuhlmann, Special Teams Coach, Indianapolis Colts
Indianapolis, Indiana

Sweet Potato Souffle

3 large sweet potatoes
1 1/2 cups sugar
1/4 cups light brown sugar
2 eggs
1/2 teaspoon salt
1 stick margarine
1 teaspoon vanilla

Topping:
1/3 stick margarine
1/4 cup brown sugar
1/2 cup chopped pecans

Peel and cut up sweet potatoes. Cover with water and cook until tender. Beat cooked potatoes. Add sugar, light brown sugar, eggs, salt, margarine and vanilla. Mix well. Pour into sprayed casserole dish. Bake at 400 degrees until set in pan, approximately 30-40 minutes. Separately, mix margarine, brown sugar and pecans. Sprinkle on top of casserole. Brown for 10 minutes.

Alan Jackson
Country Singer of the Year
Nashville, Tennessee

Carrot Layer Cake with Coconut Frosting

1 3/4 cups whole wheat
    pastry flour
2 1/4 ounces yellow cornmeal
1 1/2 teaspoons baking powder
1 1/2 teaspoons baking soda
1 teaspoon ground allspice
1 teaspoon cinnamon
1/2 teaspoon ground nutmeg
1/4 teaspoon ground cloves
1/4 teaspoon salt
2 cups shredded carrots
1 1/4 cups water
3/4 cup golden raisins
1/2 cup honey
2 tablespoons vegetable oil
1 teaspoon vanilla extract

Coconut Frosting
1 pound plus 2 ounces tofu
2 tablespoon plus 1 teaspoon honey
1 teaspoon grated orange peel
1/4 teaspoon orange extract
1/4 cup shredded coconut, toasted

Preheat oven to 350 degrees. In a large bowl, in order given, combine all ingredients. Pour 1/2 of batter into each of two 9 inch round layer cake pans sprayed with nonstick cooking spray. Bake for about 25 minutes or until knife inserted comes out clean. Cool cakes on racks while you prepare the frosting. To assemble cake, place one layer on cake plate, spread half of coconut frosting evenly to edges, top with second layer. Spread evenly with remaining frosting. Leave sides bare. Sprinkle top evenly with toasted coconut. Makes 12 servings.

Frosting: In work bowl of food processor or blender container, process in batches, if necessary, first 4 ingredients until perfectly smooth and creamy. Cover and refrigerate until ready to use as directed above.

JULIE ANDREWS

Julie Andrews, Actress

Lemon Cake

2 sticks of butter
3 cups of sugar
3 cups plus 3 tablespoons of
    cake flour
6 eggs
1 cup heavy whipping cream
2 tablespoons of vanilla extract
2 tablespoons of lemon extract

Cream butter and sugar. Add eggs, whipping cream, vanilla and lemon extract. Add flour and mix well. Bake in greased and floured tube pan at 325 degrees for 1 hour.

Ann and Vernon Jordan,
Civil Rights Leader
Washington, D.C.

Larry's Favorite Butterscotch Brownies

1 box light brown sugar
1 tablespoon vanilla
3 eggs
1 stick margarine (melted)
2 cups self rising flour
Optional: Chopped nuts, 1 cup
    oatmeal, 6 ounces chocolate
    or butterscotch chips

Mix together all ingredients in a medium bowl. Grease 9 x 13 pan. Pour into pan and bake at 350 to 375 degrees for 28 to 30 minutes.

Larry Rinker, Professional Golfer
Winter Park, Florida

One Bowl Brownies

2 cups sugar
1/4 cup melted cocoa
1 cup melted butter/margarine
4 eggs
2 teaspoons vanilla
1 1/2 cups flour
1 teaspoon salt
1/2 cup walnuts (optional)

Frosting:
1/3 cup melted butter/margarine
1 1/2 tablespoons cocoa
1 1/2 cups powdered sugar
2 tablespoons milk
1/2 tablespoon vanilla

Mix sugar and cocoa together, stir in butter. Add eggs, vanilla and beat. Add flour and salt, fold in walnuts. Bake 25 minutes at 375 degrees in a greased 9 x 13 pan.

Frosting: Beat together all ingredients until smooth. Spread on brownies.

Theodore M. Hesburgh, C.S.C.,
President Emeritus University of Notre Dame
South Bend, Indiana

Vacuum Cleaner Cookies (Neiman Marcus Squares)

1/2 cup margarine (not butter) melted
1 (18.25 ounce) box yellow cake mix
3 eggs
1 8 ounce package cream cheese softened
1 1 pound box powdered sugar
1/2 cup flaked coconut
1/2 cup chopped walnuts or pecans

NOTE: Do not use cake mix with pudding added. And do not use whipped margarine. Combine margarine, cake mix, and one egg. Mix together until dry ingredients are moistened. Pat mixture into bottom of well greased 15 x 10 jellyroll pan. Beat remaining eggs lightly, then beat in cream cheese and powdered sugar. Stir in coconut and nuts. Pour over mixture in pan, spreading evenly. Bake at 325 degrees for 45 to 50 minutes or until golden brown. Cool pan on wire rack to room temperature. Makes 4 dozen bars.

John Mellencamp, Singer and Musician
Bloomington, Indiana

Peachey Crisp

8 whole fresh peaches (peeled and sliced)
1 cup sugar
1 stick of butter or margarine softened (may use reduced calorie)
1 cup flour
cinnamon sugar

Preheat oven to 350 degrees. Wash, peel, and slice peaches and fill glass 9 x 13 baking dish. Combine butter and sugar until well blended, add flour until blended (mixture will be crumbly). Top peaches with mixture, sprinkle cinnamon sugar over the top and bake approximately 30 minutes or until fruit is tender. Serve warm with ice cream. Other seasonal fruit may be substituted (apples, pears, cherries, blackberries, etc.) or frozen fruit may be used.

Donnie Walsh, President/General Manager, Indiana Pacers
Indianapolis, Indiana

Fried Bologna Sandwiches

1 to 2 slices Oscar Mayer Bologna
Whole Wheat Bread
Slice of Tomato
Mustard

Heat the pan (not too hot). Fry bologna, spread mustard on bread, add slice of tomato and bologna.

Dorothy, David Letterman's Mother
Indiana

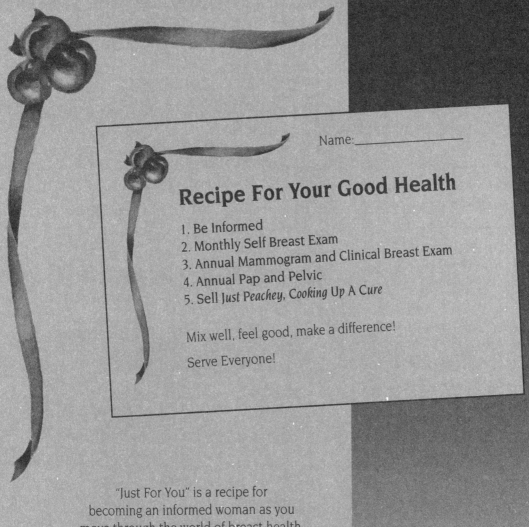

Name:_____

Recipe For Your Good Health

1. Be Informed
2. Monthly Self Breast Exam
3. Annual Mammogram and Clinical Breast Exam
4. Annual Pap and Pelvic
5. Sell *Just Peachey, Cooking Up A Cure*

Mix well, feel good, make a difference!

Serve Everyone!

"Just For You" is a recipe for
becoming an informed woman as you
move through the world of breast health.

"Just For You" is not just for the times of
crisis when a woman finds a "lump."
We hope that each woman will read this chapter
and choose to become a member of the
generation of women that changes the
course of history and wins the
War Against Breast Cancer.

JUST FOR YOU

Examining Your Breasts Only Takes a Few Minutes

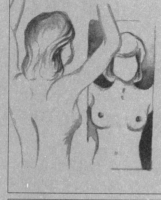

○ In front of a mirror, observe your breasts. To begin, put both your hands above your head. Look for differences in breast size, shape, or contour.

○ Look for any skin changes such as dimpling or changes in skin color or texture.

○ Put your hands on your hips and press. Continue to look for changes.

○ Lie down on your bed and place one hand under your head. Use the soft pads of your fingers to apply firm pressure to your breasts.

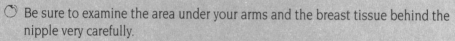

○ Cover the entire area of each breast in a circular pattern or move your fingers in an up-and-down motion. Move from the outer edge of the breast in towards the nipple until the whole breast has been examined.

○ Be sure to examine the area under your arms and the breast tissue behind the nipple very carefully.

○ Feel for lumps or any thickening or changes you have not felt before.

○ Squeeze the nipple to see if there is any fluid that comes out.

○ Now examine your other breast using the same method.

○ In the tub or shower, when you are soapy, take a moment to once again examine your breasts and underarm area. Press firmly on all areas of the breasts and be sure to feel the area around and behind your nipple.

○ Report any lumps or changes to your doctor and be sure that the cause of the lump or change is clearly determined.

Disclaimer: This information contains suggested guidelines and does not by any means replace professional medical examination and treatment.

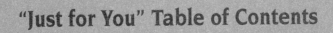

"Just for You" Table of Contents

Heroes

These women give us a way to make a difference

*There can be no Victory without a Beginning
and no Beginning without Courage.*

Florence Houn, M.D., M.P.H.
Director
Division of Mammography Quality and Radiation Programs
Office of Health and Industry Programs
Center for Devices and Radiological Health
U.S. Food and Drug Administration
Washington, D.C.

"These are exciting times for everyone concerned with breast cancer control and for those engaged in mammography. The Mammography Quality Standards Act of 1992 (MQSA) and the interim final regulations issued by the Food and Drug Administration (FDA) on December 21, 1994, usher in a new era of mammography quality in the United States."

Chocolate Cheese Cake

Crust
1 package ice box cookies
    (often called chocolate wafers)
1/4 teaspoon cinnamon
1/4 pound of melted butter

Filling
3 large eggs
3/4 cup sugar
1 1/2 pounds of cream cheese
2 tablespoons of cocoa
1 teaspoon vanilla
1/4 cup melted butter
8 ounces melted German
    sweet chocolate
3 cups of sour cream

Process cookies to crumbs. Melt butter, add cinnamon. Mix crumbs. Press firmly into a spring pan against bottom and as high up the sides as possible.

Process eggs and sugar until light. Gradually add cream cheese. Stir in cocoa and vanilla. Add to cream cheese the melted butter and melted German chocolate. Beat in sour cream. Bake 45 - 50 minutes at 350 degrees in oven. Chill overnight.

Amy S. Langer
Director
National Alliance of Breast Cancer Organizations
New York, New York

"We have made great progress in the fight against breast cancer, so we can now examine the landscape and focus our efforts. We must empower women to take care of themselves, listen to their bodies, and demand the best from their medical teams. We must find ways to communicate with women in language they will hear and can understand, crossing barriers of language, culture and fear. And, of course, we must learn how to prevent this disease, and how to cure it."

Amy's Marinated Flank Steak

1 to 2 pounds flank steak

Marinade:
1/2 cup low salt soy sauce
    (Kikoman)
3 tablespoons Dijon mustard
2 tablespoons grated,
    fresh ginger or 1 teaspoon
    powdered ginger
1 teaspoon cumin powder
freshly ground black pepper
2 tablespoons tomato paste
    or catsup
3 tablespoons olive oil
2 small garlic cloves, smashed
    or chopped
1/4 cup orange juice
1/4 cup red wine or sherry

Make the marinade by mixing all ingredients together with a fork. Pour into a large ziplock plastic bag. Pat the flank steak dry and remove any excess fat. Put the flank steak in the plastic bag. Fold over if necessary. Marinade for at least four hours with bag on plate in refrigerator, turning the bag over every half hour. Take out and let stand at least one-half hour before cooking. Grill over medium high heat. For medium rare meat, cook about five minutes per side on the grill, or until the thickest part of the steak resists your thumb slightly and the outside is nicely browned. Slice thinly on the diagonal and serve with its own juice. Serves 4.

Fran Visco, Esquire
President
National Breast Cancer Coalition
Washington, D.C.

"Our strength lies in you. We will continue to wage the war and speak out as long as women continue to live in fear of breast cancer."

Our mission is to work to eradicate breast cancer, the most common form of cancer among women in the United States, through focusing national attention on breast cancer and by involving patients and caring others as advocates for action, advances and change.

We inform, support, and direct patients and concerned others in knowledgeable and effective advocacy efforts. Nationwide, women and men are bringing about meaningful progress in breast cancer policy through legislative and regulatory input, promotion of media coverage and participation in activities such as marches and campaigns.

Seared Shrimp

12 large shrimp - clean and
　　devein (leave tails on)

Sauce
1/3 cups white wine
1/3 cup light cream or half & half
1 teaspoon Dijon mustard
tarragon, freshly chopped

Place a few drops of oil into a skillet and heat. Place the shrimp in the skillet and sear shrimp until they are pink; remove shrimp from the skillet.

Sauce: In the same skillet in which you seared the shrimp, add 1/3 cup of white wine and reduce, then add 1/3 cup light cream or half and half, reduce again, then add 1 teaspoon Dijon mustard and blend into the sauce. Next, add freshly chopped tarragon. Sauce is done when it coats the back of the spoon. Put sauce on serving plate, arrange shrimp on top and garnish with fresh sprig of tarragon.

National Breast Cancer Coalition
1707 L. Street, Suite 1060
Washington, D.C. 20036
For further information call 202-296-7477 or fax 202-265-6854

Recipe for Breast Health

 Beginning around the age of 18, every woman should:

↻ Check your breasts each month. Your doctor or nurse should show you how.

↻ Have a clinical breast exam by your doctor or a nurse practitioner when you have your regular annual physical exam.

 Beginning around the age of 35, every woman should:

↻ Have a mammogram as often as your doctor recommends. Ask your doctor when to schedule your next mammogram.

♥ You do not need permission to schedule a mammogram. Follow your heart. ♥

 Call your doctor if you notice:

↻ A lump or thickening of the breast.

↻ A discharge from the nipple that stains your bra or bedclothes.

↻ Skin changes in the breast.

These changes may be normal, but you should always have them checked as soon as possible.

Recipe for Responsibility

Your breasts are Your Responsibility: *Know Your Breasts - Notice Changes*

 When should you examine your breasts?

↻ Each month you should examine your breasts about a week after your period ends.

↻ If you are no longer having periods—choose the same week each month to check your breasts for changes.

 What is a Clinical Breast Exam?

↻ Once a year your physician or a nurse practitioner should examine your breasts for you.

↻ This is a good time to ask questions about what **you** feel when you do your breast exams.

What should you do when you or your doctor feels a "breast change" but your mammogram *does not* show that you have a problem?

⟳ You should know your breasts better than anyone else.

⟳ Not all "changes" in your breasts mean that you have a possible "Breast Cancer."

⟳ When *you* feel a change in your breast—*you* need to be sure that the change is looked at *carefully* by your doctor.

⟳ Do not believe that because you are 30 or 40 years old your breast change is "only a cyst." *No one* can be sure that a lump is a cyst by just feeling the area that concerns you.

⟳ You are responsible for demanding that your concern is taken seriously. Insist that you be examined by mammography or ultrasound or by a Fine Needle Aspiration Biopsy, Core Biopsy, or Open Biopsy depending on the lump or area of concern. (See Glossary of Terms in this section.)

⟳ Women find approximately 50% of Breast Cancers themselves. Women often report having mentioned their lump or area of change two to three years before being diagnosed with Breast Cancer. **You need to be heard.**

⟳ Make your survival your responsibility. If you are not satisfied that you have been given a true diagnosis—seek help in finding a doctor who specializes in breast health.

⟳ It is "OK" to ask for a copy of your mammography, ultrasound or biopsy results. These reports are legally yours. Be a good consumer of health care services.

♥ You do not need permission to schedule a mammogram. Follow your heart. ♥

Measuring Your Responsiblity

◯ Do you expect your best friend to examine her breasts regularly?

◯ Do you expect your sister, daughter or mother to examine their breasts regularly?

◯ Can you take the chance of missing a breast lump because you won't examine your breasts?

◯ How can you make examining your breasts easier for you and a friend?

Make a *promise* and a *phone* call.

A promise between two friends to call each other once a month,
place the phone on the table and examine their own breasts, could save a life.

Mammography Makes Sense!

◯ Mammography is still our best tool for discovering Breast Cancer when it is small enough to be cured up to 90% of the time.

◯ A mammogram is a safe, low-dose X-ray picture of the breast.

◯ Mammograms are taken during a mammography exam. There are two kinds of mammography exams—Screening and Diagnostic.

◯ A Screening Mammogram is a quick, easy way to detect Breast Cancer early when treatment is more effective and survival is high. Usually two X-ray pictures are taken of each breast. A physician trained to read X-ray pictures—a mammographer examines them later.

◯ It is generally agreed that screening mammography decreases deaths from breast cancer in women 50 and over. There is a range of opinion about the value of screening mammography for women under 50. The American Cancer Society (ACS) recommends that women have their first mammogram by age 40. At age 40-49, ACS recommends having a mammogram every 1 to 2 years; from age 50 and over, have a mammogram every year.

♥ *You do not need permission to schedule a mammogram. Follow your heart.* ♥

◯ Have a Screening Mammogram as often as your doctor or other health care provider suggests. A screening mammogram often can show breast changes, like lumps, long before they can be felt.

◯ A Diagnostic Mammogram is used if there may be a problem. It is also used if it is hard to get a good picture because of special circumstances (for instance, in women with breast implants). Diagnostic mammography takes a little longer than screening mammography because more X-ray pictures usually are taken. A mammographer may check the X-ray pictures while you wait.

◯ If you have sensitive breasts, try having your mammogram at a time of month when your breasts will be least tender. Try to avoid the week right before your period. This will help to lessen discomfort.

121

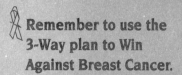 **Remember to use the 3-Way plan to Win Against Breast Cancer.**

○ Examine your breasts at least once a month.

○ Have an annual breast exam by your doctor or nurse practitioner.

○ Schedule your mammograms!

A Mammogram at the Right Facility with Caring Medical Professionals Should Be a Positive Experience

○ Understanding what happens during a mammogram will help reduce any anxious feelings you might have. It is important to know that only a small amount of radiation is used in mammography.

○ When you have a mammogram, you stand in front of a special X-ray machine. The radiologic technologist lifts each breast and places it on a platform that holds the X-ray film. The platform can be raised or lowered to match your height.

○ The breast is then gradually pressed against the platform by a specially designed clear plastic plate. Some pressure is needed for a few seconds to make sure the X-rays show as much of the breast as possible.

○ This pressure is not harmful to your breast. In fact, flattening the breast lowers the X-ray dose needed.

○ Studies show that most women do not find a mammogram painful for the short time needed to take the picture. Try to relax. If the pressure becomes painful, you can tell the radiologic technologist to stop.

○ If there is an area of your breast that appears to have a problem, the mammographer or radiologic technologist may examine the breast.

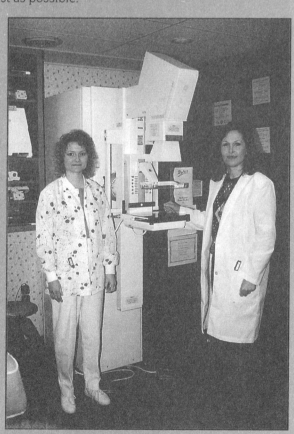

Janet Arnett, R.T. (M), Carole Cross, R.T.

You Are a Customer at Your Mammography Site—
You Have Rights and Responsibilities

○ Learning the results of your mammogram is very important.

○ Chances are your mammogram will be normal. *But do not assume that your mammogram is normal just because you have not received the results.* If you have not received your screening results within 10 days, ask your doctor or call the mammography facility.

○ If your screening mammogram shows anything unusual, talk to your doctor as soon as possible about what you should do next. Your doctor may schedule a diagnostic mammogram, or you can schedule it yourself—but have it done soon. Discuss the results with your doctor.

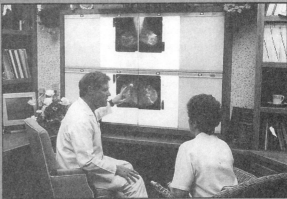

Dr. R.W. Cross with a patient.

○ When a diagnostic mammogram shows something abnormal, the mammographer may recommend another type of exam. Sometimes a biopsy is needed because of something your doctor found in checking your breast even though the mammogram appears normal. A biopsy is a way to obtain a small piece of breast tissue for study under a microscope.

○ Whenever a mammogram uncovers a problem or a need to check something further:

  • Make sure you understand what you need to do and how soon you must act.

  • Always get results of any test that you have.

  • Ask questions about your results if something is hard to understand.

○ If you do not have a doctor or other health care provider, you will need to find one if you have an abnormal mammogram. Ask the mammography facility to help you find a doctor. Make an appointment right away so you can discuss your results and what should be done next.

○ Mammography is very effective, but it does not detect all breast problems. If you find something unusual in your breast, see your doctor.

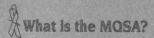

What is the MQSA?

⟳ Many hospitals, clinics, and imaging or X-ray centers perform mammography. Mobile units (often vans) offer screening at shopping malls, community centers, churches and offices. All of these facilities must meet the same quality standards.

⟳ Your doctor may refer you to a mammography facility or you may select the one that is most convenient for you.

⟳ Make sure the mammography facility you choose is certified by the Food and Drug Administration (FDA) unless it is a Veterans Health Administration (VHA) facility.

⟳ A new law, called the *Mammography Quality Standards Act*, requires all mammography facilities except those of VHA to be FDA certified beginning October 1, 1994. To be certified, facilities must meet standards for the equipment they use, the people who work there, and the records they keep. VHA has its own high-quality mammography program, similar to FDA's.

⟳ If the facility is not FDA certified, get your mammogram in a facility that is certified.

⟳ The MQSA Certificate must be clearly displayed for each woman to see.

⟳ To find a certified mammography facility, ask your doctor or call the National Cancer Institute's Cancer Information Service toll free at 800-4-CANCER (1-800-422-6237).

How Can I Learn More About Mammography?

⟳ Most mammography facilities have printed information and videotaped instructions on breast care. You can read or watch them when you go for a mammogram.

○ For general information on Breast Cancer and mammography, contact:

Cancer Information Service
(a service of the National
Cancer Institute)
800-4-CANCER

Food & Drug Administration (FDA)
MQSA Consumer Inquiries
1350 Piccard
(HFZ-240)
Rockville, MD   20850
301-443-4190

American Cancer Society
800-227-2345

○ Portions of the mammography information in this chapter are taken from "Things to Know about Quality Mammograms" - a publication of the U.S. Department of Health and Human Services, AHCPR Publication No. 95-0634.

○ For more information about guidelines or to receive copies of this booklet, call toll free (800-358-9295) or write to: Agency for Health Care Policy and Research, Publications Clearinghouse, P.O. Box 8547 Silver Spring, MD 20907.

Terms You Need to Know

Our glossary of terms is designed to help women understand the language of breast care. Women can take control and be less afraid when we understand what we are told by our medical providers.

Use these terms to help yourself write out questions when discussing your care with your doctor or nurse practitioner.

abscess: Infection that has formed a pocket of puss.

adenocarcinoma: Cancer arising in gland-forming tissue. Breast cancer is a type of adenocarcinoma.

adjuvant chemotherapy: Anticancer drugs used in combination with surgery and/or radiation as an initial treatment before there is detectable spread, to prevent or delay recurrence.

alopecia: Hair loss; a common side affect of chemotherapy.

amenorrhea: Absence or stoppage of menstrual period.

anesthesia: Entire or partial loss of feeling or sensation produced by drugs or gases.

antiemetic: A medicine that prevents or relieves nausea and vomiting used during chemotherapy.

areola: Area of pigment around the nipple.

aspiration: Withdrawal of fluid from a cyst with a hypodermic needle.

atypical cell: Mild to moderately abnormal cell.

atypical hyperplasia: Cells that are not only abnormal but increased in number.

autologous: From the same person. An autologous blood transfusion is blood removed and then transfused back to the same person at a later date.

axilla: The underarm area.

axillary lymph node dissection: Surgical removal of lymph nodes found in the armpit.

axillary lymph nodes: Lymph nodes found in the armpit area.

benign: Noncancerous (usually not life-threatening).

bilateral: Involving both sides, such as both breasts.

biopsy: Removal of suspicious tissue for examination under a microscope and diagnosis.
> *excisional biopsy*: removal of an entire growth
> *fine needle aspiration*: removal of cells with a needle and syringe.
> *incisional biopsy*: removal of a section of a growth.
> *needle biopsy*: removal of a plug of tissue using a needle.

bone marrow: Soft inner part of large bones that make blood cells.

bone scan: Test to determine if there is any sign of cancer in the bones.

bone (skeletal) survey: X-rays of the entire skeleton.

breast cancer: A potentially fatal tumor formed by the uncontrolled growth of abnormal breast cells that can invade and destroy surrounding tissue and can spread to other parts of the body.

breast implant: A round or tear-drop shaped sac inserted in the body to restore a breast form.

breast self-exam: The process in which women examine their own breasts every month in an effort to detect problems at an early stage.

breast reconstruction: Creation of an artificial breast after mastectomy by a plastic surgeon.

calcifications: Small calcium deposits in the breast tissue which can be seen by mammography.

carcinoembryonic antigen (CEA): Non-specific (not specific to cancer) blood test used to follow women with metastatic breast cancer to help determine if the treatment is working.

carcinogen: Substance that can cause cancer.

carcinoma: Cancer arising in the epithelial tissue (skin, glands and lining of internal organs). Most cancers are carcinomas.

cellulitis: Infection of the soft tissues.

chemotherapy: Treatment with drugs to destroy cancer cells; often used to supplement surgery and/or radiation or to treat recurrent cancer.

colostrum: Secretion from the breast during pregnancy or after birth before milk comes in.

cyclical: According to a cycle, such as the menstrual cycle.

cyst: A fluid-filled mass, usually harmless which can be reduced by aspiration.

cytology: Study of cells.

cytotoxic: Cell-killing.

differentiated: Clearly defined. Differentiated tumor cells are similar in appearance to normal cells.

doubling time: Time it takes the cell population to double in number.

ductal carcinoma in situ: Ductal cancer cells that have not grown outside of their site of origin; sometimes referred to as precancer.

ductal papillomas: Small noncancerous finger-like growths in the mammary ducts that cause a bloody nipple discharge. Commonly found in women forty-five to fifty.

eczema: Skin irritation characterized by redness and open weeping.

edema: Swelling caused by a collection of fluid in the soft tissues.

embolus: Plug of tumor cells or clot within a blood vessel.

endocrine manipulation: Treating breast cancer by changing the hormonal balance of the body instead of using cell-killing drugs.

estrogen: Female sex hormones produced by the ovaries, adrenal glands, placenta and fat.

estrogen receptor: Protein found on some cells to which estrogen molecules will attach. If a tumor is positive for estrogen receptors, it is sensitive to hormones.

estrogen receptor assay (ERA): A test that must be done on cancerous tissue to see if a breast cancer is hormone-dependent and may be treated with hormone therapy.

fat necrosis: Area of dead fat, usually following some form of trauma or surgery; a cause of lumps.

fibroadenoma: Benign fibrous tumor of the breast; most common in young women.

fibrocystic: A noncancerous breast condition in which multiple cysts develop in one or both breasts. It can be accompanied by discomfort or pain that fluctuates with the menstrual cycle. Often called lumpy breast disease.

fibroid: Benign fibrous tumor of the uterus (not in the breast).

flow cytometry: Test that measures DNA content in tumors.

frozen section: Freezing and slicing tissue to make a slide immediately for diagnosis.

galactocele: Milk cyst or clogged milk duct sometimes found in a nursing mother's breast.

genetic: Relating to genes or inherited characteristics.

hematoma: Collection of blood in the tissues. Hematomas may occur in the breast after surgery or trauma.

heterogeneous: Composed of many different elements. In relation to breast cancer, heterogeneous refers to the fact that there are many different types of breast cancer cells within one tumor.

hormone: Clinical substance produced by glands in the body which enters the blood stream and causes effects in other tissues.

hot flashes: Sudden sensation of heat and flushing associated with the menopause.

hyperplasia: Excessive growth of cells.

hypothalamus: Area at the base of the brain that controls various functions, including hormone production in the pituitary.

hysterectomy: Removal of the uterus. Hysterectomy does not necessarily mean the removal of ovaries (oophorectomy).

immune system: Complex system by which the body is able to protect itself from foreign invaders.

immunotherapy: Treatment by modifying the body's immune system.

infiltrating cancer: Cancer that can grow beyond its site of origin into neighboring tissue. Infiltrating does not imply that the cancer has already spread outside the breast. Infiltrating has the same meaning as invasive.

informed consent: Process by which the patient is fully informed of all risks and complications of a planned procedure before agreeing to proceed.

in situ: In the site of. In regard to cancer, refers to tumors that are not invasive.

intraductal: Within the duct. Intraductal can describe a benign or malignant process.

intraductal papilloma: Benign tumor that projects like a finger from the lining of the duct.

inverted nipple: The turning inward of the nipple. Usually a congenital condition, but if it occurs where it has not previously existed, it can be a sign of cancer.

invasive cancers: Cancers that are capable of growing beyond their site of origin and invading neighboring tissue. Invasive does not imply that the cancer is aggressive or has already spread.

lactation: Production of milk from the breast.

liver scan: A way of visualizing the liver by injecting into the bloodstream a radioactive substance which lights up the organ during the X-ray.

lobular: Having to do with the lobules of the breast.

lobular carcinoma in situ: Abnormal cells within the lobule that do not form lumps. Can serve as a marker of future cancer risk.

lobules: Parts of the breast capable of making milk.

local treatment of cancer: Treatment only of the tumor in the breast.

lump: Any kind of abnormal mass in the body.

lumpectomy: Surgery to remove lump with small rim of normal tissue around it.

lymphatic vessels: Vessels that carry lymph (tissue fluid) to and from lymph nodes.

lymphedema: Milk arm. This swelling of the arm can follow surgery to the lymph nodes under the arm. It can be temporary or permanent and occur immediately or any time later.

lymph nodes: Glands found throughout the body that help defend against foreign invaders such as bacteria. Lymph nodes can be a location of cancer spread.

malignant: Cancerous.

mammary duct ectasia: A noncancerous breast disease most often found in women during menopause wherein the ducts in or beneath the nipples become clogged with fat, producing a lump.

mammography/mammogram: An X-ray of the breast that can detect tumors before they can be felt.

mammogram (baseline): A mammogram performed on healthy breasts, usually at age 35 - 40 years, to establish a basis for comparison later.

mastectomy: Surgical removal of the breast and some surrounding tissue.
> *modified radical mastectomy*: The most common type of mastectomy performed today. The breast, breast skin, nipple, areola and underarm lymph nodes are removed, while the chest muscles are saved.
> *prophylactic mastectomy*: A procedure sometimes recommended for patients at very high risk for developing cancer in one or both breasts.
> *subcutaneous mastectomy*: This is done before cancer is detected, removes the breast tissue but leaves the outer skin, areola and nipple intact. (This is not a suitable cancer operation.)
> *radical mastectomy (halsted radical)*: The surgical removal of the breast, breast skin, nipple, areola, chest muscles and underarm lymph nodes. Rarely done today.
> *segmental mastectomy* (partial mastectomy): A surgical procedure in which only a portion of the breast is removed, including the cancer and a surrounding margin of healthy tissue.

mastitis: Infection of the breast. Mastitis is sometimes used loosely to refer to any benign process in the breast.

mastodynia: Pain in the breast.

mastopexy: Uplift of the breast through plastic surgery.

menarche: First menstrual period.

menopause: The time in a woman's life when the menstrual cycle ends and the ovaries produce lower levels of hormones. Usually occurs between the ages of forty-five and fifty-five.

metastasis: Spread of cancer to another organ, usually through the bloodstream.

microcalcification: Tiny calcifications in the breast tissue usually seen only on a mammogram. When clustered can be a sign of ductal carcinoma in situ.

micrometastasis: Microscopic and as yet undetectable but presumed spread of tumor cells to other organs.

necrosis: Death of tissue.

nodular: Forming little nodules.

nuclear magnetic resonance (NMR): Another name for magnetic resonance imaging (MRI).

oncogenes: Tumor genes that are present in the body. These can be activated by carcinogens and cause cells to grow uncontrollably.

oncology: The study of cancer.

one-step procedure: A procedure in which a surgical biopsy is performed under general anesthesia and, if cancer is found, a mastectomy or lumpectomy is done immediately, as part of the same operation.

oophorectomy: Removal of the ovaries.

palliation: Act of relieving a symptom without curing the cause.

palpation: Examining the breasts by feel.

pathologist: Doctor who specializes in examining tissue and diagnosing disease.

permanent section: A technique in which a thin slice of biopsy tissue is mounted on a slide to be examined under a microscope by a pathologist in order to establish a diagnosis. Usually takes one or two days for results.

phlebitis: Irritation of a vein.

polymastia: Literally, many breasts. Existence of an extra breast or breasts.

progesterone: Hormone produced by the ovary. Involved in the normal menstrual cycle.

progesterone receptor assay (PRA): A test that must be done on cancerous tissue to see if a breast cancer is hormone-dependent and can be treated by hormone therapy. Used as a check on the results of the estrogen receptor assay.

prognosis: Expected or probable outcome.

prophylactic subcutaneous mastectomy: Removal of all breast tissue beneath the skin and nipple, to try to prevent future breast cancer.

prosthesis: Artificial substitute for an absent part of the body, as in breast prosthesis.

protocol: Research designed to answer a hypothesis. Protocols often involve testing a specific new treatment under controlled conditions.

pseudolump: Breast tissue that feels like a lump but when removed proves to be normal.

quadrantectomy: Removal of a quarter of the breast.

radiation oncologist: A physician specially trained in the use of high-energy X-rays to treat cancer.

radiologist: A physician who specializes in diagnosis of diseases by use of X-rays.

randomized: Chosen at random. In a randomized research study, subjects are chosen to be given a particular treatment by means of a computer programmed to choose at random.

reconstruction: A way to recreate the breast's shape after a natural breast has been removed; various surgical procedures are available. Sometimes performed immediately (at the same time of mastectomy) but usually delayed several months or years.

recurrence: Return of cancer after its apparently complete disappearance.

remission: Disappearance of detectable disease.

sarcoma: Cancer arising in the connective tissue.

sebaceous: Oily, cheesy material secreted by glands in the skin.

seroma: Collection of tissue fluid.

side effect: Unintentional or undesirable secondary effect of treatment.

silicone: Synthetic material used in breast implants because of its flexibility, resilience and durability.

staging: Certain tests and examinations that should be done before any type of definitive treatment is decided upon to determine the site of the tumor, whether the lymph nodes are involved, and if the cancer has spread through the blood-stream or the lymphatic system (metastasized). Your physician should discuss patient's stage based upon test results.

systemic treatment: Treatment involving the whole body, usually using drugs.

tamoxifen: Estrogen blocker used in treating breast cancer.

thermography/thermogram: A technique in which heat from the breast is measured by special photography to identify "hot spots" which may indicate an abnormal condition. So far, not reliable in detecting breast cancer.

titration: Systems of balancing. In chemotherapy titration means using the largest amount of a drug possible while keeping the side effects from becoming intolerable.

trauma: Wound or injury.

tumor: Abnormal mass of tissue. Strictly speaking, a tumor can be benign or malignant.

two-step procedure: When surgical biopsy and breast surgery are performed in two separate stages.

ultrasonography/ultrasound: A noninvasive procedure (a procedure that does not require cutting into the skin) using a sound-wave imaging technique to examine a part of the body, or to further evaluate a breast lump or other abnormalities seen on a mammogram. Also used to evaluate liver.

xeroradiography: Type of mammogram taken on a Xerox plate rather than an X-ray film, used infrequently today.

x-rays: Electromagnetic radiations which can, at low levels, produce images that can diagnose cancer and, at high levels, can destroy cancer cells.

When Breast Surgery is Necessary— What Should You Do?

- Choose a surgeon who you know is qualified and experienced in doing breast surgery. Your primary care physician or mammographer can help you find a surgeon with whom you will feel comfortable.
- Have your surgeon explain to you carefully *why* you are having breast surgery.
- Have your surgeon supply you with literature that explains the different types of breast surgeries. Refer in the glossary to: mastectomy, lumpectomy, quadrantectomy, biopsy, one-step procedure, two-step procedure.
- Contact the American Cancer Society and ask for a visit from a Reach to Recovery Volunteer before your surgery.
- Refer to the "Where to go for Help" section in this book for phone numbers to call in order to request the information you need to make the surgical choice that is right for you.
- You and your doctor should become a team that works together closely for your well-being.

Menu For Successful Arm Care After Breast Surgery

- Not every woman who has Breast Cancer surgery today will have her lymph nodes removed from the area under her arm on the same side as her breast surgery.
- For those women who *do* have their lymph nodes removed - Education is the main ingredient for maintaining a healthy arm.
- Please question your doctor about arm care after your surgery.
- The American Cancer Society Reach to Recovery program will provide you with excellent reading materials and exercises to help you keep your arm healthy and comfortable - Call -1-800-ACS-2345 to arrange for a Reach to Recovery visit with a volunteer who is a breast cancer survivor.

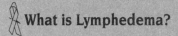

What is Lymphedema?

- Lymphedema is an accumulation of lymphatic fluid that causes swelling in the arms and legs. It can occur immediately after surgery or several years later. If you have lymph nodes removed during surgery or must undergo radiation, you should be alert to lymphedema's reality and the precautions necessary to prevent the swelling

and infections which could result.
Surgical procedures may interfere with the regular transport of lymph (a clear fluid composed of proteins, bacteria, fats and water) to and from the bloodstream. The lymph may not be able to drain properly from the limb affected by surgery, causing "edema," or swelling, in that extremity—for example, in a breast cancer patient's arm.

○ You should be alert to early signs of edema: tightness, heaviness or pain in the extremity and rings that cease to fit. If redness, swelling, pain and/or fever develop, an infection may be present and your doctor should be called immediately. The sooner lymphedema is recognized, the more effective treatment will be.

Action!

*For more information on lymphedema and its treatments, contact the
National Lymphedema Network at (800) 541-3259.*

Please Cut This Card and Carry with Your Driver's License

MEDICAL ALERT

_____
Name

In the event of an accident or medical emergency
**DO NOT
do Blood Draws, IV Treatments,
Blood Pressure or Injections on**

LEFT ARM   RIGHT ARM

Circle one or both.

Where To Go For Help!

We have not begun to list *all* of the places in Indiana that women can turn to for knowledge and assistance. These women's groups and organizations will give you assistance or help you to find help or information closer to home.

National Cancer Institute, Cancer Information Service for Michigan and Indiana: 1-800-4-CANCER (1-800-422-6237).

American Cancer Society's Indiana toll-free line: 1-800-ACS-2345

The Indiana State Department of Health's Toll Free Telephone Helpline. Call to locate information or locations for Support Groups. 1-800-433-0746

National Y-Me - Breast Cancer Information: 1-800-221-2141

The following Indiana groups are listed alphabetically by city.

DeKalb Memorial Hospital
DeKalb Unit of the ACS
Auburn, Indiana 46706
Lorraine Hines - 219-925-2594
Cheryl Clark 219-925-4600 Ext. 1024

Indiana Breast Cancer Coalition
Michele Kuntz Wood
St. Francis Hospital
1600 Albany Street
Beech Grove, IN 46107
Phone: 317-781-1281
FAX: 317-782-7978

Women's Cancer Support Group
Becky Easley
Wells Co. Health Department
223 W. Washington
Bluffton, IN 46714
Phone: 219-824-6493

Light of Hope Cancer Services of Allen County, Inc.
2925 E. State Blvd.
Fort Wayne, IN 46805
Phone: 219-484-9560

My lymphatic system was partially removed at the time of my surgery for Breast Cancer.

Please contact my physician for more information.

Physician: _____

Phone: _____

Address: _____

Fold Here

**Conquering Breast Cancer
Support Group**
Parkview Regional Oncology Center
Fort Wayne, IN   46805
Connie Goodwin, Phone: 219-637-3069
Terry Goodwin, Phone: 219-422-1503
Catherine Prange, Phone: 219-482-4139

Gary - Yes, We Can
Fay Urells
Methodist Hospital Regional
Cancer Center
600 Grant St.
Gary, IN   46402
Phone: 219-886-4328

**Indiana University Breast Care
and Research Center**
University Hospital - Room 1602
University Blvd.
Indianapolis, IN   46202
Phone: 317-274-9800

New Beginnings
Dr. Lucinda Geis Dunnaway
6820 Parkdale Place, Suite 204
Indianapolis, IN   46254
Phone: 317-328-6868
FAX: 317-328-6871

Little Red Door
Jane Ambro
1801 N. Meridian St.
Indianapolis, IN   46202
Phone: 317-925-5595

The Center for Women's Health
Dr. Chace Lottich
8920 Southpointe Dr., #B1
Indianapolis, IN   46227
Phone: 317-865-6240

Y-Me of Central Indiana
5229 Fawn Hill Terrace
Indianapolis, IN 46226
Phone: 317-240-3331

Y-Me of Wabash Valley
Coral Cochran
Phone: 812-877-3025
204 Bluebird Lane
Terre Haute, IN   47803
Carole Daugherty, Phone: 812-466-2857
Aileen Crackel, Phone: 812-235-5442

Bosom Buddies
Joan Lennon
South Bend, IN   46615
Phone: 219-234-1708

Women in Touch
Sandy Laskie
Memorial Hospital of South Bend
621 Memorial Dr., Suite 307
South Bend, IN   46601
Phone: 219-284-6944

Women Winning Against Breast Cancer
Connie Rufenbarger
%Dr. Richard W. Cross
2267 DuBois Drive
Warsaw, IN   46580
Phone: 219-269-9911
FAX: 219-269-3595

National Alliance of Breast Cancer Organizations— NABCO

*There are many places to go for help when dealing with breast problems. The National Alliance of Breast Cancer Organizations has allowed us to print a **partial listing** of resources from their Breast Cancer Resource List - 1994/95 Edition.*

NABCO, established in 1986, functions as a leading non-profit central resource for information about breast cancer, and as a network of more than 300 organizations providing detection, treatment and care to hundreds of thousands of American women. Aside from NABCO's role as a source of up-to-date, accurate information for the general public, medical professionals and the media, we spend time locally, on the state level and in Washington as advocates for regulatory change and legislation which benefits breast cancer patients.

In Fall 1993, Avon announced *Avon's Breast Cancer Awareness Crusade*, a national campaign to promote breast cancer education and access to early detection in partnership with several national organizations including NABCO, and the establishment of the *Avon Breast Health Access Fund*, enabling NABCO to distribute nearly $2 million to community programs that promote access to education and screening services. Expertise has permitted NABCO to be involved in a variety of medical, policy and media activities. NABCO representatives frequently appear on television and radio, discussing the importance of early detection and other breast cancer topics, and NABCO routinely furnishes source data and quotes to national print and broadcast media.

The following listings have been adapted from the 1994/95 NABCO *Breast Cancer Resource List* and appear here with NABCO's permission. The *List* is revised annually and can be ordered from NABCO by writing: NABCO, 9 East 37th St., Tenth Floor, New York, NY 10016.

General Information About Breast Cancer

The Breast Cancer Companion by Kathy LaTour (William Morrow & Company, Inc. New York, 1994, $22.00) This comprehensive guidebook offers readers useful tips, the insights of 75 survivors as well as background information regarding advocacy and the politics of breast cancer. **Bookstores.**

Your Breast Cancer Treatment Handbook by Judy C. Kneece, R.N., O.C.N., Breast Health Specialist (1995, $19.95) **EduCare Publishing, P.O Box 280305, Columbia, SC 29228.**

Breast Cancer Handbook: A Basic Guide for Gathering Information, Understanding the Diagnosis, and Choosing the Treatment by Linda Brown Harris (1992, $8.95; reduced rate for bulk orders). A simple, easy to understand booklet on breast cancer, from examinations through treatment for cancer. It is mostly in the form of questions to be posed to doctors. It offers tips for physical and emotional recovery and diet. 122 pages. **Melpomene Institute for Women's Health Research, 1010 University Avenue, St. Paul, MN 55104 (612) 642-1951.**

The Breast Cancer Handbook: Taking Control After You've Found A Lump by Joan Swirsky and Barbara Balaban (Harper Collins, New York 1994, $10.00) This user-friendly guide is full of practical information that will be invaluable to any woman. 232 pages. **Bookstores**.

Breast Cancer: Risk, Protection, Detection and Treatment (1990, $2.50). Reviews factors that may influence chances of having the disease, how to detect its early signs, and treatment options. A "how-to" guide to breast self-examination is included. 31 pages; also available in French. Order from **DES Action, 1615 Broadway, Oakland, CA 94612**.

Breast Cancer: The Complete Guide by Yashar Hirshaut, MD and Peter Pressman, MD (Bantam, New York, 1992, $24.50, paperback, $12.95). An easy-to-follow resource providing up-to-date medical information and practical advice on breast cancer, from suspicion of disease through diagnosis, treatment, and follow-up care. Dr. Pressman is a member of NABCO's Medical Advisory Board; the forward is by Amy Langer of NABCO. 322 pages. **Bookstores**.

The Cancer Dictionary by Roberta Altman and Michael J. Sarg, MD (Facts On File, New York, 1992, $40.00 plus shipping). This valuable resource compiles cancer-related terms with easy-to-understand definitions. Includes acronyms for chemotherapy protocols and simple anatomical illustrations. Most appropriate for patients and family as well as non-medical healthcare professionals. 352 pages. Order from **Facts on File, (800) 322-8755.**

Early Detection Brochure Published annually by the Board of Sponsors of October's National Breast Cancer Awareness Month, this leaflet discusses breast cancer facts, detection and screening guidelines. A new pamphlet was developed for 1993. 25 free; bulk orders at $8.00 per 100. Also available in Spanish. **National Breast Cancer Awareness Month, PO Box 57424, Washington, DC 20036, (202) 785-0710.**

Dr. Susan Love's Breast Book by Susan M. Love, MD with Karen Lindsey (Addison Wesley, Reading, MA, 1991, paperback, $16.00). A breast surgeon and feminist who is a member of NABCO's Medical Advisory Board discusses all conditions of the breast, from benign to malignant. A balanced view of treatment options and controversies is clearly presented in a friendly, accessible style. Good as a general reference. 450 pages. Next edition in Sept. 1995. **Bookstores.**

If You've Thought About Breast Cancer by The Rose Kushner Breast Cancer Advisory Center (Fall, 1994 edition). This updated general pamphlet will cover all aspects of breast cancer detection and treatment. Originally authored by NABCO co-founder the late Rose Kushner, it includes a section of definitions and telephone numbers for resources. 44 pages. **For ordering information, contact: The Rose Kushner Breast Cancer Advisory Center, PO Box 224, Kensington, MD 20895, (301) 949-2531.**

Make Sure You Do Not Have Breast Cancer by Philip Strax, MD (St. Martin's Press, New York, 1991, paperback, $8.95). A pioneer in mammography offers this simply written primer and his reflections on attitudes about breast cancer and the importance of its early detection. 118 pages. **Bookstores.**

Making Sense of the News About Breast Cancer by the National Women's Health Resource Center is the September/October 1992 issue of their *National Women's Health Report* on breast cancer diagnosis and treatment. 12 pages. Available for $2.00 by calling **(202) 293-6045.**

Questions to Ask Your Doctor About Breast Cancer (11/91) This 23-page booklet contains lists of questions that will help a patient ask her doctor about breast cancer. Breast cancer topics covered are early detection, diagnosis, treatment, adjuvant therapy and reconstruction. **NCI (800) 4-CANCER (1-800-422-6237).**

Understanding Breast Changes: A Health Guide for All Women (94-3536: Revised April 1994) This 56-page booklet explains how to evaluate breast lumps and other normal breast changes that often occur and are confused with breast cancer. It recommends regular screening mammography beginning at age 50, a breast exam by the doctor as part of a woman's annual checkup, and monthly breast self-examinations for the early detection of breast cancer. **NCI (800) 4-CANCER.**

What You Need to Know About Breast Cancer (94-1556, 1993). NCI's most comprehensive pamphlet on breast cancer covers symptoms, diagnosis, treatment, emotional issues and questions to ask your doctor. Includes glossary of terms. 40 pages. **NCI (800) 4-CANCER.**

Breast Examinations

A Step-By-Step Guide to BSE (1990). Detailed instruction in breast self-examination using a photographic storyboard presentation. Includes anatomical drawings of the breast. 8 pages. Also available in Spanish. **PRR Inc., 17 Prospect Street, Huntington, NY 11743, (516) 424-8900.**

Are You Age 50 or Over? A Mammogram Could Save Your Life (93-3418: Revised February 1994) This low-literacy brochure answers six questions about mammography, including who should have it, how it is done, and where it is performed. **NCI (800) 4-CANCER.**

Breast Care: You're Worth the Time it Takes (1992). Published by the Liz Claiborne Foundation in association with NABCO and ACS, this brochure discusses mammography (including guidelines), breast self-examination, nutrition and breast care. Not recommended for elderly populations, as type is faint. 10 pages. No charge, but supplies are limited. **Available by faxing request on your organization's letterhead to Hilary Finkelstein at the Liz Claiborne Foundation, Fax# (212) 626-5608.**

BSE Shower Card The AMC Cancer Research Center offers this waterproof "shower card" guide to breast self examination, with step-by-step instructions. For one free card, write to **AMC Cancer Research Center, Marketing and Public Relations Department, 1600 Pierce Street, Denver, CO 80214, (800) 321-1557 or (303) 233-6501 in Colorado.** Bulk orders available at cost; customizing available.

BSE/TSE Shower Card (2028-LE). Plastic shower card guides you through breast self examination and testicular self examination. **ACS (800) ACS-2345**.

Chances Are . . . You Need A Mammogram (PF4730, August 1991). A guide for midlife and older women published by the American Association of Retired Persons (AARP) in cooperation with the NCI. 11 pages. Spanish language version available. Up to 50 available free. Order from **AARP Fulfillment, 601 E Street, NW, Washington, DC 20049.**

How to Do BSE (2088-LE). A pamphlet that gives specific instructions on breast self-examination. **ACS (800) ACS-2345.**

Lesbians and Cancer Available in English and Spanish, this free pamphlet provides early detection information as well as addressing relevant issues for lesbians. Order from the **Mautner Project, P.O. Box 90437, Washington, D.C. 20090 (202) 332-5536.**

The Older Your Get, The More You Need a Mammogram (5020, 1993) A pamphlet that discusses the importance of early detection, especially as a woman ages, and some of the issues concerning this audience. **ACS (800) ACS-2345.**

Special Touch: A Personal Plan of Action for Breast Health (2095-LE, 1993). Lists breast cancer risk factors and gives detection guidelines mammography, clinical breast exam, and breast self examination (including the "vertical strip" and "wedge" methods.) 3-fold brochure. Also available in Spanish. A video is also available in some locations. **ACS (800) ACS-2345.**

Take Special Care of Your Breasts (2675-LE). Bilingual (English/Spanish) low-level reading card with illustrated check-up guidelines. **ACS (800) ACS-2345.**

Question and Answers About Choosing a Mammography Facility (94-3228, 1994). This 4-page brochure lists questions to ask when selecting a quality mammography facility. This publication should accompany *Are You Age 50 or Over? A Mammogram Could Save Your Life*. **NCI (800) 4-CANCER.**

Risk Factors and Benign Breast Disease

Breast Cancer and Ovarian Cancer: Beating the Odds by M. Margaret Kemeny, MD and Paula Dranov (Addison-Wesley, Reading, MA, $7.95). This book thoroughly describes the risk factors (many of them shared) for breast and ovarian cancer and what steps can be taken to reduce risk. Includes a discussion of the treatment of both diseases. 216 pages. **Bookstores**.

Challenging The Breast Cancer Legacy by Renee Royak-Schaler, PhD and Beryl Lieff Benderly (Harper Collins, New York, NY, 1993, $10.00 paperback). For the woman concerned about a family history of breast cancer, this book offers constructive approaches to coping with psychological and physical concerns. 257 pages. **Bookstores**.

DES Exposure: Questions and Answers for Mothers, Daughters and Sons (1990, $2.00). An authoritative booklet which discusses the effects of DES exposure, including the confirmed correlation between exposure and increased breast cancer risk. 20 pages. For the booklet and for additional information, write to: **DES Action 1615 Broadway, Suite 510, Oakland, CA 94612.**

The Informed Woman's Guide to Breast Health by Kerry A. McGinn (Bull Publishing, Palo Alto, CA, 1992, paperback, $12.95). A thorough overview of breast lumps and conditions that are benign: detection, treatment and need for further action. Includes a glossary of terms. 127 pages. **Bookstores.**

Questions and Answers About Breast Calcifications (91-3198, 1990). This brief brochure discusses calcifications of the breast, their significance, and what can be done about them. 3 pages. **NCI (800) 4-CANCER.**

Questions and Answers About the Breast Cancer Prevention Trial (1994). This fact sheet describes the BCPT (testing the use of tamoxifen (Nolvadex) as a means of preventing breast cancer in women at risk), who is eligible, the pros and cons of participating, and how to enroll. 8 pages. **NCI (800) 4-CANCER.**

Understanding Breast Cancer Risk by Patricia T. Kelly, PhD (Temple University Press, Philadelphia, 1992, $39.95, paperback, $18.95). Information on assessing each indivdual's risk and how to interpret study results and statistics. Discusses factors that contribute to breast cancer risk, and the active role that women should take in designing their own breast health programs. 195 pages. **Bookstores.**

Risk Counseling and Research Centers

Alta Bates-Herrick Comprehensive Cancer Center Breast Cancer Risk Counseling is offered by Patricia Kelly, author of *Understanding Breast Cancer Risk.* **Oakland CA (510) 204-4286**. Other affiliated facilities include: **Mt. Sinai Comprehensive Cancer Center, Miami Beach, FL (305) 535-3350; The Comprehensive Cancer Center at JFK Medical Center, Atlantis, FL (407) 642-3970; Komen Alliance Clinical Breast Center, Dallas, TX (214) 820-2626.**

Strang Cancer Prevention Center is a free national resource for breast cancer risk counseling and research into breast cancer risk. Strang operates a National High Risk Registry for purposes of research and educating participants. A newsletter is published. **428 East 72nd Street, New York, NY 10021 (800) 521-9356** or **(212) 794-4900.**

University of California at Los Angeles Breast Center is a risk evaluation center in a multidisciplinary setting. **(800) 825-2144.**

Women at Risk is a research, diagnosis and treatment group for women at high risk of developing breast cancer. **Columbia-Presbyterian Medical Center, Breast Service, New York, NY (212) 305-9926.**

Beyond Treatment Into Survivorship

Cancervive: The Challenge of Life After Cancer by Susan Nessim and Judith Ellis (Houghton Mifflin Co., Boston, 1992, $8.95). This book addresses some of the practical and the emotional issues faced by cancer survivors such as insurance, relationships, infertility and long-term side effects of treatment. 264 pages. **Bookstores.**

Charting the Journey: An Almanac of Practical Resources for Cancer Survivors by the National Coalition for Cancer Survivorship (Consumer Reports Books, Mt. Vernon, New York, 1990, $14.95). A collection of resources, suggestions, strategies and feelings, with a detailed Appendix directory. 225 pages. **Bookstores.**

Facing Forward: A Guide for Cancer Survivors (93-2424, 1992). Addresses the special needs of cancer survivors and their families, focusing on four major areas of need: maintaining physical health, addressing emotional concerns, managing insurance issues and handling employment problems. Resource numbers are given for each category. 43 pages. **NCI (800) 4-CANCER**.

Sources of Medical Information and Support

American Board of Medical Specialists can verify whether a doctor is board-certified and, if so, the field and year in which certification was obtained. For those seeking a board-certified doctor, you will be given the proper listing in the local phone directory. Call Monday through Friday, 9 a.m. to 6 p.m., Eastern Standard Time. **(800) 776-2378.**

National Alliance of Breast Cancer Organizations (NABCO) is a non-profit national central resource for information about breast cancer, and acts as an advocate for breast cancer patients' and survivors' legislative and regulatory concerns. Organizations and individuals who join NABCO's information network receive the quarterly NABCO *News*, customized information packets, this *Resource List* and special mailings. Membership is tax-deductible. For more information write to **NABCO, 9 East 37th Street, 10th Floor, New York, NY 10016, (212) 719-0154.**

AMC Cancer Research Center's Cancer Information Line Professional cancer counselors offer easy-to-understand answers to questions about cancer, provide advice and support and will mail instructive free publications upon request. Equipped for deaf and hearing-impaired callers. Call Monday through Friday, 8:30 am to 5:00 pm, Mountain Standard Time. **(800) 525-3777**

American Cancer Society's nationwide toll-free hotline provides information on all forms of cancer, and referrals for the ACS-sponsored "Reach to Recovery" program. **(800) ACS-2345.**

The Cancer Information Service of the National Cancer Institute can be reached toll-free at (800) 4-CANCER, and gives information and direction on all aspects of cancer through its regional network. Provides the informational brochures indicated on this *List* without charge, and refers callers to medical centers and clinical trial programs. Spanish speaking staff members are available.

The Komen Alliance is a comprehensive program for the research, education, diagnosis and treatment of breast disease. Information on screening, BSE, treatment and support, including the booklet "Caring for Your Breasts"(also available on audio cassette) is available by calling (800) I'M AWARE or contacting The Susan G. Komen Foundation, Occidental Tower, 5005 LBJ Freeway, Suite 370 LB74, Dallas, TX 75244, (214) 450-1777.

The National Coalition for Cancer Survivorship is a national network of independent groups and individuals concerned with survivorship and sources of support for cancer patients and their families. NCCS is a clearinghouse of information and advocates for cancer survivors. 1010 Wayne Avenue, 5th Floor, Silver Spring, MD 20910, (301) 650-8868.

The National Self-Help Clearinghouse will refer callers to regional self-help services, particularly in regard to insurance concerns and protection of employment rights. Send a stamped, self-addressed envelope to 25 West 43rd Street, Room 620, New York, NY 10036, or call (212) 642-2944.

The Wellness Community has extensive support and education programs which encourage emotional recovery and a feeling of wellness. All services are free. Headquarters at 2716 Ocean Park Boulevard, Suite 1040, Santa Monica, CA 90405, (310) 314-2555. Contact them for information on several additional locations around the country.

The YWCA Encore Program was designed to provide supportive discussion and rehabilitative exercise for women who have been treated for breast cancer. To find the location of the program nearest you, call (202) 628-3636.

Y-ME National Organization for Breast Cancer Information and Support, provides support and counseling through their national toll-free hotline, (800) 221-2141 (9 a.m. to 5 p.m. CST, Monday-Friday, or 24 hours at (708) 799-8228). Trained volunteers, most of whom have had breast cancer, are matched by background and experience to callers whenever possible. Y-ME offers information on establishing local support programs, and has chapters in 12 states in addition to their Illinois home office. Y-ME also has started a hotline for partners. Call or write to 212 W. Van Buren Street, Chicago, IL 60607, (708) 799-8338.

Avon Breast Cancer Awareness Crusade and the Avon Breast Health Access Fund

About the Fund

The Avon Breast Health Access Fund (the "Fund") is a program of Avon's Breast Cancer Awareness Crusade, which is raising awareness and generating funding for breast cancer programs through pink ribbon pin and key ring sales by its 415,000 U.S. sales representatives. The Fund, established in November, 1993, has as its objective to provide financial support to community-based breast cancer programs that should have a direct and immediate impact on women's access to breast health education and early detection services. The programs receiving support through the Fund are also offered hands-on assistance from the National Alliance of Breast Cancer Organizations (NABCO) and volunteer support from local Avon representatives in their communities.

These monies will enable many worthy community programs across the country to help women—especially underserved women—receive breast cancer education and early detection services. Avon provides funding to NABCO, its program partner. NABCO, together with the Fund's National Advisory Board, seeks and receives proposals for support from the breast cancer community, and selects grant recipients at a range of funding levels -- from $5,000 to $75,000.

Specific Objectives of the Fund

Through the Fund, Avon and NABCO are making financial and volunteer support available to community programs that help women access breast cancer education and early detection services. The Fund will prioritize grants to breast health programs focused on underserved women and hard-to-reach groups, such as single mothers, poor women, older women, disabled or institutionalized women and homeless women. The Fund will not support the cost of medical services themselves. It is hoped that applicants can attract funding for these services from other sources, with the Fund providing financial support for additional costs of the program. Examples of potential projects to be funded might include a multi-lingual breast health education campaign; transportation of women to screenings; and breast health seminars in comfortable settings such as a church, school or civic center.

Often, underserved women need targeted, customized approaches to bring them into breast cancer screening and care. Elements that may contribute to successful programs include specially developed educational materials, dedicated staff with specialized language or communications skills, outreach efforts that reach women where they live, work and worship, and support for child care and transportation needs that may arise during educational sessions and screenings.

Another Fund objective is to select programs for financial support that could also benefit from volunteer support from Avon's sales representatives. Representatives work together with program staff on non-medical aspects of the program, which may include distributing educational information or program announcements; identifying and contacting collaborating community organizations and groups; greeting and escorting program participants; and helping to publicize the program.

All grant recipients are given a *Program Guide* detailing how to receive assistance from NABCO and offering public relations support from Avon that assist in publicizing their programs in their communities and with the media.

Who May Apply?

Grant recipients must themselves be private, non-government, US-based not-for-profit organizations with federal non-profit status, or be chapters or units of national not-for-profit organizations. Applicants must enclose proof of their current Federal non-profit status. You may apply more than once by sending in separate applications. Publicly funded government agencies may partner with a qualified not-for-profit organization, with the non-profit filing the application.

Applicants may apply for funding for existing programs or for new programs, and funds may be requested for staff and operating expenses. However, no fund support will be available for the direct cost of medical services themselves (for example, mammograms).

NABCO would appreciate hearing from all organizations that are interested in the Fund, and encourage you to suggest that others contact us so that we can mail additional applications.

You and your organization might be eligible for an Avon grant.
Write and ask for a grant application:

> NABCO and *The Avon Breast Health Access Fund*
> 9 East 37th Street
> 10th Floor
> New York, NY   10016

Just Peachey, Cooking Up a Cure and *The Avon Breast Health Access Fund* are just two examples of women and men across America - becoming soldiers in The War Against Breast Cancer.

Please call 1-800-FOR-AVON for the location of your local Avon representative or look in your Yellow Pages for your nearest listing.

Buy Avon Pink Ribbon items!! They are working for You!!

Extension Homemakers Creed

We *believe*
in the present and its opportunities;
in the future and its promises
in everything that makes life large and lovely;
in the divine joy of living, and helping others
and so we endeavor to pass on to others
that which has benefited us;
striving to go onward and upward,
reaching the pinnacle of enconomic perfection
in improving, enlarging and endearing the
greatest institution in the world,
"The Home."

JUST
INDIANA EXTENSION
HOMEMAKERS ASSOCIATION

KITCHEN TIPS

Quiche is done when puffed up into a dome and slightly brown. Remove from oven and cool on a cookie sheet. The puff will subside, but do not be alarmed; this is not a souffle.

True quiche is strictly custard and cheese. Quiche Lorraine is made with added meats, vegetables, etc.

When carving meat, cut across the grain. If cut with the grain, long meat fibers give a stringy texture to the slice. Steaks are the exception.

Gravy made with cornstarch as a thickening agent instead of flour can be reheated many times without causing the grease to separate.

Place a piece or two of dry bread under the broiler pan. It soaks up the fat drippings and reduces smoke and fire.

Instant potatoes make a great thickening for stews and gravies—will not clump.

Add a little instant coffee powder when making gravy to give it a rich brown color and deeper flavor.

Soaking chicken in salt water before flouring to fry seals the juices in and keeps out the grease.

Before opening a package of bacon, roll it into a long tube. This loosens the slices, keeping them from sticking together.

Before frying chicken, squeeze lemon juice on it to enhance the flavor and make the meat clearer.

For a tasty topper for broiled fish, hot vegetables, toasted bread and baked potatoes: Combine 3/4 pound shredded Gruyere cheese, 1/2 cup sour cream and 1 tablespoon milk. Heat until cheese melts.

To eliminate the odor when boiling seafood, add celery leaves to the water.

For fresh caught flavor, thaw frozen fish in milk. Drain well before cooking.

Put pieces of bread in the water when cooking cauliflower or brussels sprouts to avoid an unpleasant odor in your kitchen.

To store mushrooms, place unwashed in a paper bag that is left open to allow mushrooms to breathe. Mushrooms become soggy in plastic bags. Clean mushrooms just before cooking with a damp towel.

A small pinch of baking soda will preserve the color of fresh vegetables.

Fruit Dip

1 small jar marshmallow creme
1 8 ounce package cream cheese
1/3 cup lemon juice
1 14 ounce can sweetened
    condensed milk

Mix together and serve chilled.

Dianna Hornsby - Connersville, Indiana

Ham Dip

3 celery stalks
8 ounces cooked ham
1/2 cup low fat cottage cheese
1 tablespoon lemon juice
1/2 teaspoon salt
1/4 teaspoon white pepper
1/2 teaspoon dried dill

Insert steel blade in food processor. Chop celery. Add ham, using on/off method. Add cottage cheese, lemon juice, salt, pepper and dill and process until well mixed. Yield: 2 cups - 6 calories.

Wava Fiechter - Craigville, Indiana

Party Cheese Spread

1 pound Colby cheese
    (*County Line)
6 hard boiled eggs
1 2 ounce jar pimentos (drained)
1 medium onion
2 tablespoons chopped chives
    or scallions
salad dressing (*Miracle Whip)
*may substitute low fat cheese
    and mayonnaise

Grind first four ingredients in food chopper. Add chives or scallions. Add enough salad dressing to make spreadable. May be used as a cracker or sandwich spread or as a vegetable dip.

Joy LeCount - Warsaw, Indiana

Marinated Vegetables

1 can French style green beans
1 can peas
1 can white sweet corn
1 cup chopped celery
1 cup chopped onion
1/2 cup chopped green pepper

Drain vegetables and pour into 2 quart bowl. Mix together: 1 cup sugar, 1/2 cup oil, 2 tablespoons water, 2/3 cup white vinegar, 1/2 teaspoon salt, 1/2 teaspoon pepper. Add to vegetables and refrigerate overnight.

Nancy Smith - Warren, Indiana and Mary Lou Archer - Terre Haute, Indiana

No Fat Vegetable Dip

1 24 ounce Light and Lively
   cottage cheese (no fat)
1 small envelope Hidden Valley
   Ranch Buttermilk
   Salad Dressing*

Put cottage cheese in blender and add envelope of dry powder. It may be necessary to add one tablespoon water or skim milk to get the blending process started. Blend until smooth. Best if refrigerated overnight. Great with raw vegetables.
*The envelope will state "makes 16 ounces." Disregard and use 24 ounce container of cottage cheese.

Sue Pflum - Connersville, Indiana

Spinach Dip

1 10 ounce package frozen
   spinach thawed and drained
1 cup sour cream
1 cup low fat mayonnaise
1 8 ounce can water chestnuts
   drained and chopped
1 envelope Lipton vegetable
   soup mix

Mix all ingredients together and chill. Serve with crackers, vegetables or Hawaiian bread.

Judy Edgecomb - Connersville, Indiana

Taco Dip

8 ounce cream cheese
16 ounce sour cream
16 ounce jar chunky salsa
    (mild or hot)
1 pound hamburger
9 ounce can bean dip (optional)
1 package taco mix
chopped lettuce
diced tomato

Mix cream cheese and sour cream together and spread into shallow dish then refrigerate. Meanwhile, cook hamburger and drain. Add taco mix, follow package directions, add salsa, heat until well blended, cool. Either add bean dip to meat mixture or layer separately over cheese. Spread onto cheese mixture then sprinkle chopped lettuce and tomato on top. Sprinkle grated cheese on top for added color and taste.

Mary Everett - Dugger, Indiana and Debra Certain - Marion, Indiana

Tortilla Chip Dip

1 pound ground meat
    (beef, pork, turkey)
1 can cream of mushroom soup
8 ounces Mexican Velveeta
    Cheese

Brown meat, drain off excess fat. Add soup and cheese and allow to melt. Blend and serve with tortilla chips. (OPTIONAL) Add Tabasco, chili powder, red pepper, jalapeno or salsa or green onions.

Vickie J. Hadley - Woodburn, Indiana

Cauliflower/Broccoli Soup Deluxe

1 cup sliced fresh mushrooms
1/4 cup chopped onion
4 to 5 tablespoons margarine
4 to 6 tablespoons flour
1 can chicken broth
    (14 1/2 ounces)
3 cups skim milk
2 cups thawed or cooked
    California blend vegetables
1 1/2 cups cubed cheese
    (American, Colby, Velveeta)
Salt and pepper to taste

In a heavy saucepan, saute mushrooms and onion in margarine. Add flour stirring constantly. Slowly add broth. Use a wire whip if lumps occur. Add milk and vegetables. Season to taste. Cook over low heat until thickened and hot. Do not boil. Add cheese and stir until melted. Serves 4 to 6.

Joan B. Younce - Warsaw, Indiana

Chicken and Dumpling Soup

10 3/4 ounce can chicken broth
1 can cream of chicken soup
1 cup chopped onion
1 cup chopped celery
1 small bay leaf
1 cup fresh or frozen peas
1 can Sweet Sue chicken
    and dumplings
1 can cream of mushroom soup
1 cup chopped potatoes

Put all ingredients in large pan. Simmer soup on low heat for 2 hours. Remove bay leaf before serving.

Nadine Scholz - Fort Wayne, Indiana

Italian Chicken Soup

1 whole chicken
1 large onion, minced
1 16 ounce can tomatoes,
    chopped
chicken bouillon or broth, to taste
2 to 3 carrots, sliced thin
3 stalks celery, sliced thin
Parsley, basil, oregano, salt and
    pepper to taste. (Start with
    1 teaspoon then add more
    as it cooks.)

Place chicken in 4 to 5 quarts of salted water and simmer until meat falls off bones. Remove chicken from bones and refrigerate meat in a covered container. Add to the broth, the rest of the ingredients and either packages of chicken bouillon or chicken broth if needed to make a tasty soup. Cook until vegetables are done and flavors are blended. Season to taste. Serve with chicken meat and homemade croutons.

Ruth Longroy - Fort Wayne, Indiana

Italian Sausage Soup with Tortellini

1 pound Italian sausage
2 garlic cloves, sliced
5 cups beef broth
2 cups (4 medium) tomatoes,
　　chopped, seeded and peeled
1/2 teaspoon basil leaves
8 ounce can tomato sauce
8 ounce (2 cups) frozen meat
　　or cheese filled Tortellini,
　　small ravioli or other pastas
　　as suggested below.
1 cup coarsely chopped onion
1/2 cup water
1/2 cup dry red wine
2 cups thinly sliced carrots
1/2 teaspoon oregano leaves
1 1/2 cups sliced zucchini
3 tablespoons chopped
　　fresh parsley
1 medium green pepper, cut into
　　1/2 inch slices
grated Parmesan cheese

Tortellini, an Italian word meaning "little cap," are tiny crescent shaped pastas filled with meat or cheese. These are available fresh or frozen. They add a special touch to this well-flavored soup. If Tortellini or a very small ravioli are not available, 2 cups bow-tie egg noodles or spiral macaroni can be substituted.

If sausage comes in casing, remove casing. In 5 quart dutch oven, brown sausage. Remove sausage from dutch oven, drain, reserving 1 tablespoon drippings, and saute onions and garlic until tender. Add beef broth, water, tomatoes, carrots, basil, oregano, tomato sauce and sausage. Bring to a boil. Reduce heat; simmer uncovered 30 minutes. Skim fat from soup. Stir in zucchini, Tortellini, parsley and green pepper. Simmer covered an additional 35 to 40 minutes or until Tortellini are tender. Sprinkle Parmesan cheese on top of each serving. Serves 8 - 1 1/2 cups.

Ruth Longroy - Fort Wayne, Indiana

Chunky Cream of Potato Soup

4 cups diced potatoes
1/4 cup chopped onion
1 cup water
1 teaspoon salt
1/4 teaspoon celery salt
3 tablespoons butter
　　or margarine
2 tablespoons flour
3 cups milk
1 tablespoon parsley flakes
2 chicken bouillon cubes
pepper

Cook potatoes and onions in water. Set aside half the diced potatoes and mash or whip the remaining potatoes. In heavy pan over medium heat, melt butter, stir in flour and add 1 cup of milk. Stir until thickened. Gradually add the rest of the milk and add mashed potato mixture, bouillon cubes, celery salt, salt, dash of pepper and parsley flakes. Add diced cooked potatoes last. Simmer over low heat, stirring occasionally until bouillon cubes are melted. Serves 4 to 6.

Glenda Giggy - Andrews, Indiana

Quick and Easy Vegetable Soup

1 to 2 cups left over roast beef
1 can beef broth
2 beef bouillon cubes
1 can V-8 juice (11.5 ounce)
2 cups stir fried frozen vegetables
1 cup fresh mushrooms
1 cup coleslaw from bag
Salt, pepper, garlic powder to
    taste, water for desired
    thickness.

Cook roast beef, beef broth and 2 beef cubes together for 10 minutes . Add the other ingredients in order and simmer for 15 minutes or longer. Serves approximately four.

Great flavor, low calorie and good without beef, too.

Joyce Hohman - Warsaw, Indiana

Apple Muffins

2 cups apple chopped fine
3/4 cup sugar
1 banana, mashed
1 egg
1 cup and 1 tablespoon flour
1 teaspoon soda
1 teaspoon cinnamon

Combine apple, sugar and banana. Set aside. Sift together flour, cinnamon and soda. Beat egg. Add to apple mixture. Stir in flour and mix together. Fill muffin cups 1/2 to 2/3 full. Bake at 350 degrees for 20 minutes.

Annabelle Fralick - Convoy, Ohio

Apricot Bread

1 cup snipped dried apricots
1/3 cup canned apricots (diced
    and drained)
2 cups warm water
1 cup sugar
2 tablespoons margarine
2 teaspoons baking powder
1 egg
3/4 cup orange juice
2 cups all-purpose flour
1/4 teaspoon baking soda
1 teaspoon salt
3/4 cup chopped nuts
    (walnuts or pecans)

Soak dried apricots in warm water then drain well. Cream sugar, margarine and egg. Stir in orange juice. Combine flour, baking powder, baking soda and salt. Stir in creamed mixture just until combined. Add drained apricots, dried and canned and add nuts. Pour into 9 x 5 x 3 pan. Bake at 350 degrees for 55 minutes or until bread tests done. Cool 10 minutes in pan before removing to wire rack. Yield: 1 loaf. (a good, moist bread)

Doloris Kerts - Columbus, Indiana

Banana Oatmeal Muffins

1/4 cup butter or margarine,
   softened
3/4 cup brown sugar
1 cup buttermilk
1 cup rolled oats
1 cup all-purpose flour
1 tablespoon baking powder
1/2 teaspoon salt
1 egg beaten
1/2 teaspoon allspice
2 medium bananas, mashed

Cream together butter and brown sugar. Mix in egg and buttermilk. Mix together oats, flour, baking powder, salt and allspice. Add to creamed mixture. Stir in bananas. Spoon into greased or paper-lined muffin pan, filling almost full. Bake at 400 to 425 degrees for 20 to 25 minutes, until golden brown. Makes 12 muffins.

Marsha Chenoweth - Warren, Indiana

Banana Muffins

1 egg
3 tablespoons oil
1 1/4 cups mashed bananas
1/3 cup sugar
2 cups Bisquick

Mix egg, oil and bananas. Add sugar and Bisquick. Bake in 12 muffin tins for 15 minutes at 400 degrees.

Dorothy E. Miller - Delphi, Indiana

Bran Muffins

5 cups all-purpose flour
5 teaspoons baking soda
2 teaspoons ground allspice
8 cups bran flakes with raisins
1 quart buttermilk
2 teaspoons salt
3 cups sugar
4 eggs
1 cup vegetable oil
2 teaspoons vanilla

Using a very large bowl, combine flour, soda, salt, allspice. Add the bran flakes and sugar and mix. In a mixing bowl, beat the eggs. Add oil, buttermilk and vanilla to the eggs and blend. Pour the egg mixture over the flour mixture and stir well. Transfer the batter to a large plastic container that has a tight-fitting cover and store in refrigerator until ready to use. When ready to bake, **do not stir batter**. Fill greased muffin tin or use paper liners with 1/2 cup batter. Bake in preheated 375 degree oven for 20 minutes. Note: This batter will keep in refrigerator for 6 weeks.

Mary Curry - Hope, Indiana

Butter Horns

1 package dry yeast
1 tablespoon sugar
3 eggs
1 cup warm water
1/2 cup sugar
1/2 cup shortening
1/2 teaspoon salt
5 cups flour

Mix together the yeast, 1 tablespoon sugar.
Beat in eggs with warm water. Let stand
15 minutes. Add sugar, shortening, salt and flour.
Knead well. Let stand in refrigerator overnight.
Divide into two parts; roll out in 12 inch circles.
Cut in 16 wedges. Roll up starting with wide side.
Let rise 3 to 4 hours. Bake at 400 degrees for
15 minutes. Brush with butter. Really good!

Imogene Berkenstock - Columbus, Indiana

Cheese Garlic Biscuits

2 cups buttermilk baking mix
2/3 cup milk
1/2 cup shredded cheese
1/4 cup butter, melted
1/2 teaspoon garlic powder

Combine buttermilk baking mix, milk and shredded
cheese until soft dough forms. Beat vigorously for
30 seconds. Drop dough by heaping tablespoons
onto ungreased cookie sheet. Bakeat 450 for
8 to 10 minutes or until golden brown. Combine
melted butter and garlic powder. Brush over warm
biscuits before removing from cookie sheet.
Serve warm.

Deloris L. Jennings - Sullivan, Indiana

Cracked Wheat Bread

2 cups boiling water
1 1/4 cups cracked wheat
1/2 cup brown sugar
1 teaspoon salt
2 tablespoons butter
2 cakes yeast, dissolved in
    2/3 cup warm water
1 tablespoon granulated sugar
3 3/4 cups flour, sifted

Pour boiling water over the cracked wheat. Add the
brown sugar, salt and butter. Cool. Add the granulated sugar to the yeast mixture. Combine with the
cooled cracked wheat mixture. Add flour and mix
thoroughly. Turn out on a floured board and mix
until smooth. Place in a buttered bowl, cover and
let rise for one hour. Punch down and let rise again
for thirty minutes. Punch down and turn onto a
floured board. Shape into two loaves. Place in
buttered loaf pans and let rise until the dough
reaches the top of the pans. Bake in a 350-degree
oven for one hour and fifteen minutes.

Jane Yochum - Plymouth, Indiana

Overnight French Toast

3 eggs
1/2 cup milk
2 tablespoons sugar
1/8 teaspoon baking powder
1 teaspoon vanilla extract
1/2 teaspoon almond extract
6 slices French bread
    (3/4 inches thick)
butter or margarine

Beat eggs with milk, sugar, baking powder and extracts until blended. Place bread in a shallow baking pan and slowly pour the batter over it. Press a slice of wax paper directly on the bread to cover it, and refrigerate overnight. Melt approximately 4 tablespoons butter in a skillet and over moderate heat fry bread, turning once, until golden brown on both sides. Serve with hot syrup.

Beth Myer - Greentown, Indiana

Pineapple Zucchini Bread

3 eggs
1 cup oil
2 cups sugar
2 teaspoons vanilla
2 cups shredded zucchini
1 can (8 1/4 ounce) crushed
    pineapple, well drained
3 cups flour
1 teaspoon salt
2 teaspoons baking soda
1/4 teaspoon baking powder
1 1/2 teaspoons cinnamon
3/4 teaspoon nutmeg
1 cup raisins
1 cup chopped nuts

Beat eggs, oil, sugar and vanilla until thick. Stir in zucchini, pineapple, flour, soda, salt, baking powder, cinnamon, nutmeg, raisins, and nuts. Blend well. Pour into 2 greased and floured loaf pans. Bake at 350 degrees for 1 hour or until done. Note: to cut down on fat content, use 5 egg whites in place of 3 whole eggs and 1 cup of applesauce in place of the oil.

Cindy Turner - Bedford, Indiana

Pork and Bean Bread

1 cup raisins soaked in 1 cup
  boiling water, then drained
1 can pork and beans, mashed
  but not drained
4 eggs
2 cups sugar
1 cup oil
3 cups flour
1 teaspoon cinnamon
1 teaspoon soda
1/2 teaspoon baking powder
1 teaspoon vanilla
1 cup chopped nuts

Mix eggs, sugar, and oil. Beat thoroughly. Stir in beans. Add the sifted dry ingredients. Mix well. Add vanilla, raisins and nuts. Bake 55 minutes in 350 degree oven. Makes 2 loaves.

Colleen Ladd - Greentown, Indiana

Apple and Vegetable Salad

1 pound fresh asparagus
3 Red Delicious apples
2 small zucchini
1 avocado
spinach or Romaine lettuce
1/2 cup lemon salad dressing

Lemon salad dressing:
1 lemon, quartered
1 scallion (green onion)
1/2 teaspoon dry mustard
1/2 teaspoon celery seeds
1/2 cup water
1/4 teaspoon black pepper

In blender, process inside lemon quarters and scallions until fine. Add mustard, celery seeds, water and pepper. Process until smooth. Wash asparagus, tie in bunches and stand in rapidly boiling water that has been slightly salted. Cover the stalks, leaving tips out of water. Cook 5 minutes, then cover. Cook 10 minutes longer, drain and cool. Peel and slice apples, zucchini and avocado Place asparagus in center of greens. Arrange apples, zucchini and avocado around asparagus. Chill. Serve with lemon dressing. Serves 4.

Elaine Hunt - Decatur, Indiana

Apple Salad

4 apples, chopped into
    bite-size pieces
1 cup small marshmallows
1 cup chopped nuts
1 cup celery
1/2 cup raisins
1 8-ounce container Cool Whip

Mix all ingredients together and serve.

Carol Berkey - Warsaw, Indiana

Apple Salad

1 20-ounce can crushed
    pineapple, undrained
2/3 cup sugar
1 3-ounce package lemon gelatin
1 8-ounce package
    cream cheese, softened
1 cup diced unpeeled apples
1/2 to 1 cup chopped nuts
1 cup chopped celery
1 cup low fat whipped topping

In a saucepan, combine the pineapple and sugar; bring to a boil and boil for 3 minutes. Add gelatin, stir until dissolved. Add cream cheese; stir until mixture is thoroughly combined. Cool. Fold in apples, nuts, celery and whipped topping. Pour into a 9 inch square dish. Chill until firm. Cut into squares and serve on lettuce leaves. Makes 9 to 12 servings

Juanita Smith - Middletown, Indiana

French Dressing

1 cup sugar
1 teaspoon onion powder
1 teaspoon seasoned salt
1/2 teaspoon paprika
1/4 teaspoon ground cloves
1/2 teaspoon garlic powder
1 teaspoon Worcestershire sauce
1 tablespoon cornstarch
1/2 cup cider vinegar
1/4 cup water
1 can tomato soup
1/2 cup salad oil

In medium bowl, mix sugar, onion powder, seasoned salt, paprika, cloves, garlic powder and Worcestershire sauce. Set aside. In pan, mix cornstarch, vinegar and water. Cook until clear. Boil 1 minute. Remove from heat, add first mixture and stir until sugar is dissolved. Pour into jar and add tomato soup and salad oil. Shake well and let stand to marinate flavors. Keeps well in refrigerator.

Marthanne Hensley - Fortville, Indiana

Marinated Vegetable Salad

1 can sliced black olives
1 20-ounce bag frozen
    California blend vegetables
3 stalks celery, chopped
1/2 cup sliced pimento
1 can green olives, sliced
1/2 pound sliced mushrooms
3/4 cup green onions, chopped
3 tomatoes, wedged

Dressing:

1 package Hidden Valley Ranch
    dressing mix
2/3 cup salad oil
1/4 cup vinegar

Combine all vegetables in bowl; set aside. In a small bowl, combine Hidden Valley Ranch dressing mix, salad oil and vinegar and blend well. Pour dressing over vegetables and marinate several hours before serving.

Roberta Tucker - Warsaw, Indiana

Oriental Salad

1 head lettuce, torn into
    small pieces
1 can mandarin oranges, drained
1/2 pound bacon, fried crisp
    and crumbled
5 ounces slivered almonds,
    browned in the bacon
    drippings
1 can french fried onion rings

Dressing:

2 1/2 tablespoons vinegar
2 1/2 tablespoons honey
1/2 teaspoon salt
1/3 cup sugar
1/2 teaspoon dry mustard
1/2 teaspoon paprika
1/2 small onion, minced
1/2 cup vegetable oil

Mix together all salad ingredients in large bowl and set aside. Mix together vinegar, honey, salt, sugar, dry mustard, paprika and onion. Heat until sugar dissolves. Cool and add vegetable oil. Put in blender and blend thoroughly. Just before serving, pour dressing over salad.

Nancy M. Alspaugh - Mentone, Indiana

Pretzel Salad

2 cups broken pretzels
2 tablespoons sugar
3/4 cup melted butter
1 large box orange gelatin
2 cups boiling water
1 large can peaches, drained
1 3/4 cups peach juice from
    canned sliced peaches
    (add water if needed)
1 8-ounce package cream cheese
1 cup powdered sugar
1 8-ounce container Cool Whip

Mix together pretzels, sugar and butter. Bake in 350 degree oven for 8 minutes. Set aside to cool. Dissolve gelatin in boiling water then add peach juice. Refrigerate until slightly set. Beat together the powdered sugar and cream cheese. Mix in Cool Whip and spread over pretzel crust. Set sliced peaches on Cool Whip mixture. Pour slightly set jello over peaches. Refrigerate. Serves 12 to 15. Note: may use strawberry gelatin and frozen strawberries in place of peaches.

Marcel G. Conley - Warsaw, Indiana
Nancy Barger - Warsaw, Indiana
Norma Luker - Warsaw, Indiana

Spring Salad

1 large package lime gelatin
3 cups boiling water
1 8-ounce can crushed
    pineapple, undrained
1/3 cup shredded cabbage
1/4 cup chopped celery
1/4 cup chopped radish
1/3 cup shredded carrots
1/4 cup chopped green pepper

Dissolve gelatin in water. Pour into 9 x 13 inch glass dish. Cool while preparing vegetables. Mix vegetables with a pinch of salt. Add pineapple with juice and vegetables to gelatin and refrigerate until firm. Cut into squares and serve on lettuce leaf with a dab of Miracle Whip.

Maxine Fritz - Brookville, Indiana

Tomatoes with Confetti Cottage Cheese

1 tablespoon dehydrated
    vegetable flakes
1/4 cup hot water
1 cup creamed cottage cheese
1/4 teaspoon seasoned salt
4 fresh tomatoes

Mix vegetable flakes and hot water. Let stand 10 minutes, drain. Mix flakes with cottage cheese and seasoned salt. Cut each tomato into 6 sections, but do not cut all the way through. Spoon 1/4 cup cottage cheese mixture into each tomato. Serve on bed of lettuce.

Shirley Fruechte - Decatur, Indiana

Black Beans and Rice

1 tablespoon vegetable oil
1 medium yellow onion (chopped)
1 small sweet red pepper
   (chopped)
2 cloves garlic or 1 teaspoon
   minced garlic
1 3/4 cups cooked and drained
   black beans
1/2 cup long grain rice
1 1/2 cups low sodium
   chicken broth
1/4 teaspoon red pepper flakes
1/4 teaspoon dried thyme
   (crumbled)
1 bay leaf
1/2 cup shredded Cheddar cheese

In large, heavy sauce pan, heat vegetable oil over moderate heat for one minute. Add onion and red pepper, cook until onion is soft. Add garlic, black beans, rice, chicken broth and spices; bring to a boil. Adjust heat so mixture boils gently. Cover and simmer 20 minutes or until rice is tender. Remove bay leaf and spoon rice and beans onto heated plates, sprinkle each portion with cheese. Serves 4. Variation: add browned ground turkey or chicken. For a spicier version, add hot sauce to taste.

Deb Rockenbaugh - Warsaw, Indiana

Broccoli Casserole

2 packages frozen broccoli,
   cooked, drained and chopped
1 can cream of mushroom soup
1/2 cup mayonnaise
1 tablespoon lemon juice
3/4 to 1 cup cooked rice
1 8-ounce jar Cheez Whiz
1 beaten egg
1/2 stick margarine
1/4 cup chopped onion
1/2 cup milk

Topping:
1 cup soda crackers, crushed
1/2 stick margarine

In a skillet, melt 1/2 stick margarine; add onions and saute. Add and melt Cheese Whiz, add beaten egg. In another pan, mix the mushroom soup, milk, mayonnaise, lemon juice, rice and drained broccoli. Mix and add to the skillet mixture. Pour into a 9 x 13 inch greased baking dish. Sprinkle with mixture of crushed soda crackers and melted margarine. Bake 350 degrees for 45 minutes.

Margreta Masters - Brookville, Indiana
Mary H. Roberts - Sullivan, Indiana
Dorothy E. Miller - Delphi, Indiana

California Casserole

2 pounds ground beef
1 medium green pepper,
    chopped
3/4 cup chopped onion
1 can (16 1/2-ounces)
    cream-style corn
1 can (8 ounces) tomato sauce
1 can (10 3/4 ounces tomato soup)
1 can mushrooms
1 can (10 ounces) tomatoes with
    green chilies, undrained
1 can (2 1/4 ounces) sliced ripe
    olives, drained
1 jar (4 ounces) chopped pimento
1 1/2 teaspoons celery salt
1/2 teaspoon chili powder
1/2 teaspoon dry mustard
1/4 teaspoon pepper
1 8-ounce package wide egg
    noodles, cooked and drained
2 cups (8 ounces) shredded
    Cheddar cheese

Brown meat, onion and pepper; drain off any fat.
Add remainder of ingredients, except the cheese.
Put in casserole dish. Cover and bake at
350 degrees for 50 minutes. Sprinkle with cheese
and bake additional 10 minutes to melt cheese.

Glenda Giggy - Andrews, Indiana

Cavatini

1 pound ground lean sausage
1 onion, diced
1 green or red pepper, diced
1 cup pasta shells
1 cup rotini
1 cup mostaccioli (or any 3
    different types of pasta)
3 ounces sliced pepperoni
    (separated and cut in half)
1 8-ounce can mushrooms,
    drained
1 quart prepared
    spaghetti sauce
4 ounces shredded
    Mozzarella cheese

Brown sausage, onion and diced pepper. Drain fat.
Cook pasta until tender, drain and rinse with cold
water. In large bowl, mix pasta, pepperoni,
mushrooms and spaghetti sauce. Transfer to large
baking dish and cover with mozzarella cheese. Bake
at 325 degrees for 25 minutes. Do not over-bake.

Happy Homemaker Extension Homemaker Club
Booneville, Indiana

Christy's Macaroni and Cheese

3 cups dry macaroni (cook 4 - 5 minutes and drain)
1 can Campbell's Cheddar Cheese Soup
1 soup can of milk
1/2 teaspoon dry mustard
1/2 teaspoon seasoned salt
1/4 teaspoon pepper
1/2 cup shredded Cheddar cheese
1/2 cup shredded Swiss cheese
1/2 cup Parmesan cheese (grated)
1 2.8 ounce can French fried onions

Combine soup, milk, seasonings and half of the cheeses, half of the onions and all the macaroni in a 9 x 13 inch buttered pan. Bake, covered, at 350 degrees for 25 to 30 minutes. Remove cover and top with remaining cheese and onions. Bake 5 minutes longer, or until onions brown a little bit on top.

Cathrine Marlin - Hope, Indiana

Vegetable Lasagna

1 cup chopped onion
3/4 cup chopped celery
1/3 cup chopped green pepper
1 1/2 teaspoons oregano leaves, crushed
1 teaspoon sugar
1/2 teaspoon garlic powder
3 tablespoons margarine
1 can crushed tomatoes
1 cup water
1/2 teaspoon Worcetershire sauce
1 1/2 cups shredded Mozzarella cheese
9 lasagna noodles
2 cups thinly sliced zucchini

Cook onions, celery and pepper in butter until tender. Add tomatoes, water and seasonings. Bring to boil. Reduce heat. Simmer for 30 minutes. Add 3/4 cup cheese. Stir until smooth. Preheat oven to 350 degrees. In 12 x 8 x 2 inch baking dish, spread 1 cup sauce, top with 3 noodles, 1 cup zucchini and one cup sauce. Repeat layers. Sprinkle with remaining cheese. Cover tightly with aluminum foil. Bake 45 minutes. Remove foil. Bake 15 minutes longer. Remove from oven. Let stand 15 minutes. Serves 8.

Betty L. Burkle - Rossville, Indiana

Italian Spaghetti Sauce with Meat Balls

2 6-ounce cans Italian style
    tomato paste
2 #2 1/2 cans tomatoes
    (3 1/2 cups fresh)
2 tablespoons olive oil
1/4 cup finely chopped onion
1 small clove garlic,
    finely chopped
1/4 cup celery, finely chopped
1 1/2 teaspoons salt
1 teaspoon granulated sugar
1/4 teaspoon nutmeg
1/2 teaspoon oregano
1/8 teaspoon pepper
1/4 cup chopped fresh parsley
1/4 cup grated Parmesan cheese
1/4 to 1/2 teaspoon baking soda
mushrooms

Italian Meat Balls:

1/2 pound beef, pork, lamb or
    veal, finely ground
3 slices toast, or less
2 tablespoons chopped parsley
1 small clove garlic, chopped fine
1 egg
2 tablespoons Parmesan cheese,
    grated
1 teaspoon salt
1/4 teaspoon pepper

Sauce: Brown onions, garlic and celery slowly in olive oil for 5 minutes. Put tomatoes through food strainer and discard seeds. Add tomatoes with tomato paste to onion mixture. Add all other ingredients except meat balls and baking soda. Simmer covered in a saucepan for about 1 hour, stirring occasionally. Then add browned meat balls and simmer covered for 30 minutes. Baking soda should be added last 10 minutes to neutralize acid in tomatoes, making sauce more palatable. Add soda a little at a time and cook sauce several minutes. Taste and add more soda if needed. Serve sauce over your favorite cooked pasta.

Meat Balls: Soak toast in cold water for 7 or 8 minutes, then press dry. Combine with all other ingredients and work until thoroughly blended. Form into 12 medium-sized balls and brown slowly in 2 tablespoons hot shortening until golden brown on all sides. Do not turn meat balls until absolutely brown to prevent breakage. Add meat balls and the pan drippings to the sauce. Add several table-spoons of water to frying pan, scrape drippings and add to sauce. Note: I usually double meat ball recipe and make smaller meat balls.

Joy LeCount - Warsaw, Indiana

Spaghetti Pie

6 ounces spaghetti, cooked
    according to package
3 egg whites
1 quart jar spaghetti sauce
1 can mushrooms, drained
    and rinsed
1 cup low fat cottage cheese
    (or part skim Ricotta)
3/4 cup shredded Mozzarella
    cheese (part skim milk)
1/4 cup grated Parmesan cheese

Stir Parmesan cheese and egg whites into spaghetti. Pour into a 10-inch pie plate and shape spaghetti mixture into a crust, then spread on cottage cheese. Top with spaghetti sauce and mushrooms. Bake uncovered at 350 degrees for 20 minutes. Spread Mozzarella cheese on top and bake 5 minutes longer. Let stand for 10 minutes. This may be frozen before adding cheese and baking. Serves 4 - 6.

Evelyn B. Kime - Mishawaka, Indiana

Zucchini Lasagna

1/2 pound ground beef
1/2 teaspoon oregano
1/3 cup chopped onion
4 medium-sized zucchini
1/4 teaspoon salt
1/8 teaspoon pepper
1/4 teaspoon basil
1 8-ounce container cottage
cheese
1 egg, beaten
1/4 pound Mozzarella cheese
2 tablespoons flour
1 5-ounce can tomato sauce

Preheat oven to 375 degrees. Brown ground beef and onion; drain. Add tomato sauce and spices. Heat to boiling. Reduce heat, simmer 5 minutes. Slice zucchini lengthwise in 1/4-inch thick slices. Combine cottage cheese with egg until well mixed. In 12 by 8-inch baking dish, arrange half of zucchini in layers; sprinkle with 1 tablespoon flour. Top with cottage cheese mixture and half of meat mixture. Repeat with zucchini and flour. Sprinkle with Mozzarella cheese. Add last of meat mixture. Bake 40 minutes. Let stand 10 minutes. Serve 6.

Coleen Mankey - Decatur, Indiana

Skillet Rice and Sausage Meal

1 pound smoked sausage links
3/4 cup long grain rice
3/4 cup water
1 can cream of celery soup
1 small onion, chopped
1 or 2 stalks celery, chopped
1 tablespoon Worcestershire
    sauce

Into a 10 inch skillet, add rice, water, soup, onion, celery and Worcestershire sauce. Stir together. Cut sausage into small pieces and place on top of the mixture. Bring to a boil; reduce heat and cover. Cook for 20 to 25 minutes.

Connie Atkinson - Terre Haute, Indiana

Barbecued Meatballs

Meatballs:
3 pounds ground beef
1 can (12 ounces) evaporated milk
1 cup oatmeal
1 cup cracker crumbs
2 eggs
1/2 cup chopped onion
1/2 teaspoon garlic powder
2 teaspoons salt
1/2 teaspoon pepper
2 teaspoons chili powder

Sauce:
2 cups catsup
1 cup brown sugar
1/2 teaspoon liquid smoke
    or to taste
1/2 teaspoon garlic powder
1/4 cup chopped onion

Sauce #2:
1 - 12 ounce Delmonte Chili Sauce
1 cup brown sugar
1 16 ounce whole cranberry sauce
1 can sauerkraut - well drained

Meatballs: combine all ingredients (mixture will be soft) and shape into walnut-size balls. Place meatballs in a single layer on wax paper-lined cookie sheets; freeze until solid. Store frozen meatballs in freezer bags until ready to cook.

Sauce: Combine all ingredients and stir until sugar is dissolved. Place frozen meatballs in 13x9x2 inch baking pan; pour on the sauce. Bake at 350 degrees for one hour. Yield: 80 meatballs.

Sauce #2: Combine all ingredients and stir until sugar and cranberry are dissolved.

Connie Whitcomb - Angola, Indiana
Nancy Barger - Portland, Indiana

Beef Stew

1 tablespoon olive oil
1 tablespoon chopped onion
1 tablespoon chopped carrot
1 tablespoon chopped celery
1 pound beef round,
    cut into 1 inch cubes
1 cup chopped canned
    tomatoes, with juice
1/2 teaspoon dried thyme
1 bay leaf
salt and pepper to taste
2 bunches green onions,
    chopped
2 medium carrots, pared and
    cut into 1 inch chunks
1 pound potatoes, pared and
    cut into 1 inch cubes
1 cup hot water
1 cup green beans, cut into
    1 inch pieces (fresh
    or canned)
1 tablespoon parsley flakes
1 tablespoon chopped mint
    (optional)

In medium casserole or heavy sauce pan, heat oil over medium heat. Saute chopped onion, carrot, and celery until onion is transparent. Add beef, raise heat to medium-high and saute, stirring for 5 minutes. Add tomatoes, thyme, bay leaf, salt and pepper. Bring to boil and lower heat. Simmer approximately 45 minutes. Add onion, carrots, potatoes and hot water. Cover and cook another 40 minutes. (If using fresh green beans, add when adding the above vegetables; if using canned green beans, add after cooking the above vegetables). Add parsley (and mint); remove bay leaf before serving.

Ruth Ann Livezey - Swayzee, Indiana

Elegant Rump Roast

1 (4-6 pound) rolled rump
1 can beef bouillon or 2 bouillon
    cubes in 8 ounces water
1 large bay leaf
cracked pepper
celery salt
3 tablespoons bacon fat
    or olive oil
2 stalks celery cut coarsely
1/2 cup burgundy
1 small can mushrooms or 1 pint
    sauteed fresh mushrooms

Brown roast on all sides in fat or oil. Season heavily with cracked pepper and celery salt on all sides while browning. Pour off drippings and add bouillon, water, bay leaf, celery and wine. Cover and bake at 325 degrees about 4 hours. When done, let stand about 15 minutes and slice thinly. Add an additional 1/3 cup wine and drained mushrooms to the liquid. Heat and serve along with sliced beef.

Leland Andrews - Champaign, Illinois
Aggie Justice - Indianapolis, Indiana

Korean Marinated Beef

1 pound beef (round steak
    works well)
4 tablespoons sugar
2 tablespoons peanut oil
6 tablespoons soy sauce
dash of pepper
1 green onion, diced
1 clove garlic, minced
4 tablespoons sesame seed

Cut beef into thin slices (3 inch square). Add sugar and oil, mix well. Then add soy sauce, pepper, green onion, garlic and sesame seed. Mix well. Let stand for an hour. Cook in skillet until meat is browned. Add small amount of water; cover and steam until meat is tender. Serve hot over cooked rice.

Betty Johnson - Brookville, Indiana

Pizza Casserole

1 pound ground beef
1 onion, chopped
1/2 cup water
2 cups macaroni, cooked
1 small can mushrooms
2 6-ounce cans tomato paste
1 teaspoon garlic salt
1/2 teaspoon oregano
1 package smoked sausage
1 pound sliced
    Mozzarella cheese

Brown onion and ground beef; drain off fat. Return to pan and add 1/2 cup water, mushrooms and cooked macaroni. Mix tomato paste, garlic salt and oregano together. Alternate layers of tomato paste mixture, ground beef, and cheese, beginning with tomato sauce, and ending with cheese. Top with sliced smoked sausage. Bake covered at 350 degrees for 50 minutes, uncover, add mozzeralla cheese and bake additional 10 minutes to brown cheese.

Jackie Reeves - Terre Haute, Indiana

Sloppy Joes

1 pound ground beef
1 cup celery, diced
1 cup onion, diced
1 can tomato soup
1/4 cup catsup
1 tablespoon
    Worcestershire sauce
1 teaspoon Tabasco sauce
1 tablespoon sugar
salt and pepper to taste

Brown together ground beef, celery and onions. Add remaining ingredients and simmer for 10 - 15 minutes. Serve on buns.

Linda Hamilton - Jonesboro, Indiana

Sweet and Sour Pot Roast

3 to 5 pound pot roast
3 tablespoons fat or suet
1 or 2 onions, sliced
3/4 cup brown sugar
1 cup vinegar
1/2 teaspoon nutmeg

Cook onions in vinegar in heavy saucepan until transparent. Remove onions and save. In large pan, brown meat well on both sides. Add onions, vinegar, brown sugar and nutmeg. Stir liquid around meat. Cover and bake in oven at 325 degrees until done. Note: also works well with venison.

Betty Johnson - Brookville, Indiana

Breakfast Ham Casserole

12 slices bread
6 slices ham (or shaved ham)
6 slices Cheddar cheese
6 eggs
3 cups milk
1 cup corn flakes
1/4 cup melted butter
salt and pepper to taste

Butter a 9 x 12 inch dish. Lay 6 slices of bread in dish. Top with the ham and cheese. Lay remaining bread on top, making a sandwich. Sprinkle with salt and pepper. Beat eggs and mix with milk. Add butter and corn flakes and pour over all. Refrigerate several hours or overnight. Bake at 325 degrees for 1 hour.

Alberta Thomas - Fort Wayne, Indiana

Breakfast Pizza

1/2 pound bulk pork sausage
   (or ground turkey)
1 tube refrigerated crescent rolls
1 cup frozen shredded
   hash brown potatoes
1 tablespoon dried onion flakes
4 ounces shredded
   Cheddar cheese
5 eggs
1/4 cup milk
1/2 teaspoon salt
1/8 teaspoon pepper
2 tablespoons grated
   Parmesan cheese

In a skillet, brown sausage, drain and crumble. Separate crescent roll dough into eight triangles and place on an ungreased 12-inch round pizza pan with points toward center. Press over bottom and up sides to form a crust. Seal perforations. Spoon sausage over crust. Mix onion flakes and hash browns together and spread over sausage and top with Cheddar cheese. In a bowl, beat eggs, milk, salt and pepper; pour evenly over all Sprinkle with Parmesan cheese. Bake at 375 degrees for about 25 minutes.

Ruth Ann Livezey - Swayzee, Indiana

Ham Loaf

2 pounds ground ham loaf
   mixture
2 eggs
1 cup milk
1 cup bread crumbs
1/4 teaspoon pepper
2 teaspoons dry mustard

Glaze:
1/2 cup water
1/3 cup brown sugar
1/4 cup vinegar
2 tablespoons dry mustard

Mix together all ingredients for ham loaf, form into small individual loaves and place in baking dish. Mix together ingredients for glaze and pour over and around loaves. Place in 350 degree oven for 1 1/2 hours. Brush glaze over loaves from time to time while baking.

Maxine Fritz - Brookville, Indiana

Red Raspberry Vinegar Pork Chops

1 tablespoon margarine
1 tablespoon vegetable oil
   or olive oil
3 pounds pork chops, 1-inch thick
1/2 cup raspberry vinegar, divided
3 cloves garlic, sliced
2 tomatoes, seeded and chopped
1 teaspoon dried sage, or thyme,
   or tarragon, or basil
1/2 cup chicken stock
salt and pepper to taste
1 tablespoon fresh
   or dried parsley
sage to garnish
fresh red raspberries to garnish

Melt margarine in large skillet; add oil. Brown chops on each side over high heat. Pour off oil; reduce heat to medium low. Add 2 tablespoons vinegar and garlic. Cover; simmer for 10 minutes. Remove chops to heated container; cover and keep warm. Add remaining vinegar; stir up browned bits from bottom of skillet. Raise heat and boil until vinegar is reduced to a thick glaze. Add the tomatoes, sage, parsley and chicken stock. Boil until liquid is reduced to half of original volume. Strain sauce, season with salt and pepper. Spoon over chops. Serves 8. Note: Chicken breasts may be substituted.

Nadine Scholz - Fort Wayne, Indiana

Scalloped Sausage and Potatoes

1 pound sausage
8-10 medium potatoes, sliced
1/4 cup flour
Velveeta or American
    cheese slices
1 cup milk

In skillet, cook sausage slowly and break into small pieces. Brown and drain. In 9 x 13 inch baking dish, layer potatoes and sausage in two layers. Cover with cheese and pour milk mixed with flour over all. Cover with foil and bake at 350 degrees for 45-60 minutes. Serves 4-6.

Shirley Padgett - Terre Haute, Indiana

Baked Chicken Reuben

4 whole chicken breasts,
    boned and halved
1/4 teaspoon salt
1/8 teaspoon pepper
16 ounces sauerkraut; drain and
    squeeze out all liquid
4 slices natural Swiss cheese
    (4x6 inches)
1 1/4 cups bottled
    Thousand Island Dressing
1 tablespoon chopped
    fresh parsley

Place chicken in a greased baking pan. Sprinkle with salt and pepper. Add sauerkraut over the chicken. Top with Swiss cheese. Pour dressing evenly over cheese. Cover with foil and bake in 325 degree oven for about 1 1/2 hours or until fork can be inserted in chicken with ease. Sprinkle with chopped parsley to serve.

Pauline Baatz and Ruth Longroy
Fort Wayne, Indiana

Chicken Broccoli Casserole

2 10-ounce packages
    frozen broccoli
2 cans cream of chicken soup
2 cups diced cooked chicken
1 cup cooked rice
1 cup mayonnaise
1 teaspoon lemon juice
1/2 cup shredded sharp
    Cheddar chese
1 tablespoon butter
1/2 cup bread crumbs or
    crushed Ritz Crackers

Butter 9 x 11 baking dish. Line with cooked broccoli, then chicken. Can repeat as many times as desired. Cover with rice mixture of cream of chicken soup, mayonnaise and lemon juice; then sprinkle cheese and top with bread crumbs. Bake 45 minutes at 350 degrees. Can use crushed Ritz Crackers or bread crumbs.

Rachel M. Stultz - Portland, Indiana

Chicken Noodle Almondine

2 cups noodles
1 green onion, sliced
1 tablespoon margarine
1 can cream of chicken soup
1/4 cup milk
2 cups or more diced chicken
    or turkey (cooked)
1/2 cup sliced almonds, toasted

Cook noodles in salted water until tender. Drain. Cook onion in margarine 2 or 3 minutes. Stir in soup, then milk. Heat until bubbly. Add chicken and heat through. Stir in almonds. Mix in noodles and put in casserole dish to reheat.

Ruth Murray - Terre Haute, Indiana

Chicken Coq Au Vin

2 chicken breasts
2 chicken thighs
1 tablespoon olive oil
1/4 pound minced bacon
1/2 cup pearl onions
1 sliced carrot
3 minced shallots
1 clove garlic minced
2 tablespoons flour
2 tablespoons minced parsley
1 tablespoon marjoram
1/2 bay leaf
1/2 teaspoon thyme
1 teaspoon salt
1/2 teaspoon pepper
1/2 cup sherry
1/2 cup dry red wine
1/2 pound sliced mushrooms

Brown bacon, pearl onions, carrot, shallots and garlic in olive oil. Brown chicken. Add flour, parsley, marjoram, bay leaf, thyme, salt and pepper. Add cup sherry, cup dry red wine. Simmer one hour. Add sliced mushrooms 5 minutes before done. Serve over cooked rice.

Charles and Sarah Watson - Springfield, Illinois

Chicken Casserole

1 large package frozen
 California mixed vegetables
2 cups cut-up chicken
2 cans cream of chicken soup
1 cup salad dressing
1 teaspoon lemon juice
1/2 cup shredded
 Cheddar cheese
1/2 cup bread crumbs
1 tablespoon butter

Combine cream of chicken soup, salad dressing, lemon juice, and shredded cheese and then add the chicken. Pour over California blend vegetables. Pour into buttered casserole dish. Mix together butter and bread crumbs and sprinkle on top of casserole. Bake for 25 to 30 minutes at 350 degrees.

Margaret Rybolt - Swayzee, Indiana

Chicken Casserole

1 6-ounce package long grain
and wild rice, cooked
according to package
directions.
2 cups diced cooked chicken
1/4 pound sliced
 fresh mushrooms
1 10 3/4 ounce can creamy
chicken mushroom soup
1/2 cup milk
1 4-ounce can sliced black olives
2 cups grated Cheddar cheese
1/3 to 1/2 cup slivered almonds

Spread cooked rice in greased 3-quart oblong baking dish. Top with chicken and mushrooms. Combine soup and milk; pour over ingredients in casserole. Add layer of olives and cheese. Sprinkle with almonds. Bake uncovered in 350 degree oven for 40 to 45 minutes. If browning occurs, cover loosely with foil.

Imogene Emmert - Hope, Indiana

Honey Mustard Baked Chicken

1-3 pieces chicken cut-up
1/2 cup butter or margarine
1/2 cup honey
1/4 cup Dijon mustard
1/2 teaspoon salt
1/4 teaspoon pepper

Preheat oven to 350 degrees. Place chicken pieces in a baking dish. Combine butter, honey, mustard, salt and pepper and spread over chicken. Bake one hour, basting with pan juice every 15 minutes until chicken is tender and golden brown.

Sharon Clay - Warsaw, Indiana

172

Chinese Barbecue Stir Fry

1/2 cup bottled haisin sauce
    (haisin is a sweet, rich sauce
    found in the oriental
    food section)
2 tablespoons balsamic vinegar
2 teaspoons brown sugar
1/4 teaspoon garlic powder
1/4 teaspoon black pepper
1 pound skinless, boneless
    chicken breast, cut in
    bite-size pieces
2 tablespoons cooking oil
1 medium sweet pepper,
    cut in strips
1 large onion, halved and
    separated in rings
1 large carrot, thinly bias sliced
2 teaspoons cornstarch
2 cups coarsely chopped cabbage
Hot cooked rice

In medium bowl, combine haisin sauce, vinegar, brown sugar, garlic powder, black pepper. Rinse chicken and add to previous ingredients. Toss to coat. Cover and refrigerate for 1 to 24 hours. Heat 1 tablespoon oil in wok or large skillet over medium heat. Add green pepper, carrots and onion. Stir fry 3 to 4 minutes or to crisp-tender. Remove from skillet. Drain chicken, reserving liquid. Stir cornstarch into liquid and set aside. Heat remaining oil and add half of the chicken. Stir fry for 2 to 3 minutes. Repeat with remaining chicken. Put all ingredients in wok and add cabbage. Heat through. Serve over hot cooked rice. Makes 4 servings.

Ruth Worthman - Ossian, Indiana

Crispy Elegant Chicken

4 cups cut-up chicken
1 10 3/4-ounce cream of
    chicken soup
1 small can drained
    water chestnuts
1 quart of drained green beans
1 cup of light mayonnaise
1 medium onion, chopped
1 4-ounce can pimentos
    (drained and diced)
1 6-ounce box of long grain
    wild rice (prepared as
    directed on package)
Cheddar cheese and
    bread crumbs for topping

Preheat oven to 350 degrees. Combine ingredients, except Cheddar cheese and bread crumbs, and place in a greased 9 x 13 inch baking dish. Top with bits of Cheddar cheese and dry bread crumbs. Note: You may divide into two 8 x 8 inch cake pans and freeze one pan for future meal.

Mrs. Dale Arnholt - Columbus, Indiana

Moo Goo Gai Pan

1/2 cup juice drained from can of
 juice pack chunk pineapple
1 medium green pepper,
 cut into strips
1 cup thinly sliced celery
1 cup sliced mushrooms
1 small onion, sliced
 into thin wedges
1/2 teaspoon salt
1/4 teaspoon ground ginger
1/8 teaspoon white pepper
14 ounces chicken meat,
 cut into bite-sized pieces
1 tablespoon soy sauce
1/2 cup chunk pineapple,
 drained

Spray electric wok or large skillet with non-stick vegetable spray. Using medium heat (350 degrees for wok), add vegetables. Stir-fry for 2 minutes or just until tender-crisp. Use small amounts of pineapple juice if vegetables become too dry to fry. Remove vegetables to another bowl. Add 1/4 cup pineapple juice, chicken and combined spices. Stir-fry until chicken turns white. Add remainder of juice, vegetable mixture, soy sauce and pineapple; stir-fry until hot. Serves 2.

Shirley Fruechte - Decatur, Indiana

Sweet and Sour Chicken

3/4 pound boneless
 chicken breast, cubed
1 tablespoon oil
1 cup green and red pepper strips
1 tablespoon cornstarch
1/4 cup light soy sauce
1 can (8 ounces) pineapple
 in own juice
3 tablespoons vinegar
3 tablespoons brown sugar
1/2 teaspoon ground ginger
1/2 teaspoon garlic powder
1 1/2 cups Instant Minute
 Brown Rice

Cook chicken in large skillet until browned. Add pepper strips. Cook and stir 1 to 2 minutes. Mix soy sauce and cornstarch; add to pan with pineapple and juice, vinegar, sugar, ginger and garlic powder. Bring to full boil. Meanwhile, prepare rice as directed on package. Serve chicken over rice.

Mrs. Betty Roupp - Edinburg, Indiana

Taco Pie

1 pound ground turkey,
   browned and drained
1 cup water
1 package taco seasoning
1 cup celery
1 cup chopped onion
1 cup chopped tomatoes
1 cup chopped green pepper
3/4 cup self-rising flour
1 cup skim milk
4 egg whites
2 cups shredded
   Cheddar cheese

Simmer cooked ground turkey, water and taco seasoning until thick. Mix together the celery, onion, tomatoes and green peppers and sprinkle over meat mixture. Mix together flour, milk and egg whites. Pour over meat/vegetable mixture. Top with cheese. Bake at 350 degrees for 35 minutes.

Melinda Hauri - Connersville, Indiana

Thyme Chicken Marsala

2 skinless, boneless chicken
   breast halves (4 ounces each)
1 tablespoon all purpose flour
2 tablespoons olive oil
1 small red or yellow pepper,
   cut in strips
1 medium carrot, cut in strips
2 cloves garlic, minced
1/4 teaspoon salt
1/4 teaspoon pepper
1/3 cup Marsala wine (or water)
1 tablespoon fresh thyme or
   1/4 teaspoon crushed thyme
hot cooked linguine

Rinse and dry chicken; place bone side up between two pieces of plastic wrap. Pound flat to 1/4 inch thickness. Coat chicken with flour and set aside. In a large skillet heat oil and add carrots for 3 minutes. Add red pepper, garlic, salt, and pepper and cook, stirring for 5 minutes. Arrange on two dinner plates and keep warm. In same skillet heat 1 tablespoon olive oil over medium heat and add chicken; cook for 2 to 3 minutes each side or until no pink remains. Place chicken on top of vegetables. Add wine (or water), thyme and heat for one minute, scraping up browned bits from skillet. Pour over chicken. Makes two servings.

Ruth Worthman - Ossian, Indiana

Baked Fish

2 chicken bouillon cubes
1/2 to 3/4 cup water
4 to 5 pared carrots, cut julienne
1 pound or more fish
onion salt to taste
garlic salt to taste
large onion, sliced

Preheat oven to 350 degrees. Dissolve the cubes in water; line 9 x 13 inch pan with foil. Place water and carrots in bottom. Lay fish on carrots and season. Put onion on fish. Cover with foil and seal. Bake 1 to 1 1/2 hours.

Helen Miller - Monroe, Indiana

Cod Southwestern Style

Fish:
2 pounds fresh or frozen cod fillets
   (use other fish fillets
   if preferred)
1/4 teaspoon salt
1/4 teaspoon pepper
1/3 cup white wine
1/2 cup chicken broth

Sauce:
4 tablespoons margarine
1/2 cup chopped onion
1 1/3 cup diced sweet
   green pepper
3 large tomatoes, peeled
   and diced
2 tablespoons lemon juice
1 teaspoon chili powder
1/2 teaspoon salt
1/8 teaspoon pepper
1/4 teaspoon garlic powder
1/4 teaspoon thyme
1/4 teaspoon oregano
6 slices (about 1/2 ounce each)
   Mozzarella cheese

Thaw fish, if frozen. Preheat oven to 350 degrees. Divide fish into six equal portions. Place fish in a large frying pan, season with salt and pepper, pour wine and chicken broth over fish and cover. Bring to a boil, turn heat to low and poach fish for 10 minutes. Meanwhile, prepare the sauce. Melt margarine; saute onions, add the green pepper, and cook gently for 3 minutes. Add the remaining ingredients except the cheese slices; simmer for 10 minutes. Place fish on oven-proof platter. Cover fish entirely with sauce. Place a thin slice of cheese over each portion of fish. Place in oven for a few minutes, just long enough to melt cheese.

Roberta Tucker - Warsaw, Indiana

Hot 'N Crunchy Tuna Salad

2 6 1/2-ounce cans tuna, drained
1 1/2 cups diced celery
1 cup mayonnaise or
    salad dressing
1 cup Rice Chex or
    Corn Chex cereal
1 teaspoon lemon juice
1 4-ounce can drained,
    sliced mushrooms
1/2 cup sliced black olives
1 tablespoon grated onion
1/2 cup shredded Cheddar cheese
1 tablespoon melted margarine
1 cup Chex cereal, crushed

Combine tuna, celery, mayonnaise, Chex cereal, lemon juice, mushrooms, olives and onion. Pour into greased casserole dish and bake 15 minutes at 350 degrees. Remove from oven and sprinkle cheese on top. Mix together the melted margarine and crushed Chex cereal and sprinkle on top of cheese. Bake another 10 minutes until cheese melts and topping is crisp.   Note: My husband hates all casseroles - except this one!

Linda Woodhouse - Hope, Indiana

Odd Boil

2 gallons water
4 teaspoons seafood seasoning
8 ears corn, fresh or frozen
8 medium Irish potatoes
2 pounds smoked sausage,
    cut into 2-inch pieces
3 pounds shrimp in the shell

Let water come to a hard boil. Add seasoning, corn and potatoes. Cook about 15 minutes. Add shrimp and sausage and boil until shrimp are pink (2 - 3 minutes). Remove everything to large tray.

Jill Brechbill - Terre Haute, Indiana

Corn Casserole

1 can whole kernel corn, drained
1 can creamed corn
1 box Jiffy corn muffin mix
1 cup sour cream
1 stick butter or margarine,
    melted
2 eggs, beaten

Mix together. Bake at 400 degrees for one hour in greased casserole dish. Delicious!

Brenda Ummel - Argos, Indiana

Au Gratin Potatoes

8 cups cubed, peeled potatoes
1/4 cup butter or margarine
2 tablespoons all-purpose flour
3/4 teaspoon salt
1/8 teaspoon pepper
1 1/2 cups milk
1 pound process American cheese, cubed
Minced fresh parsley

In a large saucepan, cook potatoes in boiling water until done. Drain and place in a greased 2 1/2 quart baking dish. In a saucepan melt butter; add the flour, salt and pepper; stir to form a smooth paste. Gradually, add milk, stirring constantly. Bring to a boil. Boil and stir one minute. Add cheese and stir until melted. Pour over potatoes. Cover and bake at 350 degrees for 40 - 45 minutes or until bubbly. Sprinkle with parsley. 12 servings.

Caroline Murphy - Putnam County, Indiana

Florentine Scalloped Potatoes

1 10 3/4-ounce can condensed
    Cheddar cheese soup
1 16-ounce can tomatoes,
    drained and chopped
1 10-ounce packaged frozen
    chopped spinach, thawed
1/2 cup sliced onion
1 tablespoon chopped
    fresh parsley
4 cups shredded Swiss cheese
dash of pepper
1/2 teaspoon lemon juice
1 clove garlic, minced
4 cups thinly sliced potatoes

Preheat oven to 375 degrees. Stir together all ingredients, except 1/2 of cheese and potatoes. Layer into buttered 2 quart casserole dish; sprinkle top with reserved cheese. Cover and bake for one hour and 10 minutes. Serves 6 - 8. Note: Low fat cheese may be used—save a few sprinkles of cheese to put on top uncovered and back into oven for ten minutes.

Jeannette Fivecoat - Elizabethtown, Indiana

Hot Potato Salad

8 to 10 potatoes
1 medium onion, chopped
1 cup Hellmann's mayonnaise
1 1-pound package
    Velveeta cheese
1/4 to 1/2 cup bacon bits
1 pound bacon, cooked
    and drained

Make a day ahead of time. Boil potatoes with skins on until not quite done. Cool and cut into pieces. Add onion, mayonnaise, cheese, bacon and bacon bits. On the day you serve, bake 1/2 hour at 350 degrees.

Bernice Mathison - Pendleton, Indiana

Mushroom Casserole

1 stick butter or margarine
1/2 cup chopped onion
2 pounds fresh mushrooms,
    washed and drained
1/2 teaspoon marjoram
1/4 cup rounded flour
1 can Campbell's beef broth

Crumb Topping:
1 stack Ritz crackers
2 tablespoons Parmesan cheese
1/2 stick butter or margarine

Simmer in skillet, butter and onion until onion is tender. Add mushrooms and cook until they change color. Add marjoram and flour, distributing evenly over all. Stir well, but gently to incorporate flour, Add beef broth and cook until thick. Pour into 2 quart casserole (at this point mixture may be refrigerated until next day, if desired). Remove from refrigerator and allow to come to room temperature before baking. Mix crumb topping: crush Ritz crackers to crumb mixture and mix with Parmesan cheese and melted butter. Mix well and sprinkle over casserole. Bake at 350 degrees for 15 to 20 minutes or until it boils and crumbs are golden brown. Serves 6 to 8.

Joy LeCount - Warsaw, Indiana

Sweet 'n' Sour Brussel Sprouts

1 1/2 cups brussel sprouts
    (1 9-ounce frozen package)
2 slices bacon
2 tablespoons vinegar
1 1/2 teaspoons sugar
1/2 teaspoon salt
1/4 teaspoon garlic powder

Cook brussel sprouts according to package directions and drain thoroughly. Fry bacon until crisp, drain and crumble. Combine vinegar, sugar and seasonings. Stir into sprouts. Sprinkle bacon over sprouts. Heat through.

Marie Winan - Indiana

Scalloped Tomatoes

4 tablespoons extra virgin olive oil
2 cups French bread, cut into
    1/2 inch cubes
16 ripe plum tomatoes, cut into
    1/2 inch cubes
2 cloves of garlic, minced
1 tablespoon sugar
Salt and black pepper, to taste
1/2 cup shredded basil leaves
2 tablespoons Parmesan cheese

Preheat oven to 350 degrees. Place 2 tablespoons of olive oil in a large non-stick skillet. Add the bread crumbs and stir to coat. Saute over medium heat 5 - 7 minutes, or until bread is slightly browned. Add tomatoes and garlic to the bread. Sprinkle with the sugar. Cook, stirring frequently for 5 minutes. Season with salt and pepper, then stir in basil and remove from heat. Transfer the tomato mixture to a 1 1/2 quart casserole. Sprinkle the Parmesan cheese over the top and drizzle with the remaining olive oil. Bake until bubbling and lightly browned, 35 - 40 minutes. Serve at once.

Helen H. Cooper - Tell City, Indiana

Zucchini - Eggplant Medley

1 small zucchini, 1/4 inch slices
1 small green bell pepper,
   (cut in strips)
1 small onion, sliced
1 small egg plant, cut in cubes
1/4 teaspoon garlic pepper
dried basil leaves
salt
1 tablespoon parsley flakes
2 tablespoons water
2 medium tomatoes, cut into
    small wedges

Cook all ingredients, except tomatoes, over low heat in large skillet for 15 minutes. Add tomatoes and stir. Remove from heat, cover and let stand for 3 minutes. Serves: 6

Sula E. Foss - LaPorte, Indiana

Amy's Cake

1 box yellow cake mix
4 eggs
1/2 cup margarine, softened
1 8-ounce package
   cream cheese, softened
1 pound powdered sugar

Combine cake mix, 2 eggs and margarine. Spread into a greased 9 x 13 inch pan. Beat together powdered sugar, cream cheese and 2 eggs. Pour over batter. Bake at 350 degrees for 30 - 40 minutes.

Dee Loftin - Warsaw, Indiana

Apple Cake with Sauce

2 cups diced apples
1 cup sugar
1/8 teaspoon salt
1 cup flour
1 1/2 teaspoons cinnamon
1 teaspoon baking soda
1/8 teaspoon nutmeg
3/4 cup chopped walnuts
1 egg, beaten
1/2 cup butter, melted

Sauce:
1/2 cup brown sugar
1/2 cup white sugar
2 tablespoons flour
1/4 cup butter
1 cup water
1 teaspoon vanilla

Mix together apples and sugar. Let set until sugar dissolves and it makes liquid. Meanwhile, sift together the salt, flour, cinnamon, soda and nutmeg. Add dry ingredients to apples. Add egg, melted butter and walnuts to mixture. Pour into 9 x 9 inch greased pan. Bake at 350 degrees for 35 - 40 minutes, or until done. Mix all ingredients together for sauce and cook until thick and clear. Make holes in cake and pour sauce over hot cake.

Mildred Kingseed - Kokomo, Indiana and
Pauline Baatz - Fort Wayne, Indiana

Coca-Cola Cake

1 cup cola (Coke)
2 sticks butter or margarine
3 tablespoons cocoa
2 cups flour
2 cups sugar
2 eggs, well beaten
1/2 cup buttermilk
1 1/2 teaspoons vanilla
1 teaspoon baking soda
1 1/2 cups tiny marshmallows

Icing:
1/2 cup butter
3 tablespoons cocoa
6 tablespoons cola drink
1 box powdered sugar
1 cup chopped nuts

Heat butter, cola and cocoa to a boil. Set aside. Combine sugar and flour together. Add to cocoa mixture. Add buttermilk, eggs, soda and vanilla. Pour into greased shallow baking pan. Put marshmallows on top. Bake at 350 degrees for 30 to 40 minutes.

Icing: Combine butter, cocoa and cola; heat to a boil. Pour over powdered sugar and nuts. Spread over cake while hot.

Ruth H. Higbie - Marysville, Indiana

Fruit Crunch

1 - number 2 1/2 can crushed
    pineapple
1 can Thank You brand pie filling
    (cherry, peaches, etc.)
1 box yellow cake mix
1 1/2 sticks butter or margarine
1/4 cup chopped nuts, optional

No mixing. Just place all ingredients in layers into glass baking dish in order listed, slicing butter over top and sprinkle with nuts. Bake for about 50 minutes at 350 degrees.

Lois Bogue - Greentown, Indiana

German Chocolate Upside Down Cake

1 cup pecans
1 cup coconut
1 box German chocolate cake mix
    (prepared according to
    package directions)
1 8-ounce package cream cheese
1 stick margarine
1 1-pound package
    powdered sugar

Mix together pecans and coconut and spread in bottom of 9 x 13 inch pan sprayed with non-stick cooking spray. Pour cake batter over top of pecan/coconut mixture. Set aside. Melt together in a heavy saucepan cream cheese and margarine. Remove from heat and stir in powered sugar until smooth. Pour over cake mixture. Bake 45 - 50 minutes at 350 degrees. Cool before cutting. Cake is best if cooled for 10 - 12 hours.

Karen Von Dielingen - Noblesville, Indiana and
Florence Fraze - Brownstown, Indiana

Hawaiian Cake

1 package yellow cake mix (light)
3 egg whites
1 11-ounce can mandarin
    oranges - don't drain
1 1/3 cups water

Topping:
1 20-ounce can crushed
    pineapple - don't drain
9 ounces Lite Cool Whip
1 package sugar free instant
    banana pudding mix

Blend cake ingredients for 30 seconds on low. Then mix another 2 minutes on medium. Pour batter into 9 x 13 inch pan sprayed with vegetable spray. Bake for 35 minutes or until done at 350 degrees. Let cool. Spread with topping which is prepared by mixing together pineapple and pudding. Beat well. Add Cool Whip. After adding the topping, refrigerate cake.

Marjorie Mickley - Huntington, Indiana

Hummingbird Cake

Cake:
3 cups flour
1 teaspoon baking soda
1 1/2 teaspoons vanilla
1 1/4 cups oil
1 can crushed pineapple
    undrained
2 cups chopped bananas
2 cups sugar
1/2 teaspoon salt
1 teaspoon cinnamon
3 beaten eggs
1 cup chopped nuts (optional)

Frosting:
2 8 -ounce packages
    cream cheese, softened
1 cup butter softened
2 teaspoons vanilla
2 boxes or one pound of
    confectioners sugar
1 cup chopped nuts

Combine flour, sugar, salt and baking soda and cinnamon. Add eggs and oil stirring until dry ingredients are moistened. Add in vanilla, pineapple or nuts. Add chopped bananas. Spoon the batter into three well greased and floured 9 inch round cake pans or a 9 x 13 loaf pan. Bake in 350 degree oven 25 to 30 minutes or until cake tests done. Cool in pan for 10 minutes.

To prepare frosting: Beat cream cheese and butter, add sugar, nuts and vanilla. Beat with electric mixer. Frost top, sides and between layers.

Roberta Hinkle - Columbus, Indiana

Lemon Cake

1 box Duncan Hines Lemon
    Supreme cake mix
1 box lemon Jello diluted in
    1 cup boiling water (let cool)
4 eggs
2/3 cup Crisco oil.

Glaze:
2 tablespoons butter, softened
2 teaspoons water
1/3 cup lemon juice
2 cups powdered sugar

Blend together all ingredients for cake. Mix and bake at 350 degrees for 30 - 45 minutes. Let cake cool. Mix together glaze ingredients. Punch holes in cake and pour glaze over it. Cool Whip can be dolloped on cooled cake.

Alberta Offutt - Columbus, Indiana

Mawmaw's Chocolate Cake

1 cup shortening or margarine
1 1/2 cups sugar
2 eggs, sightly beaten
4 tablespoons cocoa
cold water
1 teaspoon vanilla
1 teaspoon soda
1 cup buttermilk
2 cups flour

Dissolve 4 tablespoons cocoa in enough cold water to make a paste and set aside. Blend the shortening, sugar, and eggs. Add vanilla, then the cocoa paste. Add flour, alternating with the buttermilk to which 1 teaspoon soda has been added. Mix well. Bake in two 9 inch round greased and floured cake pans at 350 degrees for 25 to 30 minutes. A moist cake and oh, so good! Icing of your choice.

Nadean Hensley - Anderson, Indiana

Mayonnaise Cake

1 cup sugar
4 tablespoons cocoa
2 cups flour
2 teaspoons soda dissolved
   in 1 cup cold water
1 cup mayonnaise
1 teaspoon vanilla

Mix sugar, cocoa and flour. Add soda (dissolved in 1 cup cold water), mayonnaise and vanilla. Mix well and pour into 7 x 12 inch glass baking dish. Bake 25 - 30 minutes at 350 degrees.

Karen Fear - Montpelier, Indiana

Mom's Cheese Cake

3 ounces cream cheese
1 package graham crackers, crushed fine
2/3 cup sugar
1 small box lemon Jello dissolved in 1 cup boiling water
1 teaspoon vanilla
2/3 stick butter, melted
1 carton Cool Whip
1 small container cottage cheese

Mix together butter and the graham cracker crumbs. Place 1/2 of the crumb mixture in bottom of baking dish. Set aside. Pour dissolved Jello over cream cheese and mix until smooth. Add sugar, vanilla, cottage cheese and mix. Fold in Cool Whip and pour batter on top of graham cracker crust. Sprinkle the remaining graham cracker crumb mixture on top. Chill.

Nancy Barger - Portland, Indiana

Red Raspberry Cake

1 12-ounce package frozen
    unsweetened red raspberries,
thawed or 1 pint fresh
1 package white cake mix
3/4 cup water
3 egg whites
1/3 cup vegetable oil

Buttercream icing:
3/4 cup butter or margarine,
softened
1 1-pound box powdered sugar
1 tablespoon milk, or more to
make frosting consistency

Grease and flour two 8 inch round cake pans.
Process raspberries in blender until smooth. Strain
and discard seeds. Mix cake using water, egg whites
and oil following package instructions. Gently fold
in raspberry puree. Pour into pan. Bake at
350 degrees for 30 minutes or until cake springs
back when touched.

Icing: Mix butter and sugar. Add milk. Cool and
frost with buttercream icing.

Pauline Rhine - Bunker Hill, Indiana

Texas Chocolate Sheet Cake

2 cups flour
2 cups sugar
1/2 teaspoon salt
2 sticks margarine
1 cup water
3 tablespoons cocoa
2 eggs, well beaten
1 teaspoon baking soda
1/2 cup buttermilk
1 teaspoon vanilla
1 teaspoon cinnamon

Icing:
1 stick margarine
1 tablespoon cocoa
5 tablespoons milk
1 1-pound box powdered sugar
1 teaspoon vanilla
1/2 cup pecans, if desired

Sift together in large bowl the first 3 ingredients
and set aside. Boil together margarine, water and
cocoa. Pour over flour and sugar mixture and mix
well. Beat together the eggs, baking soda, buttermilk, vanilla and cinnamon and add into other
ingredients. Stir well. Bake in greased 15 x 10 x 1
inch pan 20 minutes at 350 degrees. Ice while warm
with 1 can of frosting or prepare icing by boiling
together margarine, cocoa and milk. Add powdered
sugar, vanilla and chopped nuts. Beat thoroughly
and spread over warm sheet cake.

Betty Stutzman - Indiana

Buttered Toffee Apple Pie

Pie dough to make a double
    9 inch pie crust

Filling:
1/3 cup light corn syrup
3 tablespoons granulated sugar
1 tablespoon melted butter
1 tablespoon cornstarch
1 1/2 teaspoons ground cinnamon
1/2 teaspoon salt
6 tart apples, peeled, cored
    and sliced

Toffee Topping:
1/2 cup plus 2 tablespoons
    packed dark brown sugar
1/4 cup chopped walnuts
3 tablespoons light corn syrup
3 tablespoons melted butter
2 tablespoons all-purpose flour

Preheat oven to 425 degrees. Prepare pie crust and line bottom of 9 inch pie plate. Mix corn syrup, sugar, butter, cornstarch, cinnamon and salt in large bowl. Add apples and mix well. Pour apple mixture into unbaked pie shell. Top with dough. Crimp and flute edges, make 4 large slashes in top to vent steam. Bake in preheated oven for 10 minutes. Reduce oven to 350 degrees and bake until crust is golden (about 30 minutes). Meanwhile, mix topping ingredients in small bowl. Remove pie from oven and pour topping over it. Return to oven immediately and bake 5 minutes. Cool slightly on rack. Serve warm with ice cream.

Patricia Rogers - Metamora, Indiana

Crumb Pie

1 1/2 cups brown sugar
2 cups flour
1 teaspoon cinnamon
1 stick margarine
1 cup buttermilk
1 teaspoon soda

Make sugar, flour, cinnamon and margarine into crumbs. Take out 1 cup crumbs to put on top of batter. To remainder of crumbs, add buttermilk with soda. Mix well. Put into two medium-sized greased and floured pie pans. Sprinkle the cup of reserved crumbs over top of batter. Bake at 350 degrees for 30 minutes.

Carolyn Burkle - Carroll County, Indiana

Easy Apple Cobbler

1 frozen, unbaked apple pie
3/4 cup sugar
1/3 cup butter
1 1/2 cups water

Remove pie from pan onto cutting board. Chop pie up into bite-sized pieces. Place in a greased 9 x 13 inch pan. Sprinkle sugar and butter over top of chopped pie. Then pour water over this. Bake pie according to directions on box. Serve with ice cream. Serves 8 to 10 people.

Shelly Judy - North Webster, Indiana

Million Dollar Pie

1 can Eagle Brand
　Condensed Milk
1/3 cup of lemon juice
1 small can crushed pineapple
　with juice
1 cup coconut
1 cup pecans
1 family size Cool Whip -
　16 ounces

Mix together and pour into graham cracker crusts. Makes 3 pies.

Irene Koch - Angola, Indiana

Peach Cobbler

1/2 cup sugar
1 tablespoon cornstarch
1/4 teaspoon lemon juice
1/4 teaspoon ground cinnamon
3 tablespoons shortening
4 cups sliced peaches
1 cup flour
1 tablespoon sugar
1 1/2 teaspoons baking powder
1/2 teaspoon salt
1/2 cup milk

Heat oven to 400 degrees. Mix 1/2 cup sugar, the cornstarch and cinnamon in a 2-quart saucepan. Stir in peaches and lemon juice. Cook, stirring constantly until mixture thickens and boils. Boil and stir 1 minute. Pour into ungreased 2-quart casserole, keep peach mixture hot in oven. Cut shortening into flour, add 1 tablespoon sugar, baking powder and salt until mixture resembles fine crumbs. Stir in milk. Drop dough by 6 spoonfuls onto hot peach mixture. Bake until topping is golden brown, 25 to 30 minutes. Serve warm and, if desired, with cinnamon and whipped cream. 6 servings.

Pleasant Hill Home Economics Club - Booneville, Indiana

Perfect Apple Dumplings

2 cups sugar
2 cups water
1/4 teaspoon nutmeg
1/4 teaspoon cinnamon
1/4 cup butter
6 "Rome" apples, pared
    and cored
2 cups all-purpose flour
    (or 1 1/2 cups enriched flour
    and 1/2 cup whole wheat
    pastry flour)
2 teaspoons baking powder
1 teaspoon salt
3/4 cup butter-flavored Crisco
1/2 cup milk

Sauce: Combine in saucepan: sugar, water, nutmeg and cinnamon. Cook for 5 minutes over medium heat. Add 1/4 cup butter and set aside.

In mixing bowl, sift together the flour, baking powder and salt. Cut in butter-flavored Crisco, then add 1/2 cup milk all at once to make dough into a log. Divide into 6 equal portions. Dust work area with flour. Using 1 portion at a time, roll dough 1/4 inch thick. Place apple on rolled dough, dot with butter, sprinkle with additional spices and brown sugar. Wrap dough up around apple, fold corners; pinch edges. Continue with remaining dough and apples. Place in 9 x 13 inch baking dish. Pour sauce over all. Bake at 375 degrees for about 35 minutes. Best served warm with ice cream or milk. (I bake these in small baking dishes, individually, then cool and wrap for the freezer. They thaw wonderfully in the microwave for a quick dessert!) Note: depending on the size of the apples, the dough can be rolled thinner.

Ruth Reese - Rochester, Indiana

Pumpkin Pie (with Brown Sugar)

1 1/4 cup mashed,
    cooked pumpkin
1/2 teaspoon salt
1 1/4 cups milk
2 eggs
1/2 cup brown sugar
1 1/2 tablespoons white sugar
1 teaspoon cinnamon
1/3 teaspoon ginger
1/3 teaspoon nutmeg
1/4 teaspoon cloves
1 teaspoon whiskey

Beat together all ingredients and pour into a 9 inch unbaked pie shell. Bake at 425 degrees for 45 to 55 minutes. Serves 6. For a pie with lighter color and milder flavor, use all white sugar and omit cloves. Low fat milk may be subsituted.

Dorothy Burley - Patriot, Indiana

Perfect Pie Crust

2/3 cup Crisco
2 cups sifted flour
1 teaspoon salt
1/4 cup water

Mix flour and salt in bowl. Take out 1/3 cup of flour and set aside. Cut Crisco into remaining flour with pastry blender. Add 1/3 cup flour to the 1/4 cup of water in a one-cup measure. Stir lightly to dampen flour. Add to Crisco and flour mixture and mix until dough holds together and can be shaped into a ball. Divide into two parts. Double crust for 8 inch pie.

Inice Blunk - Tell City, Indiana

Vinegar Pie

1 cup sugar
4 tablespoons flour
2 tablespoons butter
2 cups water
1 1/2 tablespoons vinegar
1/2 teaspoon lemon extract
1/2 teaspoon nutmeg

Cook all ingredients together, as any filling, and place in a 9 inch baked pastry shell.

This recipe is 140 years old and appeared in the Huntington County Cookbook in 1854.

Dallas Trip Home Extension Club - Huntington, Indiana

Zucchini Pie

3 eggs
1 1/2 cups sugar
2 tablespoons flour
2 teaspoons lemon flavoring
1/2 stick butter or margarine
    melted
2 teaspoons coconut oil
    (the kind used in
    making candy)
1 cup grated, raw zucchini
1 9-inch pie shell, unbaked

Beat eggs. Mix sugar and flour together. Add to eggs. Add margarine or butter, flavorings and zucchini. Pour mixture into pie shell. Bake at 350 degrees for 45 minutes.

Madeline Zickmund - Rensselaer, Indiana

100 Good Cookies

1 cup brown sugar
1 cup white sugar
1 cup cooking oil
1 cup margarine
1 egg
3/4 teaspoon salt
1 teaspoon soda
1 teaspoon cream of tartar
1 teaspoon vanilla
3 1/2 cup flour
1 cup Rice Krispies
1 cup cooked quick oats

Cream together sugars, oil, vanilla and margarine. Add egg. Add dry ingredients to wet ingredients and mix well. Fold in gently 1 cup Rice Krispies and 1 cup cooked quick oats. Drop by spoonfuls onto ungreased cookie sheets. Bake 12-15 minutes in 350-degree oven.

Pauline Hall - Columbus, Indiana

Apple Oatmeal Cookies

4 cups wholewheat flour
    (may need more flour
    if apples are real juicy)
2 teaspoons baking soda
1 teaspoon salt
2 teaspoons cinnamon
1/2 teaspoon nutmeg
2 cups quick-cooking oatmeal
1 cup brown sugar
1 cup canola oil
2 eggs
2 teaspoons vanilla
2 cups peeled apples,
    chopped in processor
1 cup baking raisins
1 cup chopped pecans

Combine in large bowl: whole wheat flour, baking soda, salt, cinnamon, nutmeg, oats and brown sugar. Add and mix well canola oil, eggs and vanilla. Stir in apples, raisins and pecans. Drop by rounded teaspoonfuls onto greased cookie sheets. Bake until lightly browned. Carefully transfer to wire racks to cool. Yield: 8 dozen cookies.

Linda Hathaway - Claypool, Indiana

Coffee Cake Cookies

2 packages yeast
8 cups flour
1/2 cup sugar
1/2 cup warm water
4 eggs, beaten
2 teaspoons salt
1 pound margarine
2 cups milk, scalded and cooled

Sugar mixture:
2 cups sugar
2 tablespoons cinnamon

Dissolve yeast in warm water. In large bowl, combine flour, salt and sugar. Cut in margarine. Combine eggs, milk and yeast and add to flour mixture. Combine lightly. Cover tightly and refrigerate overnight. Divide dough into 4 parts. Roll out each part. Spread with sugar mixture, roll up and cut in 1-inch pieces. Place cut-side down on greased baking sheet. Flatten with palm of hand. Bake at 350 degrees for 12 to 15 minutes. Remove from baking sheet and while still warm, ice with powdered sugar frosting (fairly thin).

Pauline Baatz - Fort Wayne, Indiana

Kolacky

1 package dry yeast dissolved in
    2 tablespoons warm water
4 cups flour
1/4 cup sugar
1 teaspoon salt
1 teaspoon grated lemon peel
3/4 cup butter, softened
3 egg yolks
1 cup heavy cream
* Assorted solo fillings

Combine lemon rind and the yeast mixture; blend in butter and egg yolks. Then add the heavy cream. Sift together flour, sugar and salt. Add flour mixture until well blended. Cover and refrigerate overnight. Roll out on floured surface to 1/4 inch thickness, cut with round cutter. Place on ungreased cookie sheet. Cover and allow to rise till doubled. When they have risen, make a dent in the center and fill with solo filling. Bake at 375 degrees for 8 to 10 minutes until lightly brown. When cool, dust with powdered sugar. * Fillings: apricot, poppy seed, cherry, raspberry.

Jean Buczek - Rensselaer, Indiana

Lo-Cal Cookies

1 package angel food cake mix
1/2 cup diet red pop
1 1/2 teaspoons almond extract
7 ounce package coconut

Combine cake mix, pop and extract. Blend 1 1/2 minutes. Fold in coconut. Cover cookie sheet with foil and spray with Pam spray. Drop by spoonsful. Bake at 350 degrees for 10-12 minutes. Let cool on foil. 25 calories per cookie.

June Witte - Decatur, Indiana

Nutty Noodle Clusters

2 6-ounce packages
    chocolate chips
2 6-ounce packages
    butterscotch chips
2 cans chow mein noodles
1/2 cup peanuts or cashews

Combine chips and melt. Stir in noodles and nuts. Mix quickly to coat evenly. Drop by teaspoonful onto wax paper and cool. Yield: 24 Nutty Noodle Clusters.

Nancy M. Alspaugh - Mentone, Indiana

Sugar Cookies

1 cup butter or margarine,
    softened
1 1/2 cups confectioner's sugar
1 egg, slightly beaten
1 teaspoon vanilla
1 teaspoon almond extract
2 1/2 cups all-purpose flour

In a mixing bowl, cream butter and sugar. Add egg, vanilla and almond extracts. Stir in flour; mix well. Chill several hours. On a lightly floured surface, roll dough to 1/4 inch thickness; cut with a 2 1/2 or 3 inch cookie cutter. Place on ungreased baking sheets; sprinkle with sugar if desired. Bake at 375 degrees for 8 to 10 minutes or until lightly browned. Yield: 3 1/2 dozen.

Caroline A. Murray - Putnam County, Indiana

Blueberry Special

1 6-ounce package
    raspberry Jello
2 cups boiling water
1 20-ounce can crushed
    pineapple with juice
1 can blueberry pie filling
1/4 cup chopped pecans

Topping:
1 8-ounce package cream cheese
1/2 cup sour cream
1/4 cup sugar
1/4 cup chopped pecans

Dissolve Jello in boiling water; while hot, add pineapple and juice, pie filling and nuts. Pour into 9 x 13 inch pan and chill until set. Mix together topping ingredients and spread on top of Jello. Sprinkle with 1/4 cup chopped pecans. NOTE: use cherry Jello and cherry pie filling for Cherry Special.

Marceil Conley - Warsaw, Indiana

Fruit Soup

6 cups fruit juice (apple, orange
    or whatever you like)
1/4 cup tapioca
2 tablespoons cornstarch
4 cups fruit (peaches, canned or
    frozen, or any fruit you like)

Mix together fruit juice, tapioca and cornstarch. Bring to boil and let cool. Add fruit. Can be served warm or cold, with a whipped cream topping.

Iris Green - Jasonville, Indiana

Lemon Lush

1 cup flour
1 stick margarine
1 8-ounce carton Cool Whip
1 8-ounce package cream cheese
1 cup powdered sugar
2 3-ounce packages instant
    lemon Jello pudding
3 cups milk
1 cup chopped pecans

Crumb flour and margarine together. Press in bottom of a 9 x 13 baking pan. Bake for 15 minutes at 350 degrees. When cool, beat 1 cup Cool Whip, cream cheese and powdered sugar together and spread on crust. Fix pudding according to package directions. Spread on top of cream cheese. Put rest of Cool Whip and nuts on top. Note: can use any flavor pudding.

Mardel Budreau - Earl Park, Indiana

Fudge Nut Freeze

1/2 cup butter or margarine
1 cup flour
1/4 cup cocoa
1/4 cup sugar
1/2 cup almonds

Topping:
1 large container Cool Whip
1 quart vanilla ice cream
  (softened)
1/2 cup cocoa
1/2 cup or more marshmallows
1/2 cup almonds

Melt butter in skillet. Combine flour, cocoa, and sugar with butter. Heat over medium heat. Stir for 5 minutes. Cool. Add nuts. Sprinkle in 13 x 9inch pan. Reserve 1/2 cup.

In bowl mix Cool Whip, cocoa, ice cream and nuts. Beat well. Fold in marshmallows. Pour over crust. Sprinkle with 1/2 cup of the reserved topping. Freeze 6 hours.

Sharon Clay - Warsaw, Indiana

Peaches and Cream Bars

1 package yellow cake mix
2 eggs
1/2 cup melted margarine
1 package coconut pecan or
  coconut almond frosting mix
1 1-pound, 13-ounce can
  sliced peaches, drained
2 cups sour cream
1 egg

Combine dry cake mix, 2 eggs, margarine and dry frosting mix. Mix by hand. Press into ungreased 9 x 13 inch baking pan. Bake at 350 degrees for 10 minutes. Remove from oven. Combine sour cream and egg in small bowl. Pour over crust. Top with peach slices and sprinkle with cinnamon. Bake 10 to 15 minutes longer. Serve with whipped topping or ice cream.

Beverley Steinerd - Connersville, Indiana

Peanut Butter/Pineapple Dessert

3 cups crushed graham crackers
3 tablespoons sugar
2/3 cup melted margarine
2/3 cup peanut butter
2 cups powdered sugar
1 8-ounce package cream cheese
1 16-ounce or 20-ounce can
  crushed pineapple (drained)
1 12-ounce container Cool Whip

Combine graham crackers, sugar and margarine and press into 9 by 13 pan. Bake at 350 degrees for 12 minutes. Cream together peanut butter, powdered sugar and cream cheese. Slowly add 16 ounces or 20 ounces drained crushed pineapple. Fold in Cool Whip. Spread over graham cracker crust. Chill. (Freezes well)

Sue Tickfer - Indiana

"Cathy taught us not about

how to win a battle, but

how to fight one."

Barbara Shoup

The Gathering Trio
*. . . a friend on either side through
thick and thin for life.*
Sharon Sims, Artist

JUST US
WOMEN WINNING AGAINST
BREAST CANCER & FRIENDS

*Julie Walsh Seiler, Connie Rufenbarger, and Pam Kolter, Indiana State Fairgrounds
5 a.m. QVC Interview*

Our special thank you to our friends at

QVC

who are helping
us to raise research dollars for the
War Against Breast Cancer.

Asparagus Roll-Ups

20 slices of white bread
    (cut off crust)
4 ounces bleu cheese
8 ounces cream cheese
1 egg
20 spears canned asparagus
    (do not cook)
2 sticks real butter (melted)
toothpicks

Mix together the bleu cheese, cream cheese, and egg. Spread mixture on bread slices. Lay one asparagus spear on end of bread and roll up. Secure with two toothpicks. Brush with melted butter and place on cookie sheet. Cover with Saran Wrap and freeze. Cut frozen rolls into 3 sections. Place in baggie or container and freeze until needed or bake in 400 degree oven for 15 minutes. Serve warm. Makes a lot.

Connie and Stephanie Rufenbarger
Warsaw, Indiana

Cheese Ball

2 packages cream cheese
1 jar each - Roko, Old English,
    pimento
2 tablespoons Worcestershire
1 tablespoon Tabasco
2 tablespoons mayonnaise
1 tablespoon garlic salt
1 teaspoon minced onion
2 jars sharp Cheddar cheese

Mix all ingredients well. Chill and roll into a ball.

Dorothy Snyder
Warsaw, Indiana

Crab Clam Spread

6 ounces cream cheese
4 tablespoons butter
1/4 cup salad dressing
1 10 1/2 ounce can
    mixed clams (drained)
1 6 1/2 ounce can crab
    (can use frozen crab)
Worcestershire sauce
Tabasco

Blend cream cheese with butter and salad dressing (soften butter and cheese first to make mixing easier). Add clams and crab, mixing in lightly. Season to taste with Worcestershire and Tabasco. Spread on rounds of rye (party rye) and broil until bubbly (6 to 7 minutes).

JoAnn Waldo
Fort Collins, Colorado

Chilies Rellenos Foise

1 can (1 pound 10 ounces)
      whole green chilies
1 pound Monterey Jack cheese
      cut 1/4 inch x 3 inches
1/2 pound Cheddar cheese, grated
5 large eggs
1/4 cup flour
1 1/4 cups milk
1/2 teaspoon salt
black pepper to taste
liquid red pepper to taste
paprika

Salsa:
tomatoes, onions,
dash of hot pepper

Rinse seeds from chilies with cold water. Spread on paper towel and pat to dry. Slip piece of Monterey Jack cheese into each. Beat eggs, gradually add flour, beat until smooth. Add milk, salt, pepper, and liquid red pepper. Beat smooth. Arrange half stuffed chilies in well greased 9 x 13 pan. Sprinkle with half Cheddar and paprika. Repeat layers, ending with cheese. Pour egg mixture over all. Bake uncovered at 350 degrees for about 45 minutes or until knife inserted comes out clean. Serve with salsa which is chopped tomatoes, onions, and dash of hot pepper.

Carole Cross, R.T., A.R.R.T. - A.S.R.T.
Warsaw, Indiana

Flying Taco

1 can refried beans
1 16 ounce container sour cream
1 bottle taco sauce
thin layer of onions
      (I use green) chopped
sliced black olives
sliced green olives
small chunks of tomato
shredded Cheddar and
      Monterey Jack cheeses

Spread one can of refried beans out on plate. Cover with the sour cream. Cover sour cream with taco sauce. Then layer onions, olives, and tomatoes, topping with cheeses. Cover and chill. Serve as a dip with nacho chips. Makes one generous plate full.

Gary Moore - Augusta, Georgia

Crescent Spinach Roll Appetizer

6 packages Pillsbury
   crescent roll mix
3 pounds ground chuck
5 packages frozen
   chopped spinach
2 teaspoons salt
1 1/2 teaspoons black pepper
1 1/2 teaspoons garlic powder
4 tablespoons McCormicks
   minced onion
1 container Kraft Parmesan cheese

Brown and drain chuck reserving 2 tablespoons of fat in the mixture. Thaw/defrost spinach. Squeeze any moisture out of spinach and chop it further. Mix together the drained ground chuck, spinach, salt, black pepper, garlic powder, and minced onion. Split the mixture into 12 piles (each pile is about 1 to 1 1/4 cups. Open two sections of rolls onto a rectangle sheet of Reynolds Wrap. Press together the sections of dough to make a rectangle. The sections should be joined vertically. Put one pile of mixture on the dough. Spread the mixture evenly over the dough. Sprinkle with lots of Parmesan cheese. Roll up the dough, tucking the ends in so the filling does not come out when you are rolling it up. Wrap the roll in the foil, twisting the ends so the roll will stay firm. Freeze the roll. Continue making the remainder of the rolls (12 in all). To bake, unwrap the roll from the foil. Bake at 375 degree oven for 20 to 25 minutes. Let sit about 5 minutes to cool before slicing the roll to serve. Best when served warm - on a heating tray or with a bread brick.

Patricia Trausch - Arlington Heights, Illinois

Croutons with 3 Cheeses and Sun Dried Tomatoes

1 French bread baguette,
   cut 1/4" slices
extra virgin olive oil
1/4 pound goat cheese
1/4 pound Ricotta cheese
1/4 pound Mozzarella cheese
1 large garlic minced
salt and white pepper to taste
18 sun dried tomatoes,
   drained and halved

Preheat oven to 300 degrees. Arrange bread slices in baking sheet; brush with olive oil. Bake until brown. Remove from oven—increase oven to 350 degrees. Blend cheeses, garlic, salt, and pepper. Mound 1 teaspoon cheese on bread. Top with tomato; cover with cheese. Bake until cheese melts. Serve immediately. Serves 36.

Kimberly Miller - Valparaiso, Indiana

Frosted Cauliflower

1 medium head cauliflower
1/2 cup mayonnaise
2 teaspoons mustard
3/4 cups shredded
    Cheddar cheese
paprika

Wash cauliflower and remove leaves from base. Cover and steam full head until tender in boiling salted water (12-15 minutes). Drain. Place carefully in shallow baking dish. Combine mayonnaise and mustard. Spread over full head. Bake at 375 degrees for 5 minutes. Top with shredded cheese and bake 5 minutes more. Sprinkle with paprika. Garnish with fresh parsley.

Mallory Miniear, owner of The Good Stuff Restaurant
Warsaw, Indiana

Guacamole With a Zip

8 avocados, mashed
1 finely chopped onion
2 diced tomatoes
1 teaspoon garlic salt (to taste)
juice of 2 to 3 lemons (to taste)
1/2 to 1 cup of hot salsa
1 teaspoon salt

Combine all and serve with tortilla chips.

Paula Harris - Warsaw, Indiana

Hot Crab Fondue

8 ounces cream cheese
7 1/2 ounces crab meat
15 ounces Cheez Whiz
1/2 teaspoon Worcestershire
    sauce
1/4 cup Maderia wine
1/4 teaspoon garlic salt
1/2 teaspoon cayenne pepper

Melt together in a double broiler, stirring until smooth. Serve hot with crackers.

Dane Miller - Winona Lake, Indiana

Marshmallow Fruit Dip

1 7-ounce jar marshmallow cream
1/2 cup mayonnaise
2 teaspoons grated orange rind
1 tablespoon orange juice
1 teaspoon grated lemon rind
1 teaspoon lemon juice
additional grated orange and
    lemon rinds (optional)
fresh strawberries

Combine first 6 ingredients in a bowl; beat at medium speed of an electric mixer until smooth. Spoon dip into a serving container; sprinkle with additional grated orange and lemon rinds, if desired. Serve with fresh strawberries. Yield: 1 1/2 cups.

Betty LeCount - Warsaw, Indiana

Meat Rolls (Small Egg Rolls) and Sauce

2 pounds ground beef
1 can water chestnuts (chopped)
1 cup chopped celery
1 large onion (chopped)
1 teaspoon ground black pepper
1 teaspoon Accent
1 teaspoon salt
1 beaten egg
1 package egg roll skins

Sauce:
1 cup water
1 cup white sugar
1/4 cup soy sauce
4 tablespoons flour (Wondra)
1 tablespoon chopped onion
1 teaspoon ground black pepper
1 teaspoon Crisco oil
1/4 cup vinegar
1/4 cup catsup
1/4 cup pineapple juice

Mix first 7 ingredients in a large mixing bowl with a large spoon. After mixing thoroughly, they are ready to be wrapped with the eggroll skins (egg roll skins are square, about 8 x 8 - cut into 4 squares for small egg rolls). Place approximately 2 tablespoons of the mixture on small skin and roll it. Seal with a beaten egg. Arrange on a tray until ready to fry. Deep fry until golden brown and crispy. These can be frozen to fry later. After frying, place in a colander to drain. **Mix sauce** ingredients together and simmer while stirring constantly and cook until it thickens (pancake syrup consistency or a little thicker). Strain through a colander to rid the onion pieces. This sauce can be kept for 2 to 3 months in the refrigerator. Reheat as needed.

Vivian Kelly - Warsaw, Indiana

Mexican Pinwheels

8 ounces cream cheese
8 ounces sour cream
1 cup shredded Cheddar cheese
1 small can black olives
1 small can green chilies
1 bunch green onions
1 package flour tortillas
   (approximately 10)

Mix first 6 ingredients with an electric mixer. Spread onto tortillas and roll. Wrap each roll with Saran wrap and refrigerate overnight. Slice into 1/4 - 1/2 inch slices. Arrange on large plate.

Kim Reiff - South Whitley, Indiana

Mushroom Dip

1 pound mushrooms - sliced
8 ounces cream cheese
6 slices bacon
1 cup Swiss cheese - grated
1/4 cup chopped onion
2 cups milk

Cook bacon; cut in small pieces and drain well. Blend all ingredients. Bake in oven at 400 degrees for 15 minutes. Serve hot with crackers.

Mary Louise Miller - Winona Lake, Indiana

Pretzels

1 package yeast
1 1/2 cups warm water
1 teaspoon salt
1 tablespoon sugar
4 cups flour
1 beaten egg
coarse salt (canning salt)

Dissolve yeast in water. Add salt and sugar. Blend in flour. Knead until smooth. Pull off pieces, size of a small ball. Roll between fingers. Shape into pretzel shape or your initials. Place on a cookie sheet. Brush with egg. Sprinkle with coarse salt. Bake at 425 degrees for 10-15 minutes. Serve warm.

Debbie B. and Brandy E. Allen - Warsaw, Indiana

Puff Pastry with Spinach, Red Onion Marmalade, and Gorgonzola

1 sheet prepared puff pastry
    (follow directions on box)
1 bag fresh spinach
    (wash, trim stems)
1 large red onion (thinly sliced)
1/2 stick unsalted butter
2-3 tablespoons olive oil
2 teaspoons rosemary
Gorgonzola cheese
egg white
2 teaspoons garlic

Bake puff pastry as directed, brushing with egg whites to help them brown. Do not overcook. This can be done ahead of time. Melt butter and add olive oil, rosemary and garlic. When combined, add onions and cook on low for an hour or so stirring occasionally. This can also be done ahead of time. Let stand at room temperature in another container. Use same pan for quickly wilting the spinach. Be careful not to overcook.

To assemble, punch down a little of the puff pastry and loosely fill with spinach and top with onion. Then add the crumbled gorgonzola cheese and broil until heated through and browned just a bit more. Serve while warm. I usually get 6 to 8 servings per sheet of puff pastry.

Father Michael Basden - Warsaw, Indiana

Roasted Garlic and Almond Spread

2 to 3 garlic cloves
1/4 cup olive oil
2 teaspoons Worcestershire sauce
1 1/2 teaspoons Dijon mustard
1 1/2 cups blanched almonds
    (chopped)
1 cup sour cream
1 cup mayonnaise
1/4 cup minced fresh parsley
1 teaspoon rosemary
salt (to taste)
pepper (to taste)

Remove outer skin of garlic cloves and place in pan with olive oil. Roast in 350 degree oven until cloves are golden brown. Combine Worcestershire sauce and mustard in food processor. Add cooled garlic cloves and process well. Stir in large bowl garlic mixture and remaining ingredients. Store in refrigerator 24 hours before serving.

This is from an Italian friend and is for garlic lovers. Serve with toasted baguette slices, hearty crackers, or melba toast. The spread is also good stuffed into mushrooms and baked.

Father Michael Basden - Warsaw, Indiana

Sausage Balls

1 roll Tennessee Pride
hot sausage
2 cups Bisquick
2 cups sharp Cheddar cheese
(shredded)

Preheat oven to 350 degrees. Mix all of the ingredients in large mixing bowl until sausage is completely saturated in Bisquick. Roll into tiny balls (about 1 inch). Place on an ungreased cookie sheet and bake at 350 degrees for 15 to 17 minutes. Take out and enjoy!

Jason Cross and Adam Small - Warsaw, Indiana

Shrimp Dip

small can cocktail shrimp
8 ounces cream cheese
3 tablespoons horseradish sauce
1 tablespoon chopped onion
1 teaspoon lemon juice
dash of salt

Mix all ingredients together and serve.

Ann Franklin - Indianapolis, Indiana

Shrimp Mold

2 cups shrimp (1 pound)
1/2 cup celery, cut fine
1 medium onion
2 1/2 packages Knox gelatin
1/2 cup water
1 cup cream of tomato soup
(from can undiluted)
2 large packages cream cheese
2 cups mayonnaise
1 tablespoon Worcestershire
sauce
1 teaspoon salt
2-3 dashes of Tabasco

Beat cheese until fluffy. Soften gelatin in water. Heat soup. Add cheese and gelatin water to soup. Beat until smooth. Fold in rest of ingredients. Add mayonnaise and chill overnight. Fills 6-7 cup mold.

Harriet Chalfant - New Albany, Indiana

Spanicopita (Spinach-Cheese Rolls)

2 pounds fresh spinach
    (or 2 boxes frozen)
1 package phyllo
5 eggs
1/2 pound Feta cheese, crumbled
1 pound cottage cheese
1 tablespoon dill
1 teaspoon ground black pepper
1 tablespoon basil
1/2 onion, chopped
butter or margarine, melted

Cook spinach just enough to wilt or thaw and squeeze dry frozen spinach. In large bowl, combine all other ingredients. Layer 5 sheets phyllo, brushing each sheet with butter before adding the next. On the 5th sheet, pat enough spinach mixture to make a 1 1/2 inch sausage shape on long edge of phyllo. Roll up into tight roll. Repeat until the filling is used. Mark each roll with a sharp knife in 1/2-inch servings. Freeze. When serving, thaw slightly; cut into 1/2-inch slices and lay cut-side up on cookie sheet sprayed with vegetable cooking spray. Bake 15 minutes at 350 - 375 degrees. Serve warm.

Nancy Sideris, owner, Mosique Restaurant
Warsaw, Indiana

Stuffed Mushrooms

1/4 cup butter
1 pound large mushrooms,
    washed and stemmed
4 slices dry bread
1 small onion, quartered
1 tablespoon lemon juice
2 tablespoons dry wine
    (Vermouth)
1/2 cup parsley sprigs
1/2 teaspoon salt
1/8 teaspoon marjoram
1/8 teaspoon thyme
1/7 teaspoon garlic powder
salt
monosodium glutamate
    (optional)

Heat oven to 375 degrees. Melt butter in skillet. Break one slice of bread into blender. Add 1/4 of the onion and 1/2 cup mushroom stems. Cover and process two cycles at grate. Empty into skillet and repeat with remaining bread, onion, and stems. Saute 5 minutes. Put lemon juice and remaining ingredients into blender. Process two cycles at grate. Add to skillet, mix well, and cook over low heat for 5 minutes. Place caps in 9 x 13 pan. Sprinkle with salt. Fill with bread mixture and bake 10 minutes. Turn oven control to broil and place mushrooms about 4 inches from heat for 4 to 5 minutes. Mushrooms may be frozen after baking. To serve, broil about 9 inches from heat for 8 to 10 minutes.

JoAnn Waldo - Fort Collins, Colorado

Spinach Balls

1 10-ounce package
    frozen spinach
1/2 cup herb stuffing mix
3/4 cup Parmesan cheese
2 eggs, beaten
1/4 cup butter, melted
salt
pepper

Cook and drain spinach. Mix all ingredients. Chill for 30 minutes. Roll into balls. (May freeze.) Bake on cookie sheet for 10 minutes at 350 degrees.

Joyce Hawkins - West Lafayette, Indiana

Surprise Dip

1 package frozen broccoli,
    cooked as directed
1 pound ground beef,
    browned and drained
1 roll garlic cheese
1 can mushroom soup
2 cans green chilies

Combine the above ingredients in a large saucepan. Cook until the cheese melts. Keep hot.

Don't tell your guests the ingredients;
let them guess what's in it!!

Karol Piecuch - Warsaw, Indiana

Vegetable Dip

1 8-ounce package cream cheese
3 tablespoons mayonnaise
    (Hellmann's)
2 tablespoons milk
3 tablespoons Kraft
    French dressing
3 tablespoons catsup
dash celery salt
dash garlic salt
dash onion salt

Mix cream cheese, mayonaise, milk, dressing and catsup until smooth. Season to taste with garlic salt, celery salt, and onion salt. Serve with fresh vegetables (cauliflower, carrots, celery, broccoli).

Patty Weybright - South Whitley, Indiana

Taco Dip

8 ounce package cream cheese
15 ounce can chili without beans
3 ounce can chopped green
    chilies, not drained
    (optional)
4 ounces Mozzarella cheese
4 ounces Cheddar cheese

Layer in above order in a 2 quart microwave-safe casserole dish or 8 x 8 microwave dish. Microwave for 5 minutes on high.

Kim Hastreiter - Fort Wayne, Indiana

Tangy Low Fat Cheese Spread

16 ounces Knudsen's
    no fat cottage cheese
2 to 4 ounces crumbled
    Bleu cheese
2 to 4 ounces crumbled
    Feta cheese or no fat
    sour cream
1 to 2 garlic cloves, minced
    (optional) or dill weed to
    taste or Paul Prudhomme's
    Vegetable Magic or your
    favorite seasoning to taste

Mash everything together with a fork or whirl in a blender. Cover and refrigerate.

William H. Hindle, M.D., F.A.C.O.G
Los Angeles, California

Vegetable Pizza

2 packages crescent rolls
2 8 ounce packages
    cream cheese
3/4 cup mayonaise
1 package Hidden Valley
    Ranch Dressing (original)
3/4 cup raw broccoli, cauliflower,
    onion, celery, green
    peppers, tomatoes or
    any vegetable you like
Cheddar or Colby cheese

Open crescent rolls and lay crosswise in 11 x 16 pan. Bake 7-8 minutes or until lightly browned in 350 degree oven. Cool completely. Soften and beat cream cheese. Add mayonaise, dressing in its dry stage. (it's strong, may use only 1/2 package) Mix together and spread over cooled baked dough. Prepare raw broccoli, cauliflower, onion, celery, green peppers, tomatoes (or any preferred vegetables). May grate a carrot. Mix all raw vegetables and press on top of dough. Add shredded Cheddar or colby cheese. Cover and refrigerate for 1-2 hours for flavor. Cut and serve.

Patty (Berkey) Beachy - Warsaw, Indiana;
Barb Lembke - Rochester, Indiana;
Dorothy Snyder - Warsaw, Indiana;
Marianne Vevia - Fort Wayne, Indiana
Carole Cross, R.T., A.R.R.T. - A.S.R.T. - Warsaw, Indiana

Adam's Oyster Stew

2 pounds new potatoes,
    peeled and diced
2 onions, chopped
8 cloves garlic, chopped
4 carrots, julienned
1/4 cup green onion, chopped
1 pint cream
2 quarts whole milk
1/4 cup Pernod
6 tablespoons butter
1 teaspoon Tabasco sauce
1 teaspoon salt
1 tablespoon coarsely
    ground pepper
1 quart oysters with liquid

Saute onions, green onions, potatoes, and garlic in butter until onions are translucent. Add oyster liquid, Pernod, salt, pepper, and Tabasco sauce. Add milk and cream. Simmer but do not boil. Adjust seasonings with salt, pepper, and Pernod (just a hint). Thirty minutes before serving, add oysters and carrots.

Father Michael Basden - Warsaw, Indiana

Roasted Eggplant and Tomato Soup

1 pound eggplant
    quartered lengthwise
12 whole Roma tomatoes,
    halved length
8 whole garlic cloves
1 whole red bell pepper,
    half and seed
1 whole onion - cut into eighths
1/3 cup olive oil
2 tablespoons salt and pepper
6 cups chicken stock
2 tablespoons Balsamic vinegar
2 teaspoons fresh mint,
    finely chopped
2 teaspoons fresh oregano,
    finely chopped
2 teaspoons fresh thyme,
    finely chopped

Preheat oven to 450 degrees. Place eggplant, tomatoes, garlic, red bell pepper and onion in a single layer in a 9 x 12 inch baking dish. Drizzle the olive oil over the vegetables, bake uncovered, for about 30 - 35 minutes, until they are soft and the edges are browned. Let the eggplant cool, then scrape the flesh from the skin into a feed processor fitted with the metal blade; discard the skin. Add the remaining roasted vegetables to the food processor and puree until smooth. Pour the puree into a large saucepan and stir in the stock, vinegar and fresh herbs. Heat the soup until it simmers gently. Serve in heated soup bowls.

Note: It is important to use only fresh herbs in this soup. When used in pairs or trios dried herbs tend to blend together in a muddy nondescript way, whereas the flavors of fresh herbs remain distinct. If you can't find all three fresh, use just one. If none of these fresh herbs is available, substitute 1/4 cup chopped fresh parsley plus 1 to 2 tablespoons fresh lemon juice.

Martha Hoover, Cafe Patachou
Indianapolis, Indiana

Cold Zucchini Soup

2 tablespoons butter
2 tablespoons shallots
1 clove garlic, minced
4 cups sliced zucchini
1/2 teaspoon salt
1/2 cup cream
1 3/4 cups chicken broth
1 teaspoon curry powder

Melt butter. Saute garlic, shallots, and zucchini for 10 minutes. Add salt, cream broth and curry powder. Heat slowly. Do not overheat. Blend in blender—chill. Serve cold—chopped chives on top. Serves 4.

Stephany Mullen - Valparaiso, Indiana

Hearty New England Clam Chowder

6 slices bacon
1/2 cup finely chopped onion
1 celery stalk, finely chopped
5 medium red potatoes,
    peeled, diced
2 tablespoons all-pupose flour
1 - 6.5 ounce can minced clams
    (drain and save juice)
1 - 10 ounce can whole baby
    clams (drain and save juice)
1 - 8 ounce bottle clam juice
1 pint half and half
1 cup whipping cream
salt and pepper to taste
parsley

In a large heavy saucepan or skillet, saute bacon until brown and crisp. Remove bacon and drain on paper towels, and crumble. Remove all but 2 tablespoons of bacon grease from pan. Sauté finely chopped onion, celery and diced potatoes for 3 to 5 minutes. Sprinkle with flour, add clam juice from cans and bottle and stir to combine. Bring to a boil, stirring occasionally until potatoes are soft, about 15 minutes. Add half and half and season to taste with salt and pepper. Add clams and heat until simmering; do not boil. Add whipping cream. Stir in half of the bacon. sprinkle with remaining bacon and parsley. Serve immediately.

Dan and Jana Williamson - Warsaw, Indiana

Minestrone Soup

1/2 cup Gioia Ditalini, pasta
2 to 3 pounds beef soup bones
3 quarts water
1 bay leaf
1 clove garlic, minced
2 teaspoons salt
1/4 teaspoon pepper
1 onion, chopped
2 cups chopped cabbage
4 carrots, sliced
2 stalks celery, sliced
1 16 ounce can kidney beans
1 16 ounce can tomatoes
1 8 ounce can tomato sauce
2 cups fresh spinach leaves,
    chopped

In large kettle bring to a boil the soup bones, water, bay leaf, garlic, salt, and pepper. Simmer covered for 3 hours. Remove meat from bones and discard bones. Add onion, carrots, cabbage, celery, kidney beans, tomatoes, and tomato sauce. Simmer uncovered for 45 minutes. Add spinach and Ditalini and simmer an additional 15 to 20 minutes. Serve in bowls topped with 1 tablespoon Parmesan cheese. Serves 12.

Susan M. Jaskulski, R.T.(R)(M) - Rochester, New York

Cream Chicken/Asparagus Soup

1 pound fresh asparagus
3/4 cup butter, softened
3/4 cup flour
1 cup warm milk
6 cups hot chicken broth
1 cup cream
1 1/2 cups cooked chicken
    chopped
salt and pepper to taste

Cook asparagus until tender. Cut into pieces—set aside. Melt butter and stir in flour. Cook until smooth. Combine milk, two cups of broth, and cream. Add to flour slowly. Cook until blended. Add remaining four cups of broth, chicken, salt, pepper, and asparagus. Serve hot.

Kimberly Miller - Valparaiso, Indiana

Midwest Chowder

6 tablespoons margarine
1/2 cup flour
3 1/2 cups 2% milk
12 ounces shredded sharp
    Cheddar cheese
3 cups water
3 cups chopped potatoes
2 cups sliced carrots
1/4+ cup chopped onion
1/2+ cup chopped celery
1 teaspoon salt
2 cups cream style corn

Combine margarine, flour, and milk in a large pan to make a cream sauce. When thick, add cheese. Stir until it is *just* melted (don't let it boil!). In the 3 cups of water cook potatoes, carrots, onion, celery, and salt for 10 minutes. Pour veggies and water into cream sauce and add 2 cups cream style corn. Heat through. Don't let it boil or cheese will curdle.

Jane Seiler - Champaign, Illinois

Crab Soup

2 pounds crab meat
2 tablespoons Worcestershire
    sauce
1 cup dry vermouth
2 tablespoons butter
2 carrots finely chopped
1 onion chopped
46 ounces chicken broth
10 1/2 ounces tomato soup
1 quart whipping cream
salt and pepper

Toss crab meat with vermouth and Worcestershire sauce. Sauté carrots, onion in butter. Add crab mixture, chicken broth, tomato soup, cream, and salt/pepper. Cook slowly for 1-2 hours. Serve hot. Serves 8.

Carolyn Allen - Chicago, Illinois

Potato Rivel Soup

3 medium potatoes, diced
1 small onion, chopped fine
1 1/2 cups water
1/2 cup grated carrots
1/2 cup chopped celery
1 egg
1/2 cup flour
1/4 teaspoon salt
4 cups milk
1 tablespoon butter
1/2 teaspoon salt
1/8 teaspoon celery seed
parsley or chives to garnish

Cook potatoes, onion, carrots and celery in water until almost tender. While cooking, make rivels by mixing egg, approximately 1/2 cup flour and 1/4 teaspoon salt with fork until it forms little stringy lumps. Add rivels and cook with above at least 7 minutes or until vegetables are done. Add milk, butter, salt and celery seed. If a thicker soup is desired, mix 1-2 tablespoons flour with milk and add to soup. Garnish with parsley or chives.

Patchwork Quilt Country Inn - Middlebury, Indiana

Thelma's Beef Barley Soup

1 pound ground beef
1 package Lipton onion soup
1 can beef broth (2 pints
    14 fluid ounces)
4 cups water
2/3 cup barley
1/2 package frozen corn
    (optional)

Brown ground beef and drain. Add next 4 ingredients. Bring to a boil and simmer 2 to 3 hours. Optional: add corn during last 1/2 hour of cooking.

Nancy Lenke Johnson - Pittsburgh, Pennsylvania

Basil Beer Bread

3 cups self-rising flour
3 tablespoons sugar
1/2 cup chopped fresh basil
12 ounces warm beer

Mix all ingredients in medium sized bowl. Stir until smooth. Pour into greased loaf pan. Bake 50 minutes at 350 degrees. Note: other herbs or combinations may be substituted for basil. This is one of my favorites: 1/4 cup dill and 1/4 cup Parmesan cheese.   Add an extra tablespoon of sugar to this one. It counteracts the salt in the Parmesan.

Kay Niedenthal, owner, Kay's Garden and Kay's Catering
Indianapolis, Indiana

Butterscotch Coffee Cake

1 box deluxe yellow cake mix
2 eggs
1 can vanilla pudding
1/2 cup sugar
1/2 cup nuts
6 ounces butterscotch chips

Mix cake mix, eggs, and pud...
floured pan. Spread mixture o...
butterscotch chips over first mix...
degrees for 35 minutes.

Cindy Stark - Ind...
Peggy Zimmerman - W...

Cream Cheese Danish

3 ounces cream cheese
1/4 cup margarine
2 cups biscuit mix
1/4 cup milk
1/2 cup fruit preserves
4 ounces cream cheese, softened
1/4 cup powdered sugar

Icing:
1 cup powdered sugar
1-2 tablespoons milk
1/2 teaspoon vanilla

Cut cream cheese and margarine into biscuit mix until the size of peas. Add milk. Mix to form dough. Roll out dough in rectangle shape 1/4-1/2 inch thick. Transfer to baking sheet. Cut outside into 1-inch strips, leaving middle section whole. Mix together cream cheese and powdered sugar and spread over middle section. Top with fruit preserves. Pull cut strips together, closing at the middle. Bake at 375 degrees for 20 minutes or until golden brown. Cool 5 minutes and drizzle with icing. Serve warm or cold.

Chelsea LeCount - North Webster, Indiana

Hickory Cheese Loaf

1 loaf French bread
1/2 cup soft margarine or butter
1 cup shredded sharp
   Cheddar cheese
1 tablespoon snipped parsley
1/2 teaspoon hickory smoked salt
2 teaspoons Worcestershire sauce

Cut bread into 1 inch slices (not going through the bottom of loaf). Spread mixture in between slices. Wrap loaf in aluminum foil. Bake in oven at 350 degrees for 20 minutes.

Doris Wall - Syracuse, Indiana

eese Pumpkin Muffins

cups flour
1 teaspoon baking soda
1/2 teaspoon salt
1 1/2 teaspoons cinnamon
1/2 teaspoon ground coriander
2 eggs, lightly beaten
2 cups sugar
1 cup canned pumpkin
1/2 cup oil
1/2 teaspoon vanilla

Filling:
6 ounces cream cheese, softened
1 egg
1 tablespoon sugar

Topping:
3/4 cup coconut
1/2 cup pecans
1/4 cup sugar
1/2 teaspoon cinnamon

For the batter, combine flour, soda, salt, cinnamon and coriander in a large bowl and set aside. In small bowl, combine eggs, sugar, pumpkin, oil and vanilla; mix well. Add liquid ingredients to dry ingredients; stir just until moistened. To make filling, combine cream cheese, egg and sugar. To make topping, combine coconut, pecans, sugar and cinnamon. To assemble muffins, spoon 1/2 of batter into 24 greased or paper-lined muffins cups, filling 1/2 full. Spoon cream cheese mixture evenly over batter. Spoon remaining batter over cream cheese mixture carefully, spreading to edges. Sprinkle pecan topping over muffins. Bake at 350 degrees for 20-25 minutes or until toothpick comes out clean.

Betty LeCount - Warsaw, Indiana

Cream Puffs

1/2 cup water
1/2 cup flour
1/4 cup shortening
2 eggs
1/4 teaspoon salt

Chocolate Topping:
1/4 cup cocoa
2 tablespoons cornstarch
3/4 cup sugar
1 cup milk
1 teaspoon vanilla
1 teaspoon butter

Bring water to boil. Add shortening and stir until melted. Quickly add flour and salt. Cook, stirring constantly about 2 minutes or until mixture forms a smooth, compact mass. Cool slightly. Add eggs, one at a time. Beat until thick and shiny. Shape with a tablespoon and bake on greased baking sheet at 450 degrees for 10 minutes, then at 350 degrees for 20 to 25 minutes.

Chocolate Topping: Mix cocoa, cornstarch, and sugar. Add milk, vanilla, and butter and cook until thick.

Dorothy Cross - Rochester, Indiana

Elephant Ears

1 1/2 cups milk
2 tablespoons sugar
1 tablespoon salt
6 tablespoons shortening
2 packages dry yeast
4 cups flour
oil for frying
1/2 cup sugar
1 teaspoon cinnamon

In saucepan combine milk, sugar, salt, and shortening. Heat until shortening is melted. Do not let boil. Cool mixture to lukewarm. Add yeast and stir until dissolved. Stir in flour 2 cups at a time, beating after each addition until smooth. Put in greased bowl. Cover with cloth and let rise until double (about 30 minutes). Dust hands with flour. Pinch off pieces of dough about the size of a golf ball. Stretch each piece into thin 6 to 8 inch circle. Fry one at a time until dough rises to surface. Turn and fry other side. Drain on paper towel. Sprinkle with cinnamon and sugar mixture.

Ann Franklin - Indianapolis, Indiana

Foccoccia

6 cups bread flour
1 tablespoon dry yeast
1 1/2 cups water (at 115 degrees
    with a little sugar mixed in)
1 tablespoon oil
garlic
5-6 medium onions
red peppers
yellow peppers
green peppers
avocado, sliced
Parmesan cheese, grated
feta cheese, crumbled
olive oil
salt

Sprinkle yeast on water to dissolve and prove. After 10 minutes you should see a thick foam on top. Add enough flour to make a thick paste or batter Gradually add enough flour until ball forms and pulls away from sides of bowl. Add oil. Knead 10 minutes or until smooth and elastic. Cover and let rise in a warm (80-degree) place until doubled, or when a slight finger dent stays indented. Preheat oven to 500 degrees. Saute onions in olive oil until they caramelize. Set aside, lightly sauté peppers and garlic in very little olive oil and set aside. Punch down bread dough and roll into pan shape with your hands or a rolling pin. If it pulls away, cover and let rest 10 minutes. When shaped, place into a pan sprinkled with very little corn meal. With your hands, spread olive oil on flattened bread dough, sprinkle some salt, crushed garlic and Parmesan cheese onto pie. Layer first onions, peppers, avocado, Feta cheese and Parmesan cheese. Place Foccoccia low in the oven and reduce heat to 450 degrees and bake for approximately 30 minutes.

Cindy Baldauf - Indianapolis, Indiana

Idiot Rolls

1 stick margarine
3/4 cup shortening
1 cup boiling water
2 eggs
3/4 cup sugar
1 cup cold water
3/4 cup warm water
2 cakes yeast
7 cups self-rising flour

Mix margarine, shortening, boiling water in a small bowl until all are melted. Put aside. Mix in a large bowl eggs, sugar and cold water. Put aside. Mix warm water and yeast and let stand until dissolved. Add all 3 mixtures together. Stir in 7 cups self-rising flour, one cup at a time, stirring well after each addition. Store in refrigerator for 7-10 days. Allow 1 hour for rising. Bake at 400 degrees for 10-15 minutes. Yield: 4-5 dozen.

Irene Saylor - Manchester, Kentucky

International Bread

1 loaf French bread
1 pound soft margarine
1 package Swiss cheese slices
1 teaspoon dry mustard
1 teaspoon Beau Monde
1 teaspoon minced onions
1 tablespoon poppy seeds
1 tablespoon lemon juice

Slice bread into slices. Insert one slice of Swiss cheese between each slice. Mix margarine and remaining ingredients together and spread between slices and on top of loaf generously. Bake 25 minutes at 325 degrees.

Alpha Lambda Chapter of Kappa Kappa Kappa
Warsaw, Indiana

Monkey Bread

4 tubes biscuits
3/4 cup sugar
1 teaspoon cinnamon
1 cup sugar
3/4 cup butter
1 1/2 teaspoons cinnamon

Quarter biscuits and roll in cinnamon and sugar mixture. Place in buttered pan. Boil sugar, butter, and cinnamon. Pour over biscuits. Bake at 350 degrees for 40 to 45 minutes.

Carole Cross, R.T., A.R.R.T. - A.S.R.T.
Warsaw, Indiana

Kay's Cranberry Zucchini Bread

3 eggs
2 cups sugar
1 cup vegetable oil
2 teaspoons vanilla
2 cups shredded zucchini
3/4 cup fresh or frozen cranberries, chopped
3 cups flour
1 teaspoon baking powder
1 teaspoon baking soda
1 teaspoon salt
1 tablespoon cinnamon

Combine eggs, sugar, oil and vanilla in mixing bowl; beat until blended. Add dry ingredients. Mix. Add cranberries and zucchini and stir. Makes 1 bundt cake or 2 loaves. Bake at 350 degrees for 50 minutes for bundt cake, 40 minutes for loaves (or until center springs back when touched).

Kay Niedenthal, owner, Kay's Garden and Kay's Catering - Indianapolis, Indiana

Morning Glory Muffins

2 cups flour
1 1/4 cups sugar
2 teaspoons baking soda
2 teaspoons cinnamon
1/2 teaspoon salt
2 cups grated carrots
1 apple, cored and shredded
1/2 cup raisins
1/2 cup shredded coconut
1/2 cup chopped pecans
3 eggs
1 cup vegetable oil
2 teaspoons vanilla extract

In large mixing bowl, combine flour, sugar, baking soda, cinnamon, and salt. Stir in carrots, raisins, coconut, and pecans. In separate bowl, combine eggs, oil, apple, and vanilla. Add to flour mixture. Stir only until combined. Spoon into greased or lined muffin tins. Bake at 350 degrees for 15-18 minutes. Yield: 18+ muffins.

Marceil Conley - Warsaw, Indiana

Nutty Oat Wheat Bread

2 1/2 cups buttermilk
1/2 cup honey
1/3 cup margarine or butter
3 1/2 cups Pillsbury's Best
    unbleached flour
1 1/2 cups rolled oats
2 packages active dry yeast
1 tablespoon salt
2 eggs
2 1/2 to 3 cups Pillsbury's Best
    whole wheat flour
1 cup nuts, chopped
2 tablespoons margarine or
    butter, melted

Grease two 9 x 5 loaf pans. In small sauce pan heat buttermilk, honey, and margarine until very warm 120 to 130 degrees. Lightly spoon flour into measuring cup; level off. In large bowl blend unbleached flour, oats, yeast, salt, eggs, and warm liquid. Beat 3 minutes at medium speed. By hand, stir in whole wheat flour and nuts. Brush top of dough with margarine. Cover; let rise in warm place until doubled in size, 45 to 60 minutes. Stir down dough; divide and shape into two loaves. Place in prepared pans. Cover; let rise in warm place until double in size, 30 to 45 minutes. Heat oven to 375 degrees. Bake 25 to 35 minutes or until deep golden brown. If too brown, cover with foil last 10 minutes. Remove immediately from pans. Makes 2 loaves. DO NOT SUBSTITUTE ANYTHING FOR BUTTERMILK.

Karol Piecuch - Warsaw, Indiana

Oatmeal Bread

2 cups quick cooking rolled oats
2 teaspoons salt
2 cups boiling water
2 tablespoons oil
1 package dry yeast
2 tablespoons dark brown sugar,
    firmly packed
3/4 cup lukewarm water
1 cup instant non-fat dry
    milk powder
4 - 4 1/2 cups unsifted flour

Put oats in a large mixing bowl. Add salt to boiling water and stir into oats. Add oil and stir until smooth; cool to lukewarm. Dissolve yeast and sugar in lukewarm water. Combine oat mixture and yeast mixture. Add milk powder and 4 cups of flour; mix thoroughly. Cover. Let rise until doubled in bulk, about 1 1/2 hours. Punch down and place on lightly floured board to knead. If dough is sticky, add a little more flour. Shape into 2 loaves and place in 2 medium-sized greased loaf pans. Let rise in warm place until doubled in bulk. Bake at 375 degrees for 35-45 minutes or until done. Yield: 2 loaves

Betty Collins - Warsaw, Indiana

Rice Flour Pizza Dough

Rice flour
3/4 cup warm water
1 package yeast (for flavor;
    dough does not rise)
1 tablespoon margarine
2 teaspoons sugar or to taste
1/2 teaspoon salt or to taste
1 dash each, oregano, garlic
    powder, fennel seed

Put sugar, yeast, warm water together with margarine and spices. Stir in flour until dough is not too sticky to handle with floured hands. Put out on 16 inch greased pizza pan. Add favorite toppings and bake until edges are brown.

Jane Mullen - Beaufort, Missouri

Rolls

2 cups self-rising flour
3 tablespoons mayonnaise
1 cup milk

Stir and bake in muffin pans at 400 degrees for 10 minutes.

Connie Rufenbarger - Warsaw, Indiana

Rolls

5 to 6 cups flour
1/2 cup sugar
1 1/2 teaspoons salt
2 packages yeast
1 cup milk
2/3 cup water
1/4 cup margarine
2 eggs (room temperature)

In large bowl, combine 2 cups flour, sugar, salt, and undissolved yeast. Combine milk, water, and margarine in saucepan and heat until very warm (margarine does not need to melt). Gradually add this to the flour mixture, mixing with electric mixer. Add eggs and 3/4 cup flour. Mix. Add remaining flour and finish mixing by hand. Turn onto floured board. Knead until smooth. Place in greased bowl, cover, and let rest 20 minutes. Punch down and shape into desired shapes. I make about 18 large pan rolls. Place in greased pans, brush with oil and, if desired, sprinkle sesame seeds on top. Cover rolls with waxed paper and refrigerate 2 to 24 hours. When ready to bake, remove from refrigerator and let stand at room temperature about 2 hours or until raised double in size. Bake at 375 degrees for 15 to 20 minutes.

Deb (Klotz) Smalley - Warsaw, Indiana

Whole Wheat Pizza Dough

1 teaspoon sugar
1 cup warm water
1 package active dry yeast
   (1 tablespoon)
1 1/2 cups flour
1 1/2 cups whole wheat flour
1 teaspoon salt
2 tablespoons vegetable oil

In large mixing bowl, dissolve sugar in warm water. Sprinkle yeast over water and let stand for 10 minutes or until foamy. Meanwhile combine flours and salt. Stir oil into foamy yeast mixture. Stir in about half the flour mixture. Add more flour, mixing until dough can be gathered into a slightly sticky ball You may need a little more or less than 3 cups of flour. On lightly floured surface, knead dough for about 5 minutes or until smooth and elastic, adding more flour as necessary to prevent dough from sticking to counter. Cut dough in half; cover with waxed paper and let rest for 10 minutes. On lightly floured surface, use a rolling pin to roll each piece of dough into a 12 inch circle about 1/4 inch thick. Transfer rounds to 2 lightly oiled pizza pans or baking sheets. Using fingers, carefully stretch dough into large circles. Let dough rise for about 15 minutes before adding toppings. For a thicker crust, let dough rise for 30 minutes. Add toppings just before baking. Bake in lower half of 450 degree oven for 16 to 18 minutes or until crust is golden brown and cheese is bubbly. Makes two 12 inch pizza rounds.

John R. Seffrin, Ph.D., Executive Vice President
American Cancer Society, Atlanta, Georgia

Aunt Onie's Thanksgiving Dressing

equivalent of two loaves,
   assorted dried breads
1 can water chestnuts
1 small can mushrooms with
   stems
1/2 cup celery
1 small onion
2 beaten eggs
1-2 cans chicken broth

Break dried bread in a large bowl (Bread will dry overnight in the oven if spread out on the racks; leave oven off). Cook onion and celery until tender; add to bowl. Whip eggs and add to bowl. Drain water chestnuts and mushrooms and add to bowl. Add a little salt and pepper. Add a can or two of chicken broth until absorbed into the bread. Bake in a pre-heated oven at 350 degrees for approximately 45 minutes.

Susan L. Wampler
Director of Development and Campaign Communications
University of Southern California
Los Angeles, California

Stromboli

Pillsbury blue label crusty
    French bread
1 egg - beat separately
1/4 pound hard salami
1/4 pound pepperoni
1/4 pound boiled ham

Brush egg on inside of bread. Sprinkle Romano cheese and Italian seasoning on bread. Add meats. Leave one inch all around the edge. Roll and close ends. Brush rest of egg on top. Bake seam side down. Bake 350 degrees for 1/2 hour. Slice and serve.

Norma Ferguson - Warsaw, Indiana

Swedish Pancakes

1 1/2 cups sweet milk
3 eggs
1/2 teaspoon salt
2 tablespoons shortening
1 tablespoon sugar
3/4 cup flour
1/2 teaspoon baking powder

Add 1 cup sweet milk to 3 eggs. Add salt, melted shortening, sugar, flour, and baking powder. Stir into smooth batter. Add 1/2 cup milk and bake on lightly greased griddle in large cakes. When done, roll up to keep warm.

Carole Cross, R.T., A.R.R.T. - A.S.R.T. - Warsaw, Indiana

Royal Hawaiian Pineapple Bread

1/4 cup butter
1 1/2 cups brown sugar
4 eggs
2 1/2 cups sifted flour
4 teaspoons baking powder
1/2 teaspoon soda
1 teaspoon salt
2 cups canned, crushed
    pineapple with syrup
1 teaspoon vanilla
1 1/2 cups Macadamia nuts,
    chopped
1 teaspoon sugar
1/2 teaspoon cinnamon

Grease 2 - 8 1/4 x 4 1/2-inch pans. Cream together butter and sugar. Add eggs and blend. Sift together and add dry ingredients. Add pineapple, vanilla and nuts. Pour into prepared pans. Sprinkle batter with the sugar and cinnamon mixture. Bake at 350 degrees for 35-40 minutes. Cool in pans for 10 minutes before removing.

Carol Offerle - Fort Wayne, Indiana

7-Layer Lowfat Salad

1/2 pound cauliflower, chopped
1 16 ounce package frozen peas
6 cups lettuce and spinach, torn
    into small pieces
1 red onion, chopped
4 ounces Canadian bacon,
    crumbled
4 ounces lowfat shredded
    Cheddar cheese

Dressing

1 package Hidden Valley Ranch
    dressing
2 cups fat free mayonnaise
1 cup fat free sour cream

Thin dressing with skim milk or vinegar to desired consistency. Place peas in the bottom of a 9 x 13 pan and continue to layer the rest. Top with dressing and refrigerate overnight. Serves 10.

Pam Lowe - Fort Wayne, Indiana

Casa de Angelo Salad

6 anchovies
8 ounces red wine vinegar
3/4 teaspoon oregano
1 1/2 teaspoons ground pepper
1 tablespoon salt
1 1/4 ounces sugar
1 1/2 teaspoons garlic salt
1/4 cup cornstarch
16 ounces light olive oil
1 head iceberg lettuce, rinse,
    drain and shred
1 head Romaine lettuce, rinse,
    drain and shred
1 large sweet red pepper
1/2 - 3/4 cup scallions or
    green onions, chopped
1/2 cup grated Parmesan cheese
1/2 cup grated Romano cheese
1/2 cup grated Mozzarella cheese

Mix together anchovies, vinegar, spices and cornstarch in blender. Add olive oil. Blend well and set aside. Place salad greens, red pepper and scallions in large bowl and toss. Mix together all of the cheeses and sprinkle over the salad and toss. Add the dressing and toss again. Note: bacon bits and croutons may be added on top.

Tina Minnix-Kleeman - Warsaw, Indiana

Cranberry Salad

1 cup cranberries
1/2 cup sugar
1 package lemon Jello (small)
1 cup hot water
1 cup crushed pineapple
1/2 cup pecans, chopped
3/4 cup cold water

Grind cranberries, add sugar and let stand for 1/2 hour. Dissolve 1 package lemon Jello with hot water and let cool. Add together the cranberry mixture with: crushed pineapple, chopped pecans (or other nutmeats), cold water. Chill in refrigerator until mixture is firm. Recipe can be doubled for a larger amount. Especially good for Thanksgiving and Christmas holidays!

Evelyn Franklin - Freedom, Indiana

Egg Salad

4 hard boiled eggs
1/4 cup mayonnaise
1 tablespoon mustard
dash of salt
dash of pepper

Cut up eggs into medium bowl. Add mayonnaise, mustard, salt, and pepper. Mash everything together with a fork. If you like creamier egg salad, add more mayonnaise. You might also add some chopped celery, green pepper, carrot, or cheese for more taste. Cover and refrigerate for an hour.

This is from one of our younger cooks.
Laurel is in the fifth grade.

Laurel Jenks - Leesburg, Indiana

French Dressing

3 cups catsup
3 cups oil
2 cups vinegar
2 cups sugar
1 onion, grated
2 tablespoons paprika
salt
pepper

Blend well, refrigerate. Keeps a long time.

Grandma Klotz

Garden Slaw

1/2 head purple cabbage,
  shredded
1/2 head green cabbage,
  shredded
1 large red pepper (cut in
  bite-size pieces)
1 large yellow pepper (cut in
  bite-size pieces)
2 small cans mandarin oranges,
  drained
1 tablespoon celery seed
Favorite slaw dressing
1/2 cup pine nuts for garnish

Toss together the purple and green cabbage. Combine remaining ingredients and toss with your favorite slaw dressing and garnish with pine nuts. Should not be prepared until right before serving. Does not keep well. Note: purple cabbage stains everything purple.

Pam Kolter - Warsaw, Indiana

Greek Salad

1 large head Romaine lettuce
2 medium tomatoes, cut into
    1/2 inch wedges
1 large cucumber, sliced
    1/8 inch thick
6-8 radishes, thinly sliced
4 green onions, cut into
    1/4 inch slices
6 ounces Feta cheese,
    coarsely crumbled
1/4 pound black olives
1 teaspoon finely chopped
    fresh mint

Dressing:
1/2 cup olive oil
3 tablespoons fresh lemon juice
2 tablespoons red wine vinegar
1 clove garlic, crushed
1/2 teaspoon finely chopped
    fresh oregano

Tear lettuce into bite-sized pieces. Place in large salad bowl. Add tomatoes, cucumber, radishes, green onions, cheese, and olives. Sprinkle with mint. Blend all remaining ingredients in small bowl with whisk. Pour over salad and toss lightly until thoroughly mixed. Serve immediately.

Carol Clay - Warsaw, Indiana

Green Goddess Salad

1 cup mayonnaise
1/2 cup sour cream
3 tablespoons white wine
    tarragon vinegar
1 tablespoon lemon juice
1/2 cup chopped parsley
3 tablespoons finely
    chopped onion
3 tablespoons mashed
    anchovy fillets well drained
1 tablespoon chopped chives
2 teaspoons chopped capers
1 clove minced garlic
salt/pepper to taste

Combine in jar and shake. Chill 3-4 hours.
Top cleaned dried mixed greens.

Stephany Mullen - Valparaiso, Indiana

Insalatette de Pollo (Chicken Salad)

3 to 4 diced grilled
    chicken breasts
1 cup prepared pesto (basil)
1/4 cup toasted pine nuts
1/4 cup chopped black olives
5 to 6 oil-packed sun dried
    tomatoes (minced)
1/2 cup golden currants or raisins

Brush the chicken breasts with olive oil and garlic
before grilling. Grill chicken and cool in refrigerator
(can be done ahead of time). Dice and mix with
remaining ingredients, adjusting to taste and
consistency. Flavor is enhanced if prepared a day
before serving.

Father Michael Basden - Warsaw, Indiana

Layered Mozzarella and Tomato Salad

4 large tomatoes cut in
    1/4" slices
2 pounds fresh Mozzarella
    cut in 1/4" slices
4 teaspoons dried basil
    or 4 tablespoons fresh
4 teaspoons dried Italian parsley
    or 4 tablespoons fresh
1/2 cup Vinaigrette dressing
fresh ground pepper

Vinaigrette dressing:
(makes 1 cup)
1 tablespoon Dijon mustard
4 tablespoons red wine vinegar
1 teaspoon sugar
1/2 teaspoon salt
1/2 teaspoon fresh
    ground pepper
chives/parsley to taste
1/2 cup olive oil

On large platter alternate cheese and tomatoes.
Serves 6.

Kimberly Miller - Valparaiso, Indiana

Mandarin Salad

1/2 cup sliced almonds
3 tablespoons sugar
1/2 head iceberg lettuce
1/2 head romaine lettuce
1 cup chopped celery
2 whole green onions, chopped
11 ounces mandarin oranges,
    drained

Dressing:
1/2 teaspoon salt
dash of pepper
1/4 cup vegetable oil
1 tablespoon chopped parsley
2 tablespoons sugar
2 tablespoons vinegar
dash of Tabasco sauce

In a small pan over medium heat, cook sugar and
almonds, stirring constantly until almonds are
coated and sugar dissolved. Watch carefully as they
will burn easily. Cool and store in air-tight container.
Mix all dressing ingredients and chill. Mix lettuces,
celery, and onions. Just before serving add almonds
and oranges. Toss with dressing. Serves 4-6

*JoAnn Waldo - Fort Collins, Colorado and Carole Cross, R.T.,
A.R.R.T. - A.S.R.T. - Warsaw, Indiana*

Pasta Salad with Currants, Olives and Pine Nuts

1 pound penne pasta
1 garlic clove, quartered
1 teaspoon salt
1 cup parsley
1 cup fresh lemon juice
1/4 cup red wine vinegar
1 teaspoon curry powder
1 teaspoon sugar
3/4 teaspoon ground cumin
1/2 teaspoon pepper
1 cup olive oil
1 red onion, peeled and
    finely chopped
1 cup sliced pitted Kelomata
    olives (or black olives)
2/3 cup dried currants
2/3 cup toasted pine nuts
fresh parsley sprigs
cherry tomatoes

Cook pasta in large pot of boiling, salted water until just tender, but still firm to bite, stirring occasionally. Drain. Rinse under cold water; drain well. Transfer pasta to large bowl. Meanwhile, blend garlic and salt to paste in processor, scraping down sides of bowl occasionally. Add parsley and mince. Blend in lemon juice, vinegar, curry, sugar, cumin and pepper. With machine running, gradually add oil through feed tube in thin steady stream. Pour dressing over pasta. Add onion, olives, currants and pine nuts to pasta and toss. Season with pepper. Cover and refrigerate until chilled, about 2 hours (can be made a day ahead).

Nelda Coglazier - Indianapolis, Indiana

Pretzel Jello Dessert

3/4 cup butter or margarine
3 tablespoons brown sugar
2 1/2 cups crushed pretzels
1 large (6 ounce) package Jello
    (raspberry or strawberry)
2 cups boiling water
3 cups chilled raspberries or
    cut strawberries (frozen
    berries are fine)
1 8 ounce package cream cheese
1 scant cup white sugar
1 small carton (8 ounce) Cool Whip

Mix first 3 ingredients and pat into bottom of 9 x 13 cake pan. Bake 10 minutes at 350 degrees. Mix together the following 3 ingredients. Cream cheese and sugar; fold in Cool Whip. Allow crust to cool. When Jello mixture begins to thicken, pour over crust and chill. Top with cream cheese/Cool Whip mixture.

Shirley Burish - Warsaw, Indiana

Rainbow Jello

1 6 ounce package orange Jello
1 6 ounce package lemon Jello
1 6 ounce package lime Jello
1 6 ounce package cherry Jello
2 pints lowfat (or regular)
   sour cream

Dissolve orange jello in 2 cups boiling water. Stir well. Allow to cool to room temperature. To 1/2 cup liquid Jello, add 1 cup sour cream. Pour sour cream/Jello mixture into a 9 X 13 clear glass dish. Refrigerate until set. When firm, pour reserved orange Jello over first layer. Let set. Repeat with other flavors, lemon, lime, and cherry. This makes an easy but festive looking dessert or salad for the holidays or any special occasion.

Joanne Sargent - Indianapolis, Indiana

Raspberry Spinach Salad

1 pint raspberries
2 quarts torn spinach
1/2 cup walnuts

Dressing:
8 ounces Lite cream cheese
1/2 cup reserved raspberries
1/4 cup white wine vinegar or
   raspberry vinegar
3 tablespoons sugar
1 tablespoon olive oil
1/4 teaspoon salt

Reserve 1/2 cup raspberries for dressing. Arrange spinach on individual plates. Sprinkle on raspberries and nuts. Place dressing ingredients in blender. Process until well blended. Serves 8.

Sharodene Morris - Warsaw, Indiana

Raspberry Vinaigrette

2 tablespoons raspberry vinegar
2 tablespoons seasoned
   rice vinegar
2 tablespoons water
1/4 teaspoon crushed rosemary
1/4 teaspoon dried tarragon

Whisk ingredients together. Chill

Susan Jaskulski, R.T., Kodak
Rochester, New York

Romaine Salad and Dressing:

1 head Romaine lettuce
1 Granny Smith apple sliced
4 ounces grated Swiss cheese
8 ounces cashews

Dressing:
1/2 cup olive oil
3 tablespoons red wine vinegar
1 tablespoon grated onion
2 tablespoons poppy seeds
1 teaspoon dry mustard
1/4 cup sugar
1/2 teaspoon salt

Clean lettuce. Top with cheese, apple, and nuts.
Add dressing and toss.

Carolyn Allen - Chicago, Illinois

The Best Chicken Salad

chicken breasts and thighs—
    cut into small pieces.
    Can bake, roast, or boil.
2 tablespoons lemon juice
1 cup chopped celery
2/3 cup white or red grapes,
    chopped
3/4 cup light mayonnaise thinned
    with milk or 1 1/2 tablespoons
    apple butter
salt to taste
3/4 cup almonds - roasted and
    chopped in blender

Mix lemon juice and chicken. Chill one hour. Blend
in other ingredients and chill until serving time.

Mary Gathany - North Manchester, Indiana

Angel Hair Pasta with Lobster Sauce

2 quarts water
2- 10 ounce lobster tails, fresh
    or frozen, thawed
16 ounce angel hair pasta
2/3 cup sliced fresh mushrooms
3 tablespoons green onion
    chopped
2 tablespoons butter, melted
2 tablespoons flour
1 cup plus 2 tablespoons
    half and half
2 tablespoons dry white wine
1/4 teaspoon salt
1/4 teaspoon dry mustard
2 tablespoons fresh grated
    Parmesan cheese

Bring water to boil. Add lobster. Cover and cook 6 minutes. Drain and rinse with cold water. Drain. Cut lobster into 1/2 inch pieces. Cook pasta and drain. Saute mushrooms and onion in butter. Add flour and stir until smooth. Cook 1 minute. Gradually add half and half, stirring constantly. Stir in wine, salt, mustard, and lobster meat. Cook over low heat, stirring constantly. Serve sauce over pasta. Sprinkle with cheese. Serves 4.

Mary Louise Miller - Winona Lake, Indiana

Bolognese Sauce

2 tablespoons olive oil
1/2 cup diced bacon
1/2 cup Proscuitto (or ham)
1 onion minced
1 celery rib minced
1 carrot minced
1/4 pound chopped mushrooms
3 tablespoons butter
1/2 cup heavy cream
1/4 pound ground beef
1/4 pound ground veal
1/2 pound ground pork
2-3 cups beef broth
1/2 cup marsala wine
2 tablespoons tomato paste
1/2 cup dry white wine
1/4 teaspoon rosemary
salt/pepper

Heat olive oil in large skillet. Brown bacon and Proseiutto in oil. Saute onion, celery, carrot in same skillet until tender. Add beef, veal, and pork and cook until pink color is gone—about 15 minutes over low heat. Mix together 1/4 cup beef broth and 1/4 cup marsala; add to skillet and cook until liquid has almost been absorbed. Stir in tomato paste. Mix together white wine and enough beef broth to barely cover the ingredients. Add rosemary, salt, and pepper to taste. Simmer 40 minutes. Saute mushrooms in butter. Add to sauce and cook for 5 minutes longer. Mix cream with remaining 1/4 cup of marsala and stir into sauce. Serve over pasta. Serves 6-8.

Darleen Hunter - Warsaw, Indiana

Cheese Enchiladas with Beans

5 - 6 super size soft tortillas
2 16 ounce jars mild
    Pace picante sauce
8 ounces cottage cheese
8 ounces Monterey-Jack cheese,
    shredded
1/2 cup sour cream
1 can seeded cut green
    chili peppers, mild
1/4 teaspoon salt
1/8 teaspoon pepper
1 can pinto beans, rinsed and
    drained
1 can white kidney beans,
    rinsed and drained

Mix together the cottage cheese, sour cream, salt, pepper, and all but 1 cup of the Monterey Jack cheese. Dip tortilla in picante sauce (both sides). Fill with the cheese mixture and top with the green chili's. Wrap. (Put aside on cookie sheet.) Mix the beans with the remaining picante sauce and put in baking pan. Place the enchiladas on top of the bean mixture. Top with the remaining cup of Monterey Jack cheese. Bake 20 minutes at 375 degrees or until the beans are hot and bubbly.

Nancy Wooldridge - Indianapolis, Indiana

Cheese Grits Casserole

1 1/2 cups grits
6 cups boiling water
1 1/2 sticks margarine
1 pound sharp Cheddar cheese,
    grated (use New York or
    Vermont cheese)
4 teaspoons Lawry's Savory salt
1 teaspoon salt
2 dashes Tabasco sauce
3 eggs, well beaten

Cook grits in water until thick. Add remaining ingredients. Bake one hour in well-greased pan at 300 degrees. Serves 12.

Barbara Cook - West Lafayette, Indiana
Indiana Commission for Women

Chicken Manicotti with Chive Cream Sauce

12 packaged manicotti shells
2 8 ounce containers soft-style
    cream cheese with chives
    and onions
2/3 cup milk
1/4 cup Parmesan cheese
2 cups diced cooked chicken
1 10 ounce package frozen
chopped broccoli, thawed
    and drained
1 4 ounce jar diced pimento
1/4 teaspoon pepper
paprika

Cook manicotti shells in boiling salted water for 18 minutes. Drain. Rinse with cold water, then drain well. Meanwhile, for sauce, in a saucepan stir cream cheese over medium-low heat until melted. Slowly add milk, stirring until smooth. Stir in Parmesan cheese. For filling, in a mixing bowl, stir together 3/4 cup sauce, chicken, broccoli, pimento, and pepper. Using a small spoon, carefully stuff each manicotti shell with about 1/3 cup of the filling. Arrange shells in a 9 x 13 baking dish. Pour the remaining sauce over the shells. Sprinkle with paprika, Cover with foil and bake in a 350 degree oven for 30 minutes. Makes 6 servings.

Raynae Hammond - Warsaw, Indiana

Easy Chicken with Spinach Fettuccine

Vegetable cooking spray
4 4-ounce boneless, skinless
    chicken breast halves
1/4 teaspoon freshly ground
    black pepper
1 cup chopped onion
1 clove garlic, minced
1 4-ounce can mushroom stems
    and pieces, drained
1 14 1/2-ounce can stewed
    tomatoes, undrained
    and chopped
1 bay leaf
1/4 teaspoon salt
1/2 cup Chablis or other dry
    white wine
4 cups cooked spinach fettucine
    (cooked without salt or fat)
1 tablespoon minced fresh
    parsley

Coat a large skillet with cooking spray; place over medium heat until hot. Cut chicken into bite-size pieces and sprinkle with pepper; saute chicken until lightly browned. Remove from skillet; set aside. Saute onion and garlic in skillet until browned. Add chicken, mushrooms, tomatoes, bay leaf, salt and wine; stir well. Simmer, uncovered, 15 minutes. Spoon fettuccine onto serving platter. Remove bay leaf. Arrange chicken and vegetables on fettuccine; sprinkle with parsley. Yield: 6 servings.

Betty LeCount - Warsaw, Indiana

Company Lasagna

1 tablespoon olive oil
2 cloves garlic, minced
1 tablespoon minced onion
1 tablespoon parsley flakes
1 tablespoon dried basil leaves
1 teaspoon dried oregano leaves
1 pound lean ground beef
2 14 1/2-ounce cans whole
    tomatoes
1 12-ounce can tomato paste
1 8-ounce can tomato sauce
1 12-ounce carton large curd
    cottage cheese
1 15-ounce carton Ricotta cheese
1/4 teaspoon salt
1/4 teaspoon pepper
1 cup grated Parmesan cheese
2 eggs, beaten
2 tablespoon parsley flakes
1 tablespoon dried basil leaves
12 lasagna noodles
3 whole basil leaves
16 ounces thinly sliced
    Mozzarella cheese

In deep skillet, heat oil, garlic, onion and parsley flakes, and oregano. Add ground beef. Break up and stir until browned. Drain. Add tomatoes, tomato paste, tomato sauce, salt and pepper to taste. Meanwhile, combine cottage cheese, Ricotta cheese, salt, pepper, Parmesan cheese, eggs, parsley flakes and basil; mix well. Cook lasagna noodles as directed on package, adding 3 basil leaves to water. Drain. Heat oven to 350 degrees. In 9x13x2 inch pan, layer half of noodles, half of cottage cheese mixture, half of Mozzarella cheese, half of sauce. Repeat layers; sprinkle with Parmesan cheese. Bake 35-40 minutes. 12 servings. Tip: Lasagna can be made ahead and refrigerated, then bake 45-60 minutes.

Kelly Zachrich - Fort Wayne, Indiana

233

Jim's Red Sauce

2 14 ounce cans zucchini in
    red sauce
3 14 ounce cans tomatoes,
    peeled and diced
1 small can tomato paste
1 large yellow bell pepper
1 large white onion
3 cloves fresh garlic
1 tablespoon virgin olive oil
1/4 cup red wine
1 bay leaf
1 teaspoon dry basil
1/4 teaspoon crushed sage
1 teaspoon Italian seasoning
1/2 teaspoon fennel seed, whole
1/4 teaspoon salt
1/2 teaspoon pepper

This can all be done in one pan. Dice the onion. Steam or par-boil the unpeeled garlic cloves for 2 to 3 minutes, then peel, trim off hard end, and remove the center "core." Steaming makes the core easy to remove. The result is milder, but still rich tasting garlic. Dice. Add oil to preheated pan and coat bottom evenly. Add onion and garlic and saute over low to medium heat until onions just begin to turn brown. Chop pepper into bite-size chunks but not too small. When the onion-garlic mixture has begun to turn brown, pour in the wine to deglaze the pan. Add the rest of the ingredients and simmer for at least 15 minutes. You can cook a short time for a "bright" fresh tasting sauce or cook longer for a darker, "softer" sauce. Do not let the sauce boil or stick to the bottom of the pan.

Variations:
The onions and garlic in olive oil is a major key to the rich but low-fat flavor of this dish. Butter or other oils would change the recipe too much. Add other vegetables; mushrooms, sliced yellow squash, and artichoke hearts are very good. You can substitute or add green and red bell peppers. Add chopped fresh basil and other herbs from the garden as available.

Jim Seiler - Indianapolis, Indiana

Marinara Sauce

1/2 cup olive oil
6 to 8 cloves garlic, peeled
1 28 ounce can plum (Italian)
    tomatoes
1 28 ounce can tomato puree
1 teaspoon salt
1 teaspoon basil
1/4 teaspoon red pepper flakes
1/2 teaspoon garlic powder

Heat olive oil over medium high heat. Add garlic cloves and cook until soft (not brown). Add tomatoes, puree, and seasonings and bring to a boil. Reduce heat to simmer and cook for 20 minutes. Serve over pasta.

Lucinda Geis-Dunaway, M.D.
Indianapolis, Indiana

Kay's Angel Hair Pesto Prima Vera

1 cup fresh basil leaves
2 cloves fresh garlic, peeled
    and chopped
1/2 cup grated Parmesan cheese
1/3 cup parsley leaves
1/2 cup shelled walnuts
1/2 cup olive oil
2 tablespoons grated
    Romano cheese
Salt and pepper to taste
1/2 pound angel hair pasta
    or thin spaghetti
1 tablespoon salt
2 tablespoons heavy cream
1 small red pepper
1 zucchini, sliced
1 red tomato, cut into wedges
1 small red onion
1 yellow tomato, cut into wedges
1/2 pound mushrooms, sliced
Lawry's Seasoned Salt

To make a pesto, combine the basil, parsley, garlic and walnuts in a food processor or blender and chop thoroughly. Leave the motor running and add the olive oil in a slow, steady stream. Turn off motor and add cheeses, salt and pepper. Grind briefly and set aside. Cook pasta according to package directions. Stir 1 tablespoon of the hot pasta water into the pesto and heavy cream. Drain the pasta and return it to the warm pan. Stir in the pesto and toss well. Warm a large skillet with about 2 tablespoons olive oil. Slice pepper and onion and saute 2 minutes; sprinkle with seasoned salt. Add mushrooms and zucchini slices. Sauté 2 minutes. Sprinkle with more seasoned salt and cover over low heat for 5 minutes. Add tomatoes. Cover over low heat for 5 more minutes. Arrange vegetables on top of pesto pasta on large serving platter. Voila! Great dinner! Serves 2.

Kay Niedenthal, owner, Kay's Garden and Kay's Catering
Indianapolis, Indiana

Risotto with Asparagus and Porcini Mushrooms

4-5 cups chicken stock
1/2 ounce dried Porcini
    mushrooms
1/2 cup chopped onion
1 tablespoon olive oil
1 cup Arborio rice
1/2 cup white wine
1 pound asparagus
1/2 cup Parmesan cheese, grated
salt and pepper

Heat stock until it simmers. Add dried mushrooms. Saute onion in hot oil in a deep pot. Add rice and stir well. Add wine, stir and cook 2 minutes. Cut asparagus into 1/2 inch pieces. Add 1 cup simmering stock to rice, and stir often until liquid is absorbed. Continue adding stock as rice absorbs it, stirring often. Five minutes before rice is done, stir in asparagus and mushrooms. When rice is tender and slightly runny, add cheese. Season with salt and pepper. Serve immediately.

Susan Claymon - San Francisco, California

Pasta with Hot Tomato and Bacon Sauce

1/2 pound thickly sliced bacon
3 tablespoons olive oil
2 1/2 large onions, coarsely
    chopped
3 large garlic cloves, minced
1 28 ounce can tomatoes,
    chopped with liquid
1 16 ounce can tomatoes,
    chopped with liquid
1 tablespoon tarragon
    or 2 teaspoons sugar
2 teaspoons salt
1/4 teaspoon red pepper flakes
    or cayenne
1/4 cup minced fresh parsley
1 1/2 pounds pasta
unsalted butter, as needed
grated Parmesan (optional)

Fry bacon until crisp. Drain. Pour all grease except 1 tablespoon from skillet. Add olive oil and onions to skillet. Saute onions until wilted, about 5 minutes. Stir in garlic, tomatoes, salt, tarragon, and pepper. Simmer 30 minutes to reduce liquid. Crumble bacon and add along with the parsley. Remove sauce from heat. (If you like a smoother sauce, give it a whirl in a food processor, but don't overdo it.) Toss cooked pasta with a bit of butter and then some of the sauce. Top each serving with additional sauce and cheese. Serves 6.

Susan Jaskulski, R.T., Kodak
Rochester, New York

Shrimp Tortellini

1 medium onion, chopped
2 cloves minced garlic
3/4 stick butter
1 pound shrimp, cooked
1/2 cup Parmesan
1/8 cup chopped fresh parsley
1/2 pint half and half cream
1 bag cheese tortellini

Saute onion and garlic in butter. Add shrimp and heat through. Add Parmesan, parsley, and cream. Prepare tortellini according to package. Drain. Fold into shrimp mixture. Add salt and red pepper. Bake at 350 degrees until it bubbles. Sprinkle paprika on top. Enjoy.

Donnette Hall - Warsaw, Indiana

Spinach Mushroom Pasta

2 10 ounce packages frozen
    chopped spinach cooked
    and drained
1 pound fresh mushrooms
    chopped
1 clove of garlic minced
1 shallot minced
4 tablespoons butter
2 tablespoons flour
1/2 cup milk
1 cup sour cream
1 cup mayonnaise
1/2 cup fresh lemon juice
1/2 cup Parmesan cheese grated
1/2 cup Asiago cheese grated
1/2 cup Gruyere cheese grated
12 ounces Rigatoni cooked

Melt butter. Saute garlic, shallots. Add mushrooms. Saute. Remove mushrooms. Stir in flour slowly. Add milk. Blend. Add sour cream, mayonnaise, lemon juice, and cheeses. Salt and pepper to taste. Stir in spinach and mushrooms. Layer pasta and sauce. Bake 350 degrees for 30-40 minutes. Serves 8-10.

Dane Miller - Winona Lake, Indiana

Beef Broccoli Pie

1 pound ground beef
1/4 cup chopped onion
2 tablespoons all-purpose flour
3/4 teaspoon salt
1/4 teaspoon garlic salt
1 1/4 cups milk
1 3 ounce package
    cream cheese, softened
1 egg, beaten
1 10 ounce package frozen
    chopped broccoli, cooked
    and well drained
pastry for 2 crust 9 inch pie
4+ ounces Monterey Jack cheese
milk

Brown beef and onion. Drain. Stir in flour, salt, and garlic. Add cup milk and cream cheese. Stir until mixture is smooth and bubbly. Add a moderate amount of the hot creamed mixture to the beaten egg in a separate bowl. Return the egg mixture to the meat mixture in the skillet. Cook and stir over medium heat until thick (1 to 2 minutes). Stir in chopped and cooked broccoli. Set aside. Line a 9 inch pie plate with half the pastry. Spoon the hot meat mixture into the pastry shell. Cut the Monterey Jack cheese into slices. Arrange the cheese slices atop the meat mixture. Adjust the top crust of the meat pie and seal. Use a fork to make perforations in the crust in spoke-fashion or slashes to allow for escape of steam. Brush the top of the beef pie with a little milk. Bake at 350 degrees for 40 to 45 minutes. If the pastry browns too quickly, cover edge of crust with foil during the last 20 minutes. Let stand 10 minutes before serving.

Carol Montgomery - Ligonier, Indiana

Beef Casserole Delight

2 pounds ground beef
1 cup chopped celery
1/4 cup chopped green pepper
3/4 cup chopped onions
1/2 cup margarine
1 29-ounce can tomatoes
1 16-ounce can tomatoes
1 8-ounce can mushroom pieces,
    drained
1 8-ounce can chestnuts,
    drained and sliced
1 cup cubed American cheese
1/2 cup chopped green olives
1/2 cup black olives
1/2 teaspoon salt
1/4 teaspoon pepper
6 ounces egg noodles, uncooked
2 cups shredded Cheddar cheese

Brown ground beef and drain. Saute celery, green pepper and onion in margarine. Add tomatoes, and their juices. Add all remaining ingredients, except Cheddar cheese, and simmer 20 minutes. Pour into 13 x 9-inch pan. Sprinkle cheese on top and bake at 350 degrees for 40 minutes.

Jill Collins - Fort Wayne, Indiana

Prairie Meatloaf (Hoosier Meatloaf)

2 lbs. ground sirloin or beef
1 lb. ground veal
1 lb. ground pork
2 whole canned tomatoes
    (use no juice)
3/4 cup soft breadcrumbs
    soaked in 1/2 cup beef broth
1 medium onion, minced
1/2 cup chopped fresh herbs
    (parsley, dill, coriander,
    basil in any combination
    of three)
2 whole eggs, slightly beaten
1/2 teaspoon salt
1/2 teaspoon of coarsely
    ground black pepper
1 tablespoon Worcestershire
    sauce

Mix all ingredients together until thoroughly blended. Pat into loaf about 5 inches wide in large greased or oiled roasting pan and bake at 400 degrees for almost 1 1/2 hours. While cooking, add a little water if the pan becomes dry.

This recipe was first published in 1966 in "These Entertaining People" by Florence Pritchell Smith (MacMillan)

Eleanor Lambert Berkson
New York, New York

Beef Filet

7 pounds beef filet whole
1 cup soy sauce
3/4 cup oil
1/2 cup olive oil
1 1/2 cups sherry
7 cloves of garlic minced
1 1/2 tablespoons Tabasco sauce

Do not butterfly meat. Marinate meat in oil mixture for 8 hours or overnight. Bake in metal pan at 475 degrees for 30 minutes for rare meat.

Dane Miller - Winona Lake, Indiana

Beef Roll Mozzarella

1 1/2 pounds lean ground beef
1 teaspoon salt
1/4 teaspoon pepper
1 teaspoon dehydrated
     onion flakes
1 egg, slightly beaten
1/2 cup dry bread crumbs
1 4-ounce can mushroom stems
     and pieces
6 ounces Mozzarella, shredded
1 15-ounce can tomato sauce
2 tablespoons dry vermouth

Combine meat, salt, pepper, onion, egg and bread crumbs in a large bowl. Drain mushrooms, reserving liquid. To mushroom liquid add enough water to make 1/2 cup and add to meat mixture. Mix lightly, just until well-combined. Press mixture into one 14 x 10-inch rectangle on a piece of waxed paper. Sprinkle surface with Mozzarella, leaving a 1/2-inch border. Roll up, jelly roll fashion starting with one of the short sides. Place, seam side down in 13 x 9-inch baking dish which has been lightly greased. Cover and refrigerate until ready to bake. Remove from refrigerator and preheat oven to 375 degrees. Combine tomato sauce and vermouth. Spread half the sauce over the roll. Bake 45 minutes. Combine remaining sauce with mushrooms; spread over roll; bake 10 minutes longer. Lift onto heated platter using two wide spatulas. Yield: 6 servings.

Jill Collins - Fort Wayne, Indiana

Beef Stroganoff

3 tablespoons flour
1 1/2 teaspoon salt
1/4 teaspoon pepper
1 pound beef (round cut)
1 cut clove garlic
1/4 cup butter
1/2 cup minced onion
1/4 cup water
1 can condensed mushroom
    soup
1 pound sliced mushrooms
1 cup sour cream
1/4 cup sherry (optional)
snipped parsley, chives, or dill

Combine flour, salt, and pepper. Rub meat with garlic. With rim (plate) pound flour into both sides. Cut into 1 1/2 x 1 strips. In hot butter in dutch oven, brown strips, turning often. Add onion; saute until golden. Add water. Stir to dissolve brown bits in bottom. Add soup, mushrooms and sherry (optional). Cook uncovered over low heat until mixture is thick and meat is fork tender (about 20 minutes). Just before serving, stir in sour cream. Heat but do not boil. Sprinkle with parsley. Serve with noodles.

Carole Cross, R.T., A.R.R.T. - A.S.R.T. - Warsaw, Indiana
and Delores Basney - Fountaintown, Indiana

Beef with Stout

Use your favorite stout (Guiness
    or Murphy for example)
2 pounds lean stewing beef
flour
3 tablespoons olive oil
2 thinly sliced onions
2 teaspoons sugar
1 teaspoon dry English mustard
1 tablespoon concentrated
    tomato puree
1 strip dried orange peel
a bouquet garni made of 1 bay
    leaf, 1 sprig of fresh thyme,
    and 4 parsley stalks
1 pint stout
8 ounces mushrooms
1/2 ounce butter

Cut meat into 1 1/2 inch cubes and toss in flour. Heat some oil in a hot pan and fry the meat in batches until it is brown on all sides. Transfer the meat into a dutch oven and add a little more oil to the frying pan. Fry the thinly sliced onions until browned, deglaze with the stout and add to meat. Add sugar, mustard, tomato puree, orange rind,and bouquet garni. Season with salt and pepper. Bring to boil, cover, and simmer for 2 to 2 1/2 hours. Meanwhile, wash and slice the mushrooms. Sauté in very little melted butter in a hot pan. Season with salt and pepper. Set aside. When the stew is cooked, add the mushrooms and simmer for 2 to 3 minutes. Taste and correct the seasoning. Serve sprinkled with chopped parsley.

Mary Darling

Chateau Briand with Cabernet Pepper Brown Sauce

2 pounds whole beef tenderloin
   (trimmed)
1 cup coarse ground pepper
1 cup Cabernet Sauvignon
1/2 cup butter
1/2 cup flour
4 cups beef bouillon
2 cups water

Roll beef in pepper and coat well. Brown in skillet over medium heat. Put in oven at 250 degrees for 1 hour (rare); 1 1/2 hours (medium). In a medium sauce pan, make roux with butter and flour. Separately mix bouillon and water. Add together with salt and pepper to taste and add Cabernet. Keep on moderate low heat to thicken. Slice beef 1/4 inch thick; place on plate, Cabernet pepper sauce to taste.

*Kirk Dieckamp, Executive Chef, St. Elmo Steak House
Indianapolis, Indiana*

Country Ribs

1 can beer
1 bottle Liquid Smoke
3-4 pounds ribs
favorite barbecue sauce

Boil ribs in beer until tender. Add more beer if needed. Turn off; let set 3 hours. Put in baking dish with barbecue sauce. Bake 45-60 minutes at 350 degrees until really tender.

Kelly Zackrich - Fort Wayne, Indiana

Goulash

1 pound ground beef
chopped onion to taste
salt, pepper
1 can tomato soup, undiluted
1 can mushrooms (stems/pieces
   will do) and the juice
1/2 pound or more Velveeta
   cheese - shredded
1/2 to 3/4 package noodles,
cooked, drained, rinsed in
   cold water
chopped green pepper if desired

Brown ground beef with onion, salt, and pepper. Drain and place in a baking dish. Add remaining ingredients. I use flat noodles about 1/2 inch wide. Top with dry buttered crumbs 1 to 2 inches thick. Cover casserole loosely with foil (tent type). Crumbs stay crisp but stop browning. If casserole is room temperature, cook at 375 degrees for 1/2 to 3/4 hour in a preheated oven. If casserole is cold it will take much longer. Must be served very hot. Will hold heat well.

Nita Oppenheim - Warsaw, Indiana

241

Flank Steak with Brandy Cream Sauce

2 pounds flank steak
2 tablespoons butter, softened
2 tablespoons dijon mustard
1 1/2 teaspoons Worcestershire
    sauce
3/4 teaspoons curry powder
1/4 teaspoon dry mustard
1 clove garlic, crushed
salt and pepper to taste
1/4 cup sherry or Madeira
1/4 cup wine vinegar
2 tablespoons butter
1/2 pound fresh mushrooms,
    sliced
1 shallot, minced
3/4 cup sour cream
3 tablespoons brandy
fresh parsley, minced

Either the night before or early in the day, place flank steak in shallow glass baking dish. Combine softened butter, mustard, Worcestershire sauce, curry, dry mustard, garlic, salt and pepper and mix to a paste. Spread this mixture evenly over meat. Pour sherry and vinegar over meat. Cover loosely and refrigerate for at least 8 hours, or let stand at room temperature for 2 hours. If refrigerated, allow meat to reach room temperature before cooking. Broil meat in a pre-heated broiler 2-3 minutes per side for rare. While meat is broiling, melt 2 tablespoons butter in a skillet over medium heat. Add mushrooms and shallots. Sauté until tender. Remove from heat. Transfer meat to warm platter. Place broiler pan with juices over medium-high heat. Gradually stir in sour cream and brandy. Blend well. Simmer for about 4 minutes, stirring constantly. Blend in mushroom and shallot mixture and heat thoroughly. Cut steak diagonally into very thin slices. Spoon sauce over steak and sprinkle with minced parsley before serving.

Jill Collins - Fort Wayne, Indiana

Hamburger Pie

1 pound ground beef
1/2 cup onion, chopped
1/2 teaspoon salt
1/2 teaspoon pepper
1 16 ounce can cut green beans
1 10 3/4 ounce can tomato soup
5 medium potatoes, cooked
    and hot
1/2 cup warm milk
1 egg, beaten
1/2 cup shredded American
cheese

Brown hamburger and onion. Drain. Add salt and pepper. Drain beans and add with soup. Put in casserole dish. Mash potatoes. Add milk and egg. Put on top of other ingredients and sprinkle with cheese. Bake at 350 degrees for 25 to 30 minutes. NOTE: Instant potatoes may be used.

Mary Smoker - Warsaw, Indiana

Grilled Lamb With Rosemary Garlic Butter Sauce

4 small shallots, finely chopped
2/3 cup olive oil (more if desired)
2 tablespoons chopped
    fresh rosemary
4 small garlic cloves or
2 teaspoons prepared
    minced garlic
salt and pepper
leg of lamb, bone and
    butterfly

Rosemary Garlic Butter Sauce:
lamb bone reserved from lamb
3 cups chicken stock or canned
low-salt broth
1/3 cup rice vinegar
2 shallots, finely chopped
2 bay leaves
1 garlic clove, pressed or
    1 teaspoon prepared
    minced garlic
1 tablespoon finely chopped
    fresh rosemary
1/2 cup (1 stick) chilled unsalted
    butter, cut into 8 pieces

Combine first 6 ingredients and pour over lamb in a large dish or zip lock bag. Marinate at least 6 hours or overnight. Grill lamb to desired doneness (medium to medium-rare).

Place reserved lamb bones in heavy large pot. Pour stock over and cook over medium-high heat until liquid is reduced to 1/4 cup (about 30 minutes) Strain stock into heavy medium saucepan. Add vinegar, shallots, bay leaves, garlic and rosemary. Simmer until liquid is reduced to 1/4 cup (about 8 minutes) Remove from heat and whisk in 2 pieces of butter. Set pan over low heat and whisk in remaining butter 1 piece at a time, removing pan from heat briefly if drops of melted butter appear. If sauce breaks down at any time, remove from heat and whisk in 2 tablespoons cold butter. Keep sauce warm in top of double boiler over warm water or in a vacuum bottle. Makes 1 1/2 cups.

Father Michael Basden - Warsaw, Indiana

New York Strip Steak with Roquefort Butter

4 New York strip steaks
    (cut to desired size)
1/4 pound (1 stick) salted butter
2 ounces crumbled
    Roquefort cheese
2 tablespoons cognac or brandy
1/8 teaspoon pepper
1 teaspoon granular garlic

Cook steak to desired doneness. Put butter in small mixing bowl. Add Roquefort cheese and blend until smooth. Add cognac brandy. Add pepper and garlic and mix until well blended. Place cooked steaks on broiling pan and mound Roquefort butter on top. Place under broiler until butter melts and browns slightly. Place steaks on serving plate and pour remaining butter over top. Serves: 4.

Jim Adams, owner, Adams Rib and Seafood House
Zionsville, Indiana

Ground Beef and Green Beans

Sauce:
6 tablespoons cornstarch
1 cup cooled broth
3 tablespoons soy sauce
3 tablespoons dry sherry
3 teaspoons cider vinegar

Main ingredients:
1 tablespoon oil
1 pound green beans, trimmed,
    sliced diagonally into
    2 inch lengths
2 teaspoons minced fresh ginger
2 teaspoons minced garlic
    (2 large cloves)
1/4 teaspoon hot red
    pepper flakes (optional)
1/2 pound lean ground beef

Combine all the sauce ingredients. Make sure cornstarch is completely dissolved. Set mixture aside. In a wok or large skillet, heat the oil for 30 seconds over high heat and add green beans. Stir fry the green beans for 4 minutes. Remove the green beans with a slotted spoon and set aside. Add the ginger and garlic to the pan, cook them for 30 seconds and add pepper flakes and beef, crumbling the meat with a spatula. Stir fry the mixture just until the beef loses its pinkness. Drain off all the excess fat from the pan. Stir the reserved sauce once more and add to the meat. Cook mixture, stirring it, until the sauce thickens. Fold in the reserved green beans. Heat for one minute and serve.

Kelly Zachrich - Fort Wayne, Indiana

Pappy's Braciole in Red Sauce

1 slice round steak, 3/4 inch thick
1 cup Italian seasoned
    bread crumbs
1/2 cup grated Romano
    or Parmesan cheese
3 hard boiled eggs
1/4 cup fresh parsley
3 cloves garlic, minced
1 teaspoon salt
1 teaspoon coarse pepper
1/4 cup olive oil

Using a mallet, pound round steak on bread board to tenderize. Slice down the center to form two pieces of steak. Sprinkle with salt and pepper. Layer on bread crumbs, cheese, parsley, and minced garlic. Slice hard boiled eggs on surface. Beginning at the end nearest you, form each section of steak into a roll. Tie with butcher cord to secure. Place medium sized iron skillet on medium heat. Add olive oil. Do not burn oil. Place rolled round steaks into oil and brown well, turning gently. When well browned, remove from skillet and place them on paper towels. Set aside. Add the bracioles to your favorite red sauce. Cover and simmer slowly for two to three hours. To serve, place bracioles on a cutting board. Cut and remove cord. Slice into 1/2 to 3/4 inch rounds. Place on platter. Cover with sauce.

Lorees Sherman - Warsaw, Indiana

Pot Roast

rump roast (approximately
   3 pounds)
1 16 ounce can of tomato wedges
3 bouillon cubes
1 6 ounce can of V-8 juice
1 green pepper, chopped
1 red onion, chopped
4 carrots
8 - 10 small red potatoes
1 bay leaf
salt and pepper to taste
1 10 ounce box of frozen
   snap peas

Put roast in dutch oven. Add tomatoes, V-8 juice, bouillon cubes, onion, peppers, carrots, unpeeled potatoes and seasonings. Add water so that liquid is level with the top of the roast. (Approximately 4 cups.) Cover and cook at 350 degrees for four hours. Add frozen snap peas. Cook another twenty minutes.

Barbara Shoup - Indianapolis, Indiana

Seven Layer Casserole

2 large potatoes, sliced
1 pound ground beef
1/2 teaspoon salt
1/2 teaspoon pepper
1/2 teaspoon garlic powder
1/2 teaspoon dill weed
3 stalks celery, chopped
1 medium onion, sliced
1 11-ounce can whole kernel corn,
   drained
1 10 3/4-ounce can tomato soup
3/4 soup can water
1/2 pound Cheddar cheese, grated
3/4 cup bread crumbs

Heat oven to 375 degrees. Parboil the sliced potatoes for 5 minutes and drain. Place in the bottom of a greased 2-quart casserole. In skillet, brown hamburger, salt, pepper, garlic powder, dill weed and celery. Drain; place on top of potatoes. Place sliced onion on top of ground beef. Spread can of corn on top of onions. Pour tomato soup mixed with 3/4 cup water over all the layers. Add grated cheese on top of all. Put bread crumbs on top of cheese. Bake 1 hour. Tip: Seasoned crumbs may be substituted for bread crumbs.

Lee Collins - Fort Wayne, Indiana

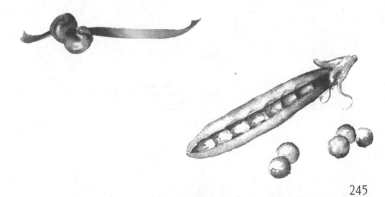

Shish Kabob

2 pounds round steak
3/4 cup oil
1 small onion, chopped
1 stalk celery, diced
1/4 cup wine vinegar
1 bay leaf
1/2 teaspoon thyme
1/2 teaspoon marjoram
1 teaspoon parsley
1/4 teaspoon salt
1/4 teaspoon pepper
1 jar pearl onions
1 pint cherry tomatoes
1 small container
    fresh mushrooms

In small saucepan, heat oil, onion, and celery for 5 minutes. Let cool. In medium bowl with cover combine oil mixture, vinegar, bay leaf, thyme, marjoram, parsley, salt and pepper. Cube meat for skewering and marinade in mixture. Refrigerate overnight. Alternate meat, onion, mushrooms, and tomatoes on skewers. Grill or broil on medium heat until meat is done to your preference.

Kristy Schmitt - Warsaw, Indiana

Venison Tenderloin

2 venison tenderloins
    fully cleaned
butter
1 bottle red wine
1 tablespoon fresh garlic
2 teaspoons salt
2 teaspoons pepper
6 green onions
3/4 cup sugar
2 shots cognac
1 cup heavy cream
1 teaspoon red current jelly

Place venison in non-reactive bowl. Stir the next six ingredients in separate bowl and cover the venison. Marinate for 24 hours. For each order, cut three medallions out of the loin and pound just enough to shape. Sauté in butter, turning once, to about medium rare and then place on a plate to hold. Drain off fat and deglaze pan with the cognac. Pour two cups of the marinade into the pan and reduce by half. Add the jelly and let dissolve. Add the cream and reduce again by half. Set the venison on a clean plate with vegetable and spoon the sauce over the venison.

Scott Grigoletti, Chef, Diamonds and Denim Dance Club
Warsaw, Indiana

Steak Diane

2 tablespoons butter
1/2 cup thinly sliced mushrooms
1 teaspoon instant onion
1/2 teaspoon garlic salt
1/2 teaspoon lemon juice
Worchestershire Sauce to taste
1 tablespoon snipped parsley
1/2 pound beef tenderloin,
    cut 1/2-inch thick
    or sirloin steak 1/2-inch thick,
    tenderized to 1/4-inch

Melt 1 tablespoon butter; cook and stir in mushrooms, onions, garlic, lemon juice and Worcestershire sauce until mushrooms are tender. Stir in parsley. Keep warm. Melt 1 tablespoon butter in a skillet. Cook meat over medium heat, turning once, 2-4 minutes each side. (May broil, but don't overcook.) Place meat on platter and spoon sauce over meat. To flame sauce, warm 2 tablespoons of brandy, pour over the meat and ignite.

Jackie Bahler, R.N., Director, Kathryn Well Center
West Lafayette, Indiana

Hearty Sausage and Pasta Stew

10 ounces turkey sausage links,
    cut into 1/8 inch rounds
2 cups chopped yellow onion
4 cloves garlic, minced
1 medium green bell pepper,
    chopped
1 10 ounce can condensed
    beef broth
1 16 ounce can chicken broth
1 cup dry red wine
1/2 cup water
1 8 ounce can tomato sauce
1 16 ounce can peeled
    whole tomatoes, chopped,
    undrained
1 teaspoon dried basil leaves
1 teaspoon dried oregano leaves
1/4 teaspoon black pepper
1/4 cup chopped fresh parsley
2 teaspoons Worcestershire sauce
1/2 teaspoon sugar
2 cups cooked penne, no butter,
    margarine, or oil used
    in cooking

Coat a dutch oven with cooking spray and place over medium high heat for 1 minute. Add sausage, brown lightly, and set aside. Add onion and garlic to dutch oven and cook, stirring occasionally, for 4 minutes. Add green pepper, beef broth, chicken broth, wine, water, tomato sauce, tomatoes and their liquid, basil, oregano and black pepper. Bring to a boil. Reduce heat, cover tightly, and simmer for 20 minutes. Stir in parsley, Worcestershire sauce, sugar, and pasta. Remove from heat and let stand, covered, for 10 minutes. Flavor is enhanced if refrigerated overnight. Serves 4.

Donna Arnett - Warsaw, Indiana

Grilled Pork Tenderloin and Pineapple

3 tablespoons soy sauce
2 tablespoons lime juice
2 tablespoons orange juice
2 tablespoons vegetable oil
1/2 teaspoon dry mustard
1/4 teaspoon garlic powder
2- 1 pound pork tenderloins
6- 1/2 inch slices
    fresh pineapple

Make marinade with first 6 ingredients. Stir well. Marinate pork for 24 hours. Turn occasionally. Remove tenderloins from marinade. Heat marinade. Grill tenderloin 45 minutes. Meat should register 160 degrees on meat thermometer, basting frequently with marinade. Grill pineapple for 5 minutes. Serve with sliced tenderloin.

Stephany Mullen - Valparaiso, Indiana

Ham and Potato Casserole

1/2 cup minced onion
1 clove garlic, mashed
1 tablespoon cooking oil
2 tablespoons butter
1 cup diced cooked ham
3 eggs
1 tablespoon minced parsley
1 tablespoon minced chives
3/4 cup grated Swiss cheese
1 1/2 cup light cream
dash cayenne
salt
pepper
3 medium potatoes
2 teaspoons butter

Cook onion and garlic in oil and 2 tablespoons butter until limp but not brown. Add ham and cook, stirring for 1 to 2 minutes. Beat eggs with parsley, chives, cheese, and cream. Season. peel potatoes and grate them coarsely. Press out liquid. Stir ham and potatoes into egg mixture. Pour in a buttered 2 1/2 to 3 quart dish. Dot with 2 teaspoons butter. Bake at 375 degrees for 30 to 35 minutes or until brown. Serves 4.

Evelyn Franklin - Freedom, Indiana

Hungarian Goulash

3/4 pounds boneless pork,
    cubed
3/4 pounds bottom round of
    beef, cubed
3 tablespoons butter
1 large onion, chopped
1 tablespoon paprika
3 cups water
1 pound can sauerkraut
1/2 pint sour cream
salt
pepper

In a 2 1/2 to 3 quart dish, cook meat in hot butter until well browned. Add onion and brown it to golden. Sprinkle all with paprika and mix. Add 1 cup water and cook until it evaporates. Continue adding water and letting it evaporate until meat is tender (approximately 1 hour). Add kraut and mix well. Stir in sour cream and season to taste. Heat but do not boil. Serves 4.

Carole Cross, R.T., A.R.R.T. - A.S.R.T. -
Warsaw, Indiana

Meal in a Squash

5 yellow squash
1/2 pound Italian sausage
    (Bob Evans)
1/2 cup onion
1 stalk celery
1/4 cup seasoned stuffing mix
3 tablespoons Parmesan cheese
1/2 teaspoon salt
1/2 teaspoon pepper
1/4 cup mozzarella cheese,
    grated
8 ounces tomato sauce

Cook whole squash in boiling water until tender (about 20 minutes). Cool. Split lengthwise, scoop out pulp and reserve. Saute meat, onion, and celery. Add squash pulp, stuffing mix, Parmesan, salt and pepper. Stuff squash shells. Place on greased 9 x 13 baking pan. Top with mozzarella. Pour tomato sauce over squash and cheese. Bake at 350 degrees for 35 minutes.

Georgia Ferguson - Warsaw, Indiana

Pork Chops with Apples and Sweet Potatoes

6 pork chops (3/4 inch)
1/4 cup bacon drippings
flour
1 medium onion, chopped
1 cup apple juice
1 tablespoon
    Worchestershire sauce
4 medium apples, peeled and
    cut into 1/2 inch slices
4 medium sweet potatoes, peeled
    and cut into 1/2 inch slices
salt/pepper to taste

Coat pork chops with flour. Brown on both sides in hot bacon drippings. Place pork chops in casserole just large enough to hold them in a single layer. Add onion to skillet. Saute until tender. Add apple juice and Worchestershire sauce and bring to a boil, stirring to loosen clinging particles. Remove from heat. Preheat oven to 350 degrees. Arrange alternate layers of apple and sweet potatoes on top of chops. Sprinkle with salt and pepper as you layer. Pour apple juice mixture over everything. Cover tightly, bake for 1 1/2 hours. Serves 6.

Marceil Conley - Warsaw, Indiana

Pork Loin Mornay

1 pound lean pork loin slices
egg
bread crumbs
tomato sauce
2 tablespoons butter
2 tablespoons flour
1 cup cream
1/8 teaspoon cayenne
salt
white pepper
1/8 teaspoon nutmeg
1 cup sharp cheese, cut up
1/2 cup grated American cheese
paprika

Flatten pork loin slices. Season and dip in beaten egg and bread crumbs. Braise until tender (about 30 minutes). Place on hot baking pan coated with tomato sauce. Melt butter over low heat. Add flour and stir until well blended. Cook over low heat stirring until mixture is smooth and bubbly. Remove from heat and gradually stir in cream and cayenne. Bring to a boil, stirring constantly. Boil for 1 minute. Stir in salt, white pepper, and nutmeg. Add sharp cheese. Pour mixture over pork slices. Sprinkle with grated American cheese and paprika. Place under broiler until hot and bubbly. Serves 6.

Arleen Koors - Warsaw, Indiana

Smoked Sausage Harvest Casserole

2 tablespoons margarine or butter
5 cups chopped green cabbage
1 medium onion, cut into halves
    and sliced
1 cup sliced carrots
1 can (15 1/2 ounces) red beans,
    drained
1 can (8 ounces) stewed tomatoes
1 tablespoon vinegar
1/3 cup grated Parmesan cheese
2 tablespoons flour
1/8 teaspoon ground black pepper
1 pound smoked sausage

Heat oven to 350 degrees Melt margarine or butter in Dutch oven over medium-high heat. Add cabbage, onion and carrots; saute for 5 minutes. Stir in beans, tomatoes and vinegar. Sprinkle cheese, flour and pepper over cabbage mixture and stir in. Spoon into greased shallow 2-quart casserole. Cut sausage into serving-size pieces. Arrange on top of cabbage mixture and push down partially. Cover and bake 40-50 minutes. Makes 6 servings.

Mary Armstrong - Warsaw, Indiana

Sweet and Sour Pork

1 pound lean boneless pork,
    cut into 1 inch cubes
1 tablespoon oil
1/2 teaspoon salt
1/2 cup water
1/4 cup sugar
1/2 cup green peppers, chopped
8 ounce can pineapple chunks,
    undrained
2 1/2 tablespoons cornstarch
2 tablespoons soy sauce
1/4 cup vinegar

Brown pork in hot oil. Add salt and water. Simmer covered for 30 minutes. Add sugar, green pepper, vinegar, and pineapple. Combine cornstarch and soy sauce. Stir into meat mixture. Heat until mixture thickens, stirring constantly. Simmer covered for 10 minutes. Serve on rice. Serves 4.

Doris Wall - Syracuse, Indiana

Tenderloin of Pork with Dried Berries, Capers and Almonds

2 tablespoons olive oil
1/2 cup and 2 tablespoons butter
1 1/2 pounds trimmed pork
    tenderloin (not pork loin)
3/4 cup port or Madeira
1/2 cup dried blueberries
2 tablespoons capers
pinch of cinnamon
salt, if desired
freshly ground pepper
1/2 cup very finely
    ground almonds
1/4 cup balsamic vinegar

Heat saute pan (large enough to accommodate pork tenderloins) until very hot. Add oil and 2 tablespoons butter. When melted, place pork into pan and allow to sear on all sides. Remove from pan and keep warm and covered. Deglaze pan with port. Add remaining ingredients, except vinegar and simmer until thickened slightly. Slowly add butter, swirling pan, until incorporated. Add vinegar. Uncover pork and add to pan any pieces that have accumulated. Slice pork diagonally into 3/4-inch slices and place on top of sauce. Cover and simmer until medium, about 5 minutes. Place slices on serving plates and pour sauce over.

Nancy Sideris, owner, Mosaique Restaurant -
Warsaw, Indiana

Wakeup Casserole

1 pound pork sausage
6 eggs
2 cups milk
1 teaspoon salt
1 teaspoon dry mustard
2 cups seasoned bread croutons
(or 7 slices bread)
1 cup shredded Cheddar cheese

Brown sausage, drain and cool. Mix eggs, milk, salt and mustard in mixer. Fold in bread (croutons), cheese, and sausage. Pour mixture into greased 13 x 9 x 2-inch baking dish. Cover and refrigerate overnight. Remove 1/2 hour before baking. Bake uncovered for about 45 minutes. Let stand for 5 minutes before serving. Yield: 8 servings.

The Thorpe House Country Inn - Metamora, Indiana
and Majorie (Klotz) Berkey

Another Chicken Broccoli Casserole

1 24 ounce package broccoli cuts
1 pound cooked diced chicken
2 cans cream of chicken soup
1 cup mayonnaise
1/2 teaspoon lemon juice
1/2 teaspoon curry powder
1 cup shredded cheese

Thaw and cook broccoli for 3 to 4 minutes in microwave. Combine all ingredients in a 9 x 13 baking dish and cook in 350 degree oven for 1 hour. Add shredded cheese on top and return to oven for 10 minutes.

June Gerth - Indianapolis, Indiana

Chicken Rolls with Mushroom

Wine Sauce
6 boned and split chicken breasts
    (allow 1 1/2 per person)
For each breast half:
1 thin slice prosciutto ham
1 thin slice Muenster cheese
1/2 teaspoon butter in wedge form
Seasoned bread crumbs
1 egg, slightly beaten

Mushroom Wine Sauce:
2 tablespoons butter
2 tablespoons flour
1 cup rich chicken stock
1/2 cup dry white wine
1/2 teaspoon tarragon
salt and pepper to taste
1 4-ounce can mushroom pieces
    (or 1/4 pound fresh sliced
    and sauteed for 5 minutes
    in butter)
1/2 cup half and half
1 egg yolk

Remove skin from breast halves and pound thin between sheets of waxed paper. Place 1 slice ham and 1 slice cheese on each one and dot with butter. Roll up, tucking in ends and tie with string. Dip in beaten egg and then roll in bread crumbs. Place on cookie sheet with seam side down and freeze until firm. Remove and put into heavy plastic bag and return to freezer. To bake: Place, not touching, in shallow baking dish which has been greased. Bake at 350 degrees for 1 1/4 hours. (If you haven't had time to freeze them, place for 4-6 hours in refrigerator and then bake without bringing to room temperature at 350 degrees for 45 minutes.) Put on heated platter, or serve from baking dish, garnished with parsley.

Mushroom Wine Sauce: Melt butter in saucepan and add flour and cook, without browning, stirring constantly for several minutes. Slowly add stock, wine and spices. Simmer several minutes and add mushrooms and simmer for 5 minutes. Remove from heat and stir in cream mixed with egg yolk and cook, stirring, until heated through. Do not let boil. May be made a day ahead of time and reheated. Preparation: 30 minute each recipe. Must do ahead. Can freeze. Baking: 1 hour, 15 minutes

Betty Menke - Greenville, Ohio

Chicken Cacciatore

1 14 1/2-ounce can Mexican-
    style stewed tomatoes
    with jalapeno peppers
    and spices
2 teaspoons sugar
1 teaspoon basil leaves
1/4 teaspoon garlic powder
1 tablespoon cornstarch
1/2 cup sliced green peppers
1/2 cup sliced mushrooms
1/2 teaspoon curry powder
1/8 teaspoon white pepper
1/2 teaspoon thyme leaves
1 tablespoon oil
1/2 cup onion, sliced
Parmesan cheese
6 unbreaded chicken breast filets

Place oil in large skillet over medium heat. Saute peppers, onion and mushrooms for 5 minutes, or until tender-crisp. Place tomatoes in medium bowl and cut up. Add remaining ingredients, except chicken and cheese. Stir until cornstarch is dissolved. Place chicken in bottom of baking dish. Place sauteed vegetables over chicken. Pour tomato mixture over all. Bake uncovered 45 minutes at 350 degrees. Sprinkle with Parmesan cheese. Serves: 6

Sue Moryl - Warsaw, Indiana

Chicken Carbonara

2 chicken breasts
1 medium green pepper
8 ounces thin spaghetti
3 tablespoons vegetable oil
1 cup heavy cream
1/2 cup Parmesan cheese
1/2 cup Hormel real bacon bits
1/2 teaspoon dried thyme
salt
pepper
parsley

Slice chicken breasts while partially frozen into 1/2 inch strips. Chop green pepper. Cook chicken and green pepper in oil until chicken is tender (approximately 10 minutes). Cook spaghetti while chicken cooks. When chicken is cooked, add cream, Parmesan cheese, bacon bits, thyme, salt, and pepper. Stir and heat until thickened. Ladle over spaghetti and top with parsley. Serves 4.

Thomas Johnson, P.T. - Warsaw, Indiana

Chicken Fingers

oil
3 whole chicken breasts, boned
    and cut into strips
1/2 cup flour
3/4 teaspoon salt
3 teaspoons sesame seeds
1 egg, beaten
1/2 cup water

Heat 2 inches of oil in skillet. Make a batter of flour, salt, sesame seeds, egg and water. Dip chicken in batter and drop into hot oil. Do not crowd pieces. Turn pieces over once. Cook until light brown on both sides, approximately 4-5 minutes.
Hint: prepare in batches and keep warm in oven. These are tasty served with Chinese hot mustard or warmed plum jelly.

Kelly Zackrich - Fort Wayne, Indiana

Chicken Roll-Ups

2 cups cooked, skinless
    chicken breasts, cubed
1/4 cup chopped onion
3 ounces cream cheese
2 tablespoons melted butter
1/8 teaspoon salt
1/8 teaspoon pepper
1 tube refrigerated
    crescent dinner rolls
3/4 cup crushed
    seasoned croutons
3 tablespoons, plus 2 teaspoons
    melted butter

In a large bowl, combine chicken, onion, cream cheese, 2 tablespoons melted butter, salt and pepper. Set aside. Open tube of dinner rolls, but do not separate. In small bowl, mix together the crushed croutons and 2 teaspoons melted butter. Set aside. Use two triangles of dough and pat together to make 1 large rectangle. (You will have 4 rectangles to work with.) Using 1 rectangle of dough at a time, place about 2 tablespoons of chicken filling in center of dough, then press dough on all sides to seal in mixture. Dip the chicken pocket in the remaining 3 tablespoons melted butter; then dip in crouton mixture until completely covered.   Place on ungreased cookie sheet. Bake at 350 degrees for 20-25 minutes.

Tina Minnix-Kleeman - Warsaw, Indiana

Chicken Spectacular

2 cups or more cooked
    diced chicken
1 package wild and white rice,
    cooked
1 1 pound can French style
    green beans, drained
1 medium onion, chopped
1 can cream of celery soup
1 medium jar pimentos
1/2 cup mayonnaise
1 can water chestnuts, diced
salt and pepper to taste

Mix all ingredients well. Pour into large casserole and cover. Bake at 350 degrees for 1 hour uncovered. Serves 8 to 10.

Peggy Zimmerman, Warsaw, Indiana
Cindy Stark, Indianapolis, Indiana

Easy Baked Chicken Breasts

8 chicken breasts halves, skinned
    and boned
8 (4 x 4) slices Swiss cheese
1 10 3/4-ounce can
    cream of chicken soup
    or cream of mushroom
1/4 cup dry white wine
1 cup herb-seasoned stuffing mix,
    crushed
2 to 3 tablespoons butter
    or margarine, melted
parsley, optional

Arrange chicken in a lightly greased 12 x 8 x 2-inch baking dish. Top with cheese slices. Combine soup and wine; stir well. Spoon sauce over chicken; sprinkle with stuffing mix. Drizzle butter over crumbs; bake at 350 degrees for 45 minutes. Garnish with parsley. Yield: 8 servings.

David Collins - Warsaw, Indiana

Ginger and Peach Chicken

Nonstick cooking spray
4 medium skinless chicken breasts
1 8-ounce can peach slices
1 teaspoon cornstarch
1/8 teaspoon ginger
1/4 teaspoon salt
1/2 cup sliced water chestnuts
2 cups hot cooked rice
1 6-ounce package pea pods,
    cooked and drained

Spray a large skillet with non-stick cooking spray. Preheat skillet over medium heat. Add chicken; cook 8-10 minutes. Drain peaches, reserving juice. Add water to juice to equal 1/2 cup. stir in cornstarch, ginger and salt. Add to skillet. Cook and stir until thickened and bubbly. Gently stir in peaches and water chestnuts; heat through. On a serving platter, arrange rice, pea pods and chicken. Spoon sauce over chicken.

Betty Menke - Greenville, Ohio

Lite Chicken Mole

4 skinless, boneless
    chicken breasts
1 medium onion, peeled
    and finely chopped
1 cup low sodium chicken broth
1 medium clove of garlic,
    peeled and minced
1 15-ounce can peeled and
    diced tomatoes, undrained
1/3 cup dark or golden raisins
1/4 cup finely chopped cilantro
2 tablespoons chili powder (hot)
2 tablespoons unsweetened
    cocoa powder
1/2 teaspoon salt
2 tablespoons sugar
1/2 teaspoon cinnamon
1/2 teaspoon ground cumin
1 tablespoon peanut butter
2 tablespoons lime juice
2 cups cooked white rice
Lime wedges
Optional: garnish - chopped
    cilantro, lime wedges

Place chicken breasts in a pan and cover with water. Bring to a boil; reduce heat; cover and simmer about 10 minutes, or until cooked through. Remove the water and cool slightly. Shred chicken and set aside. In a medium sized covered pan, set over medium heat, saute the onion in 2 tablespoons of the broth until softened, about 4-5 minutes. Uncover and add the garlic, tomatoes, raisins, cilantro, chili powder, cocoa powder, salt, sugar, cinnamon, cumin and peanut butter. Simmer for 5 minutes. Add the remaining broth and simmer 15 minutes. Stir in shredded chicken and lime juice. Heat through on medium low heat until hot. Spoon over rice and serve with lime wedges. Garnish with cilantro if desired. Serves 4.

The Tippecanoe Lake Country Club
Leesburg, Indiana

Italian Chicken Strata with Prosciutto and Pine Nuts

Italian bread, approximately
    7 to 8 1/2-inch-thick slices,
3 tablespoons unsalted butter
    (unsalted margarine), divided
1/3 cup chopped onion
8 ounces skinless, boneless
    chicken breasts, cut into
    1 inch cubes (1 cup)
4 ounces prosciutto, trimmed
    of fat and slivered into
    1/4-inch strips (1 cup)
1 cup seeded and chopped
    Italian plum tomatoes,
    3 medium
6 large eggs
    (1 1/2 cups egg substitute
    plus 3 large egg whites)
1 3/4 cups milk (low fat)
1/3 cup chopped fresh basil,
    or 1 tablespoon dried basil
2 tablespoons chopped
    fresh parsley, or 2 teaspoons
    dried parsley
1/4 teaspoon freshly ground
    black pepper
1 cup grated Parmesan cheese
1/4 cup pine nuts, toasted in a
    350 degree oven for
    5 minutes

Generously butter (or coat with non-stick vegetable spray) a 2 quart shallow baking dish. Melt 2 tablespoons of the butter and brush one side of bread slices with it. Toast in oven until golden brown. Cut into 1/2 inch cubes to equal 4 cups. Set aside. In a medium skillet over medium heat, melt the remaining 1 tablespoon butter and sauté onion until soft, 2 minutes. Add chicken and continue cooking until opaque, 5 to 6 minutes, stirring occasionally. Do not overcook. Add the prosciutto and tomatoes and cook an additional 1 to 2 minutes. Remove from heat and set aside. In a large bowl, whisk eggs. Add milk, basil, parsley, and pepper and whisk until well mixed. Place half the bread cubes in prepared pan. Top with half the chicken mixture and half the Parmesan. Repeat layering. Carefully pour custard mixture over bread and cheese. Cover with plastic wrap and press down with your hands or back of a spoon so that the bread absorbs the liquid. Refrigerate several hours or overnight. Preheat oven to 350 degrees. Remove plastic wrap from pudding. Sprinkle top with pine nuts. Bake for 40 to 55 minutes,(the depth of the dish will determine the baking time, the deeper the dish, the longer the pudding needs to cook) or until custard is set (knife inserted 1 inch from center comes out clean), pudding is puffed, and top is golden brown. Remove from oven onto a wire rack and cool for at least 10 minutes. Cut into individual servings.

Barbara Hayford and Linda Hegeman
Indianapolis, Indiana

Grilled Chicken Marinade

1 pound butter
1 cup lemon juice
4 teaspoons salt
1/2 cup vinegar
1 5 ounce jar prepared
    cream style horseradish
Tabasco to taste
lemon pepper to taste

Make marinade. Use 4-5 pound chicken pieces. Cover pieces of chicken with marinade and cook in slow oven (250 degrees) for 1 to 1 1/2 hours. Remove from oven and continue cooking on grill, basting until chicken is completely done.

Lee Walsh - Tupelo, Mississippi

Main Dish Chicken

1 1/2 pounds boneless chicken
1 10-ounce package
    frozen broccoli, thawed
    or frozen peas
8 (4 x 4-inch) slices
    Velveeta cheese
1 10 3/4 ounce can condensed
    cream of chicken soup
    or cream of celery
1 6-ounce package chicken-
    flavored Stove Top Stuffing

Heat oven to 350 degrees. Cook chicken until done; cut into bite-size pieces. Spray 2-quart casserole dish with vegetable oil cooking spray. Arrange chicken, then broccoli or peas and cheese in casserole. Spoon sauce over all. Prepare stuffing as directed on package. Spoon stuffing over top of casserole. Bake 30 to 35 minutes. Yield: 4-6 servings.

Jane Nave - Warsaw, Indiana
and David Collins - Warsaw, Indiana

Parmesan Chicken

1/2 cup Dijon mustard
4 tablespoons white wine
1 cup fresh bread crumbs
1 cup grated Parmesan cheese
3 pounds chicken breast -
    boned, skinless and
    cut in two

Thin mustard with white wine. Combine bread crumbs and cheese. Dip chicken into mustard and roll in bread crumbs. Bake on greased sheet 375 degrees for 45 minutes or until cooked. Good hot or room temperature. Serves 4-6.

Mary Louise Miller - Winona Lake, Indiana

Moist Pheasant in Sour Cream Sauce and Wine

1 pheasant, skinned and cut
    into serving pieces
1/2 teaspoon salt
1/2 cup all-purpose flour
1/2 teaspoon freshly ground
    black pepper
1/2 teaspoon celery salt
milk
4 tablespoons butter
1/2 cup game stock
    or chicken broth
2 green onions,
    cut into 1/2-inch lengths
1/2 cup sliced celery
1 orange peel, cut julienne
1 cup dry white wine
1 tablespoon honey
1 cup mushroom caps
1 cup sour cream

In a paper bag, combine salt, flour, pepper and celery salt. Dip the pheasant pieces in a bowl of milk; drop into paper bag and shake to coat. Melt the butter in a skillet. Over medium heat, brown the pieces on all sides. Transfer the pieces to a Dutch oven and keep warm. Blend some of the flour mixture with the butter remaining in the skillet until a thick paste is formed. Add the game stock, onions, celery and orange peel. Stir and cook for 3 minutes. Mix the wine with honey. Add to the sauce. Pour the sauce over pheasant in the Dutch oven. Cover and bake for 2 hours at 325 degrees. Mix the mushroom caps with sour cream. Add to the pheasant, stir in and cover; cook for an additional 30-40 minutes. Serve hot over a bed of wild rice.

Thomas W. Earhart - Warsaw, Indiana

Scalloped Chicken

3 to 4 cups diced chicken
1 1/2 cups cubed cheese
1 large chopped onion
4 cups chicken broth
2 eggs, well beaten
1 can cream of chicken soup
6 cups Ritz crackers

Mix all ingredients together, except crackers, and set aside. Crush Ritz crackers and put 3 cups in the bottom of a 9 x 13 inch pan. Put chicken mixture over cracker crumbs and cover with remaining crackers. Bake at 350 degrees for 45 minutes.

Lee Collins - Fort Wayne, Indiana

Sweet and Sour Chicken

2 whole chicken breasts,
    cut in 1 inch chunks
1/2 teaspoon salt,
    sprinkle on chicken
1 egg, beaten
3/4 cup Bisquick
2/3 cup sugar
2+ tablespoons cornstarch
1 tablespoon paprika
1 can pineapple chunks (liquid
    and water to equal 2 cups)
1/4 cup soy sauce
1/4 cup cider vinegar
1 cup green pepper strips
    (1 pepper)
1/2 cup sliced onion
2 medium tomatoes, cut in wedges
pineapple chunks

Sprinkle salt on chicken breasts. Coat chicken with egg and Bisquick. Fry in hot (400 degree) oil until brown. Remove and drain on paper towels. Keep warm in 250 degree oven. Combine sugar, cornstarch, and paprika in a 10 inch skillet. Add pineapple liquid, soy sauce, and vinegar. Cook to boiling. Boil 1 minute. Add green pepper and onion. Cover and cook until tender crisp (approximately 5 minutes). Add tomatoes and pineapple chunks. Heat well, but do not overcook. Add chicken chunks and serve over hot rice.

Twila Beahm

Teriyaki Stuffed Chicken Breasts

6 chicken breasts
1/2 cup soy sauce
1/4 cup water
1 cup pineapple juice
1/2 teaspoon grated ginger
1/2 tablespoon brown sugar
1/2 teaspoon garlic
1 cup green onions with tops,
    chopped
1 clove garlic, crushed

Mix together soy sauce, water, pineapple juice, ginger and brown sugar. Set aside 1/2 cup and pour remaining mixture over chicken breasts. Place chicken in refrigerator and allow to marinate at least 30 minutes. In microwave-safe bowl, combine: 1/2 cup reserved marinate, 1 cup chopped green onion and tops, 1 clove garlic. Cover loosely and microwave on high 1 1/2 minutes. Slice chicken breasts in half horizontally and stuff with green onion mixture. Place in baking dish and pour marinate over breasts. Bake at 350 degrees for 30 minutes or until chicken is done.

Jana Day - Fort Wayne, Indiana

Tortilla and Chicken Casserole

4-5 cups diced chicken or turkey
1 can cream of mushroom soup
1 4-ounce can chopped
    green chilies
1 7-ounce can green chili salsa
2 1/2 ounces sliced ripe olives
1 bunch sliced green onions
    and tops
1/2 teaspoon cumin
8 corn tortillas,
    cut in 1/8-inch strips
1 8-ounce package shredded
    Monterey Jack cheese
1 8-ounce package shredded
    Cheddar cheese

Combine all ingredients, except cheese and tortillas. Arrange 1/2 tortilla strips in greased 13 x 9-inch pan. Add 1/2 chicken mixture; cover with Jack cheese. Top with tortilla strips and remaining mixture. Bake at 350 degrees for 20 minutes. Add Cheddar cheese on top and bake an additional 10 minutes. Let stand for 5 minutes before cutting.

Mary Steele - Warsaw, Indiana

Coconut Shrimp with Sweet Dipping Sauce

2 pounds medium size fresh
    shrimp, peeled and deveined
2 cups flour divided
12 ounces beer
1/2 teaspoon baking powder
1/2 teaspoon paprika
1/2 teaspoon curry powder
1/2 teaspoon salt
1/4 teaspoon red pepper
14 ounces flaked coconut
vegetable oil

Sweet Dipping Sauce:
1- 10 ounce jar orange marmalade
3 tablespoons prepared
    horseradish
3 tablespoons creole mustard

Combine 1 1/2 cup flour, beer, and next five ingredients. Dredge shrimp in 1/2 cup flour. Dip in beer batter roll in coconut. Fry in hot oil about 350 degrees until golden brown.

Sweet Dipping Sauce: Combine and stir until smooth.

Kimberly Miller - Valparaiso, Indiana

Halibut with Coriander Butter

Coriander Butter:
1/2 stick (4 ounces) unsalted
    butter at room temperature
2 teaspoons lime juice
Pinch of white pepper
1/2 teaspoon granular garlic
1/2 teaspoon ground coriander

Halibut:
2 8-ounce filets of fresh halibut
    (skinless and boneless)
1 large (or 2 small) leeks
Mayonnaise

Coriander Butter: Place butter in small mixing bowl. Add lime juice, pepper, garlic and coriander. Whip until smooth and creamy. Set aside until fish is cooked.

Halibut: Coat fish with a thin layer of mayonnaise. Place on broiler grids and cook on both sides until done. Do not overcook! While fish is cooking, cut leeks in half lengthwise and place directly on broiler grids and cook, turning them often. When fish is done, melt lime-coriander butter over fish. Spread out roasted leeks on plate. Place fish on top of leeks. Pour remaining butter over fish. Serves: 2. Note: This dish can be baked if charbroiler is not available.

Jim Adams, owner, Adams Rib and Seafood House
Zionsville, Indiana

Lobster Thermidor

2 tablespoons butter
2 tablespoons chopped onion
1/2 cup sliced mushrooms
2 tablespoons flour
1/4 teaspoon salt
1/8 teaspoon pepper
1/8 teaspoon paprika
1/2 cup cream or rich milk
1/2 cup chicken stock
1/2 teaspoon Worcestershire sauce
1 egg yolk
1 tablespoon sherry
2 cups cooked lobster pieces
3 tablespoons fine buttered
    crackers or dry bread crumbs
Parmesan cheese to taste

Sauté butter: chopped onion and sliced button mushrooms. Blend in: flour, salt, pepper, and paprika. Cook over low heat, stirring constantly until mixture is smooth and bubbly. Remove from heat and stir in: cream or rich milk, chicken stock, and Worchestershire sauce. Bring to boil and boil for 1 minute, stirring constantly. Add egg yolk, sherry, and cooked lobster (in pieces) Place mixture in shell of lobster or individual baking dishes (or casserole dish if recipe is doubled) and sprinkle with fine buttered cracker or dry bread crumbs. Parmesan cheese may be mixed with these crumbs if desired. Bake at 450 degrees for 5 minutes. Serves 6.

Arleen Koors - Warsaw, Indiana

Mouth Watering Walleye

clean whole walleye
    about 3 to 4 pounds
    (excluding head and tail)
1/4 cup chopped red bell peppers
1/4 cup chopped onion
1/4 cup margarine
1 3 ounce can mushroom pieces
    (reserve liquid)
6-8 ounce can crab meat
1/2 cup Ritz cracker crumbs
2 tablespoons parsley
salt
3 tablespoons butter or margarine
3 tablespoons flour
1/3 cup dry white wine
1 cup shredded swiss cheese
dash paprika

Cook onions and red bell peppers in butter until tender, stir in drained mushrooms, flaked crab, cracker crumbs, parsley, 1/2 teaspoon salt and a little pepper. Stuff the fish, place in baking pan. In a saucepan, melt 3 tablespoons butter or margarine. Blend in flour and salt. Add enough milk to mushroom liquid to make about a cup, add wine, cook and stir until thickened. Pour over fish, bake at 350 degrees for about 3/4 to 1 hour. Sprinkle with cheese and paprika. Bake until fish flakes. Serves 6-8.

Delores Glaser - Kalamazoo, Michigan

Scalloped Oysters

1/4 cup minced onion
1/2 cup melted butter
    or margarine
3/4 teaspoon celery
    or seasoned salt
1/4 to 1/2 teaspoon red pepper
1 tablespoon
    Worcestershire sauce
1 teaspoon lemon juice
2 cups saltine cracker crumbs
1 tablespoon parsley flakes
2 12 ounce containers
    fresh standard oysters
2 eggs, beaten
1 cup half and half

Sauté onion in butter until tender. Remove from heat and stir in next four ingredients. Combine cracker crumbs and parsley flakes. Preheat oven to 350 degrees. Drain oysters, reserving 1/3 cup liquid. Sprinkle 1/2 cup crumb mixture in bottom of a lightly greased 8 inch square baking dish. Layer 1/2 of oysters and 1/2 of remaining crumb mixture. Drizzle with 1/2 of butter mixture. Repeat layers. Combine eggs, half and half, and remaining oyster liquid. Mix well. Pour over oyster layers. Bake for 40 - 45 minutes or until set. Serves 6.

Marceil Conley - Warsaw, Indiana

Okra Seafood Gumbo

3-5 tablespoons cooking oil
1/2 pound ham or veal stew
    (or both)
1 large onion, chopped fine
4-6 stalks celery, chopped fine
1/2 bell pepper, chopped fine
    (optional)
3 boxes frozen okra, thawed
    and cut into rounds
    (may use fresh okra)
1 large can tomatoes with juice
1 quart water
1-2 bay leaves
thyme - several pinches
parsley - generous amount
3 pods garlic (optional)
several dashes of Tabasco
2 pounds shrimp, cleaned
1 can fresh or frozen crabmeat
    (any white fish may be substi-
    tuted or oysters if desired)

Heat oil in large pot. Add onion, celery, bell pepper. Saute until onion is transparent. Add ham and/or veal and okra. Cook and stir until okra stops "roping", about 30 minutes. Add tomatoes, water and other seasonings. Simmer 1 1/2 - 2 hours, stirring occasionally. Salt and pepper to taste. Add shrimp and crab. Cook until shrimp is done and crab is heated through, about 15 minutes. Serve gumbo over white cooked rice in a flat bowl.

Barbara I. Cook - West Lafayette, Indiana
Indiana Commission for Women

Potato Chip Coating

1 egg, beaten
1 tablespoon milk
crushed potato chips
oil

Filet fish and remove skin. Cut filets into approximately 3 inch pieces. Dip filets into mixture of egg and milk. Crush potato chips very fine. Dip egg covered filets into crushed potato chips and let stand 20 minutes. Fry in oil at high temperature (350-380 degrees) for approximately 15 minutes.

Captain Gary - St. Martin

Salmon Loaf

1 1 pound can salmon; drained
   and flaked
2 cups soft bread crumbs
1 tablespoon chopped onion
1 tablespoon butter, melted
1/2 teaspoon salt
1/2 cup milk
1 slightly beaten egg

Piquant Sauce:
2 tablespoons chopped
   green onion
3 tablespoons butter
2 tablespoons flour
1/2 teaspoon dry mustard
1/2 teaspoon salt
dash of pepper
1 1/4 cups milk
1 teaspoon Worcestershire Sauce

In bowl, combine salmon, crumbs, chopped onion, butter and salt. Combine milk and egg. Add to salmon mixture and mix thoroughly. Shape into a loaf on a greased shallow baking pan or in 7-1/2 x 3-3/4 x 2-1/4 inch loaf pan. Bake at 350 degrees for 35 to 40 minutes. Serve with Piquant Sauce or creamed peas. Makes 3 to 4 servings.

Picante Sauce: Cook green onion in butter until tender, but not brown. Blend in flour, dry mustard, salt, and a dash of pepper. Add milk and Worcestershire Sauce. Cook, stirring constantly, until sauce thickens and bubbles.

Captain Gary - St. Martin

Seafood Gumbo

1 pound raw shelled shrimp
1 cup raw crab meat
1/2 pound raw, shucked oysters
2 cups chopped onion
2 cups chopped celery
2 cups chopped green pepper
5 cups chicken stock
3/4 cup margarine
1 1/4 cups tomato sauce
1 tablespoon paprika
1 teaspoon cayenne
1 teaspoon pepper
1/2 teaspoon dried thyme
1/2 teaspoon dried oregano

Melt the margarine in a large pot over medium heat. Add the onions, peppers, and celery. Turn the heat to high, add all the spices. Cook about 5 minutes, stirring constantly. Reduce heat to medium, add tomato sauce, cook 5 minutes, still stirring constantly. Add the chicken stock, bring the mixture to a boil; reduce heat and simmer 1 hour, stirring occasionally. Add the seafood, cover, and simmer for 3-6 minutes, until done. Serve gumbo over rice, or Louisiana Rice. Pass around the Tabasco sauce!

Nancy Wooldridge - Indianapolis, Indiana

Salmon Patties

1- 14 ounce can salmon
1 egg
chopped onion to taste
2 medium pre-cooked potatoes
    (any style)
dash of salt

Mix all ingredients together and make patties. Be sure there is enough potato so patty is firm. Instant potatoes can be added if too loose. Fry in oil or shortening until golden brown on both sides. Makes 5-6 patties. Serve hot or cold.

Jane Mullen - Beaufort, Missouri

Shrimp Diane

1 3/4 pounds medium shrimp
    with heads and shells
6 tablespoons, (in all),
    Basic Shrimp Stock
1 1/2 sticks unsalted butter
1/4 cup very finely chopped
    green onions
3/4 teaspoon salt
1/2 teaspoon minced garlic
1/2 teaspoon ground red pepper
    (preferably cayenne)
1/4 teaspoon white pepper
1/4 teaspoon black pepper
1/4 teaspoon dried
    sweet basil leaves
1/4 teaspoon dried thyme leaves
1/8 teaspoon dried
    oregano leaves
1/2 pound mushrooms,
    cut into 1/4 inch thick slices
3 tablespoons very finely
    chopped fresh parsley
French bread, pasta or basic
cooked rice.
*If Shrimp with heads are not
available, buy 1 pound of shrimp
without heads but with shells for
making the stock.*

In a large skillet, melt 1 stick of butter over high heat. When almost melted, add the green onions, salt, garlic, the ground peppers, basil, thyme, and oregano, stir will. Add the shrimp and saute just until they turn pink, about 1 minute, shaking the pan (versus stirring) in a back and forth motion. Add the mushrooms and 1/4 cup of the stock; then add the remaining 4 tablespoons butter in chunks and continue cooking, continuing to shake the pan. Before the butter chunks are completely melted, add the parsley, then the remaining 2 tablespoons stock; continue cooking and shaking the pan until all ingredients are mixed thoroughly and butter sauce is the consistency of cream.
Serve immediately in a bowl with lots of french bread on the side, or serve over pasta or rice. Makes 2 servings.

S. Chace Lottich, M.D. - Indianapolis, Indiana

Yellow Fin Tuna Fantasy

4 yellow fin tuna steaks
2 tablespoons melted butter
1 tablespoon olive oil
1 clove garlic crushed
1/2 cup match stick sliced carrots
1/2 cup match sticks
    sliced zucchini
1/2 cup sliced mushrooms
6 teaspoons stick butter
    or margarine
2 tablespoons flour
1 cup milk
2 tablespoons chopped fresh basil
1 teaspoon dried marjoram
1/4 teaspoon salt
1 6 ounce can crab meat drained
8 water packed artichoke hearts

Place tuna steaks on grill racks or broiler pan and set aside. In a large skillet heat olive oil and garlic. Lightly saute carrots, zucchini, and mushrooms, 2 to 3 minutes. Set aside. Brush tuna steaks lightly with melted butter and begin broiling. In a medium sauce pan, melt stick butter over medium heat, stir in flour until smooth and bubbly. With wire whisk, gradually stir in milk. Continue stirring constantly until mixture thickens and comes to a full boil. Boil 1 minute and reduce to simmer. Turn broiling tuna steaks. Stir in basil, marjoram, and salt. Add sauteed vegetables. Add drained crab meat and drained artichoke hearts. Simmer until heated through. Place tuna steaks on plates. Place sauce on steaks dividing artichoke hearts evenly. Serves 4.

Note: Yellow fin tuna is one of several species of tuna, all of which are part of the Mackeral family. It is a mild fish that flakes easily when cooked, with little or no odor. Tuna may be eaten raw, rare, medium rare, or cooked thoroughly through depending on your taste preferences. As a rule, cook a tuna steak as you would a strip steak. Generally, a fully cooked steak will take approximately 4-7 minutes per side depending on the steak thickness and heat used.

Debbie Allen - Warsaw, Indiana

Artichokes Cellini

1 package frozen
    artichoke hearts
3 ounces cream cheese
1/4 cup chopped chives
1/4 cup butter softened
1/2 cup shredded
    Parmesan cheese
salt/pepper to taste

Cook artichoke according to directions. Drain well. In a buttered shallow baking dish, arrange artichokes close together in single layer. Blend cream cheese with chives and butter. Sprinkle artichokes with salt and pepper. Dot cheese mixture over top. Add Parmesan cheese on top. Bake uncovered at 375 degrees for 20 minutes or until golden.

Mary Louise Miller - Winona Lake, Indiana

B-Momma's O'Fashion Corn Pudding

1 16 1/2 ounce can of golden
    cream corn
2 eggs
2 to 3 tablespoons of
    granulated sugar
1/4 pound butter or margarine
5 patties butter or margarine
    (hold till last)

Thoroughly mix ingredients in mixing bowl. Pour contents into well buttered baking dish. Place the 5 patties of butter on all four sides and one in the middle of pudding. Bake pudding for 1 hour at 375 degrees. Decrease heat to 325 degrees and bake another 1 1/2 hours or until golden brown.

Beatie Cummings - Indianapolis, Indiana

Baked Corn

2 eggs
1 can creamed corn
1 can whole corn, do not drain
1/2 cup melted butter
1 box Jiffy corn bread mix

Beat the eggs, add all the remaining ingredients and mix well. Pour into a baking dish and bake 30 to 45 minutes at 350 degrees. Remove from oven and cover with 1 cup of shredded cheese. Bake 10 more minutes.

Cindy Scott - Indianapolis, Indiana

Calico Beans

1/2 pound hamburger
1/2 pound bacon
1 cup onion, diced
1 can (20 ounces) dry lima beans,
    drained
1 can (20 ounces) red
    kidney beans, drained
1 large can pork and beans
2 tablespoons vinegar
1/2 cup catsup
1 teaspoon mustard
1/2 cup brown sugar
1/2 cup white sugar

Brown and drain hamburger, bacon, and onion. Mix all together with remaining ingredients and cook in bean pot or crock pot 3-4 hours. May also cook in casserole dish in oven until very hot.

Dorthy Cross - Rochester, Indiana

Carciofi Dorati E Fritti (Golden Fried Artichokes)

12 small, tender artichokes
2 lemons, juice and rinds
1 cup flour
2 eggs
2 egg yolks
1 cup olive oil
salt
1 lemon, cut lengthwise
    into 6 wedges

Prepare artichokes. Cut in half lengthwise and cut each half into 3 wedges; keep in the acidulated water for no longer than 15 minutes. Drain and pat dry with paper towel. Dredge with flour and shake to remove excess. Beat eggs and egg yolks together. Heat oil in small frying pan. Dip artichokes in beaten egg and fry, a few at a time, in moderately hot oil until lightly browned on all sides. Sprinkle with salt, garnish with lemon wedges, **and serve immediately.**

Marydale De Bor, President, De Bor and Associates, Inc.
Bethesda, Maryland

Carrots With Walnuts

1 pound carrots,
    cut in 1/4 to 1/2 inch slices
2 tablespoons olive oil
1/4 cup chopped walnuts,
    lightly toasted
1 teaspoon grated lemon peel
1/4 teaspoon lemon-pepper
    seasoning

Steam carrots until tender (10 minutes). Combine olive oil, nuts, lemon peel and seasoning in a bowl. Add carrots and toss. Serve warm. Serves 4.

Janie Peterson, R.N. - Fowler, Indiana

Cranberry Casserole

3 cups raw apples, unpeeled
    and chopped
2 cups raw cranberries
1 cup granulated sugar
1 cup quick-cooking oats
    (uncooked)
1/2 cup brown sugar, packed
1/3 cup flour
1/3 cup pecans, chopped
1/2 cup butter or margarine,
    melted

In a 2-quart casserole, combine apples, cranberries and granulated sugar; top with mixture of remaining ingredients. Bake at 350 degrees for 1 hour or until bubbly and light brown. Delicious served hot or cold. Can double as a dessert when served with cream or ice cream.

Sue Moryl - Warsaw, Indiana

Farm Country Eggs

2 tablespoons butter
12 ounces frozen hash browns
O'Brien (with onions and
    green peppers)
9 eggs
1/3 cup milk
1/2 teaspoon salt
1/4 teaspoon basil, optional
dash of pepper
6-8 ounces Cheddar cheese
1/8 -1/4 cup bacon bits (to taste)

Place butter and potatoes in 9 x 13 microwave safe dish (or 2 smaller casserole dishes). Cook uncovered for 6 minutes on high, stirring once. While potatoes are cooking, mix eggs, milk and seasonings. Flatten potato mixture and pour eggs over top. Cover with plastic wrap and microwave at 70 percent power for 7-9 minutes or until eggs are almost set. Stir once. Sprinkle bacon and cheese over top. Heat 1 minute to melt cheese. Remove and let stand 5 minutes before serving. Recipe may be cut in half.

Chris Hastreiter - Fort Wayne, Indiana

Onion-Herb Potatoes

2 pounds potatoes, cut in chunks
1/3 cup vegetable soup mix
2-3 tablespoons butter or oil
1 package onion soup mix

Toss in a bag with soup mixes. Melt butter in casserole. Add potatoes. Bake for 40 minutes in 375 degree oven, stir often.

Bertha Sisk - Warsaw, Indiana

Parmesan Potatoes

4 large potatoes
1/3 stick butter
1/4 cup Parmesan cheese
1/4 cup flour
salt and pepper to taste

Melt butter in oven safe 9 x 13 pan. Cube potatoes and fill bottom of pan. Add other ingredients. Bake for 1 hour at 375 degrees.

Ellen Jagger - Columbia City, Indiana

Potatoes Deluxe

2 pounds frozen hash brown
    potatoes, thawed
1/2 cup diced onions
1 can cream of chicken soup
16 ounce container sour cream
1 stick melted margerine
8 ounces grated mild
    Cheddar cheese
1 teaspoon seasoned salt
1/8 teaspoon pepper

Mix all ingredients together and put in
9 x 13 pan. Top with crushed potatoe chips.
Bake at 325 degrees for 1 hour.

Doris Wall - Warsaw, Indiana

Quiche

5-6 flour tortillas
1 pound cottage cheese
1 cup sharp Cheddar cheese
3 eggs beaten
1 tablespoon parsley
salt/pepper to taste
1/2 cup sharp Cheddar cheese

Butter each tortilla on each side. Mix cheeses, eggs,
parsley, salt, and pepper. Put tortilla on bottom of
pie plate. Layer cheese mixture between tortillas.
Last layer tortilla. Put 1/2 cup cheese on top. Cut
before baking. Bake at 350 degrees for 45 minutes.

Margaret Schilke - Springfield, Ohio

Roasted New Potatoes With Rosemary And Lemon

10-12 new potatoes
2 cloves crushed garlic
olive oil
1 teaspoon rosemary
juice of 1 lemon
butter
salt and pepper

Quarter potatoes and place in roasting pan with
bottom covered in olive oil and garlic. Toss well.
Add juice of 1 lemon, rosemary, salt, pepper
(generously),and quartered squeezed lemon.
Top with slices of butter and roast in oven
(375 degrees) at least 1 hour, maybe longer, tossing
occasionally until well browned.

Father Michael Basden - Warsaw, Indiana

Roasted Potatoes

1/2 cup crushed corn flakes
2 tablespoons margarine, melted
1/2 teaspoon thyme
1/2 teaspoon marjoram
1/4 teaspoon pepper
1/2 teaspoon salt, optional
5 large potatoes, peeled and cut into quarters

Preheat oven to 450 degrees. In shallow baking pan thoroughly blend all ingredients except potatoes. Add potatoes and turn to coat evenly with crumbs. Bake for 60 minutes or until potatoes are tender. To save time, steam potatoes in a covered dish for 10 minutes in the microwave, then roll in crumbs and bake. Reduces baking time to 15 minutes. Makes 6 one cup servings.

Veronica Bayles - Warsaw, Indiana

Southwestern Cheesecake

1 cup finely crushed tortilla chips
3 tablespoons margarine, melted
2- 8 ounce packages
    cream cheese, softened
2 eggs
1- 8 ounce package colby cheese/
    Monterey Jack cheese,
    shredded
1- 4 ounce can chopped
    green chiles, drained
1 cup sour cream
1 cup chopped orange
    or yellow pepper
1/2 cup green onion slices
1/3 cup chopped tomatoes
1/4 cup olive slices

Stir together chips and margarine and press into bottom of 9-inch springform pan. Bake at 325 degrees for 15 minutes. Beat cream cheese and eggs at medium speed with electric mixer until well blended. Mix in shredded cheese and chiles. Pour over crust. Bake 30 minutes. Spread sour cream over cheesecake. Loosen cake from rim of pan. Cool before removing from rim. Chill. Top with remaining ingredients just before serving. Serves 16-20.

Sharodene Morris - Warsaw, Indiana

ucchini Casserole

cups sliced zucchini
    (do not peel)
1 cups sliced carrots
1/4 cup chopped onion
1 can cream of chicken soup
1 cup sour cream
1 8-ounce package
    herbed stuffing
1/2 cup margarine, melted

Mix zucchini, carrots, onion in small amount of water for 5 minutes. Drain. Mix and add to vegetables the chicken soup and sour cream. Set aside. Mix stuffing and margarine. Put about half the stuffing mixture in bottom of greased 9 x 13 inch pan. Add the vegetable mixture; spread remaining stuffing on top. Bake 350 degrees for 30 minutes.

Bertha Sisk - Warsaw, Indiana

Zucchini Casserole

4 cups zucchini diced
1 small onion diced
1/2 cup Cheddar cheese shredded
1/4 teaspoon oregano
1 cup Bisquick
1/2 cup salad oil
3 eggs beaten
1/2 teaspoon salt
1/4 teaspoon pepper

Mix all dry ingredients and put in lightly greased baking dish. Add zucchini and onions. Pour salad oil and beaten eggs over dry ingredients. Put cheese on top. Bake at 350 degrees for 40 minutes or 24 minutes in microwave then brown under broiler.

Jeannine Richardson - Morgantown, Indiana

Banana Split Cake

2 1/2 cups graham cracker crumbs
3 sticks margarine
1 egg
1 pound powder sugar
1 large can drained crushed pineapple
1 large Cool Whip
chopped nuts
cherries
3 or 4 bananas

Melt 1 stick of margarine and mix with graham crackers. Press into pan. Mix egg, sugar and 2 sticks of margarine. Beat until fluffy and spread over crust. Drain pineapple and spread on crust. Slice bananas and place on pineapple. Spread cool whip over top and garnish with nuts and cherries. Chill.

Sandy Cooksey - Spencer, Indiana

Blueberry Cheescake

11 graham crackers
1/4 cup margarine melted
1/2 cup sugar
2 eggs beaten
2 8 ounce packages cream cheese
1 cup sugar
1 teaspoon vanilla
1 can blueberry pie filling

Mix and spread in pan: graham crackers, margarine and sugar. Beat eggs. Add to eggs; cream cheese, sugar, and vanilla. Beat until fairly smooth. Pour on crust and bake at 375 degrees for 25-30 minutes. Cool. Top with blueberry pie filling. Chill.

Carlla Kiser - Warsaw, Indiana

Carrot Cake

1/2 cup shredded carrots
1/2 cup brown sugar
1/2 cup white sugar
2/3 cup oil
1/3 cup nuts
2 beaten eggs
1/2 teaspoon milk
1 1/2 cups flour
1 tablespoon cinnamon
1 teaspoon baking soda
1 1/2 teaspoons baking powder
1/2 teaspoon salt

Mix all ingredients. Pour in slightly greased 8 x 8 baking pan. Bake 1 hour at 350 degrees or until done when tested with toothpick.

Mary Allen - Warsaw, Indiana

Delicious Cake

1 Jiffy yellow cake mix
1 large package vanilla pudding
1 8 ounce package
    cream cheese (softened)
1 large can crushed pineapple
1 carton Cool Whip

Layer 1: Preheat oven and prepare cake as directed. Pour into 9x13 dish. Bake and cool. *Layer* 2: Prepare pudding as directed then add cream cheese. Beat until smooth. Spread on cake. *Layer* 3: Drain crushed pineapple amd spread on pudding mixture. *Layer* 4: Top with Cool Whip and spread. May also top with nuts or marachino cherries if desired. All ingredients may be substituted for "sugar free or light".

Marilyn Botkin - Indianapolis, Indiana

Chocolate Eclair Cake

1 box graham crackers
2 3-ounce instant French
   vanilla pudding
3 cups milk
9 ounces Cool Whip

Icing:
1 2-ounce packet Liquid Chocolate
3 tablespoons butter
2 teaspoons white Karo
3 tablespoons milk
1 teaspoon milk
1 1/2 cups powdered sugar

Butter 9 x 13 inch pan and line with graham crackers. Prepare pudding with 3 cups milk. Beat Cool Whip into pudding. Put 1/2 cup pudding over layer of grahams in pan. Second layer of grahams and remainder of pudding, then graham crackers. Mix together all icing ingredients. Pour over layered ingredients in pan and spread over all. Refrigerate 24 hours.

Dorothy Snyder - Warsaw, Indiana

Chopped Apple Cake

1 1/2 cups flour
2 teaspoons soda
1 teaspoon cinnamon
1 teaspoon nutmeg
1/2 teaspoon salt
1 1/2 cups sugar
1/2 cup shortening
2 eggs, well beaten
4 cups, peeled and chopped,
   apples
1 cup 40% bran flakes

Cream Cheese Icing:
1 stick margarine,
1 teaspoon vanilla
1 package cream cheese
1 pound powdered sugar

Cream sugar and shortening. Add eggs and beat thoroughly. Sift all the dry ingredients together and add to sugar mixture. Add chopped apples and bran flakes. Bake in layer pan or in oblong baking dish at 350 degrees.

Cream Cheese Icing: Beat all together and spread on cooled cake.

Evelyn Franklin - Freedom, Indiana

Cloud Nine Shortcake (Hot Milk Sponge Cake)

1 cup flour
1 teaspoon baking powder
1/4 teaspoon salt
2 eggs
1 cup sugar
2 tablespoons butter or margarine
1/2 cup hot milk
1 teaspoon vanilla

Sift together flour, baking powder and salt. Beat eggs until thick and lemony, about 3 minutes at high speed of mixer. Gradually add sugar, beating constantly at medium speed, 4 to 5 minutes. By hand fold in quickly dry ingredients into egg mixture. Add butter and hot milk. Stir in vanilla. Blend well and pour into lined 8 x 8 pan. Bake at 350 degrees for 25-30 minutes.

Doris Wall - Warsaw, Indiana

Easy Apple Cake

3 cups flour
1 cup cooking oil
3 teaspoons baking powder
2 cups sugar
1/3 cup orange juice
2 1/2 teaspoons vanilla
4 eggs beaten fluffy
4 large apples, sliced
4 tablespoons sugar
2 teaspoons cinnamon

In separate bowl combine apples and mix with sugar and cinnamon. Grease and dust a 9x13 or tube pan. Mix all ingredients well (except for separate bowl items) Pour half of batter in pan, sprinkle with half apple mixture. Pour remaining batter in and add remaining apple mixture. Bake at 350 degrees for 1 1/2 hours or until tester comes out clean.

Barbara Rabinowitz, PhD - Long Branch, New Jersey
Founder, National Consortium of Breast Centers

Sour Cream Coffee Cake

2 cups sugar
1 cup butter
1 cup sour cream
2 eggs
2 cups flour
1 teaspoon baking powder
1 teaspoon vanilla
1 tablespoon cinnamon
2 tablespoon brown sugar
1/3 cup chopped pecans
   (or other nuts)

Cream together sugar, butter, and fold in sour cream. Add eggs, flour, baking powder and vanilla. Mix together cinnamon, brown sugar and nuts. Using bundt pan, alternate batter with sugar mixture. Using 1/3 of each and finishing with sugar on top. Bake one hour at 350.

Connie Goodwin, R.N. - Fort Wayne, Indiana

Flourless Chocolate Cake

10 ounces semi-sweet
    chocolate chips
4 ounces butter
6 large eggs, separated
1 cup sugar (reserve 1/4 cup
    for egg whites)
1 tablespoon dark rum or brandy
Confectioner's sugar
    to sprinkle on top

Butter 8 x 3-inch pan. Line bottom with wax paper, cut to fit. Spray with non-stick vegetable spray. Melt chocolate chips and butter in microwave until just melted. Beat egg yolks with electric mixer until blended. Add 3/4 cup sugar and beat until thick and pale yellow. Add chocolate and rum and beat on low until combined. Whip egg whites with electric mixer until frothy; add 1/4 cup sugar and beat until soft peaks form. Stir 1/4 cup egg whites into chocolate mixture, then fold remaining whites into mixture until just combined. Pour into prepared pan. Place pan in water bath 1-inch deep and bake at 300 degrees for 1 hour. Cool cake completely and run knife around edge to loosen. Turn cake out onto cake plate forcefully. Sprinkle confectioners sugar over cake surface. Serve with cold whipped cream on side.

Nancy Sideris, owner of Nancy's Fancies Catering
and Mosaique Restaurant
Warsaw, Indiana

Grandma Hewitt's Oatmeal Cake

1 cup oatmeal
1 1/4 cups boiling water
1 cup brown sugar
1 cup granulated sugar
1/2 cup shortening
2 eggs
1 1/3 cups unsifted flour
1 teaspoon soda
1 teaspoon salt
1 teaspoon cinnamon

Topping:
6 tablespoons butter
1/2 cup brown sugar
1/2 cup cream or milk
1 cup coconut

Soak the oatmeal in the boiling water and set aside. Cream together the brown sugar, granulated sugar and shortening. Add other ingredients, then add warm oatmeal and beat until smooth. Pour into a greased 9 x 9 inch pan; bake at 350 degrees until the cake shrinks from sides of pan. For topping, mix all ingredients; spread on warm cake. Place under broiler until bubbles.

Shannon Jenks - Leesburg, Indiana

Hawaiian Cake

2 1/2 teaspoons baking powder
1 box graham cracker crumbs
2 cups sugar
1/2 pound butter
5 eggs
1 cup milk
1 cup coconut
1 cup chopped pecans
1/2 teaspoon vanilla
Icing:
1 can crushed pineapple, drained
1 stick butter or margarine
1 pound powdered sugar
1 cup pecans

Combine baking powder and graham cracker crumbs in a small bowl. Set aside. Cream together in a large bowl, sugar, butter and eggs (one at a time). Add the graham cracker mixture, milk, coconut, 1 cup chopped pecans and vanilla. Beat together. Pour in greased and floured 13x9x2-inch pan. Bake at 350 degrees for 35-40 minutes. Mix together all ingredients for the icing and ice cake when cool.

Kelly Zackrich - Fort Wayne, Indiana

Jane's Cake

2 cups sugar
2 cups flour
2 sticks margarine or butter
4 heaping tablespoons cocoa
    (I use Ghirardelli cocoa;
    may use Hersheys)
1 cup boiling water
2 eggs
1 teaspoon salt
2 teaspoons vanilla
1 teaspoon cinnamon
1 teaspoon soda
1/2 cup buttermilk

Icing:
1 stick butter or margarine
4 heaping tablespoons cocoa
6 tablespoons milk
1 teaspoon vanilla
1 box powdered sugar

In large bowl stir together: sugar and flour. In sauce pan melt: butter or margarine, cocoa and water. Bring to a full boil and pour over flour mixture. Stir well. Add: eggs, salt, vanilla, cinnamon, and soda. Stir well and add buttermilk and stir well again. Pour into greased 10 x 15 jelly roll pan (give a sharp tap to remove bubbles). Bake 20-21 minutes at 400 degrees or until toothpick comes out just barely clean. Do not overbake.

Icing: While cake is baking, melt margarine and cocoa in a saucepan. Add milk. Bring just to a boil, and remove from heat. Add vanilla and powdered sugar. Beat until smooth and spread on cake after cake has cooled (only about 10 minutes). Arrange 35 pecan halves on top.

Jane Grossnickle - Warsaw, Indiana

Italian Cream Cake

1 stick butter
1/2 cup oil
2 cups sugar
5 egg yolks, beaten
1 teaspoon soda
1 cup buttermilk
1 tablespoon vanilla
1 small can coconut
1 cup pecans
5 egg whites, beaten
2 cups flour

Icing:
1-8 ounce cream cheese
1 box powdered sugar
1 stick butter

Cream butter, oil, sugar and vanilla. Add eggs one at a time and blend. Beat egg whites. Add flour and soda to butter mixture. Add buttermilk, coconut and pecans. Fold mixture into egg whites. Put into 2 layered pans greased and floured. Bake at 350 degrees for 30 minutes. Cool.

Icing: blend ingredients and put on cake.

Donnette Hall - Warsaw, Indiana

Kay's Chocolate Zucchini Cake

1/2 cup plus 1 tablespoon
    margarine
2 cups sugar
3 squares baking chocolate,
    melted
3 eggs
1/2 cup milk
2 teaspoons vanilla
2 cups grated zucchini
2 1/2 cups flour
1 tablespoon baking powder
1 1/2 teaspoon baking soda
1/2 teaspoon salt
1 teaspoon cinnamon
chocolate frosting:
    canned or purchased

Cream butter; add sugar and baking chocolate. Beat until fluffy. Add eggs and beat well. Beat in milk, vanilla and zucchini. Combine flour, baking powder, soda, salt and cinnamon; add to creamed mixture. Pour batter into 2 large loaf pans or 3 small loaf pans, greased and floured. Bake at 350 degrees for 45-50 minutes, or until wooden pick inserted in center comes out clean. Recipe will also make one bundt cake. Bake at 350 degrees for 1 hour. Cool cake in pan 15 minutes, then turnout onto wire rack. Drizzle with chocolate frosting that has been warmed in the microwave to thin.

Kay Niedenthal, owner, Kay's Garden and Kay's Catering
Indianapolis, Indiana

Moon Cake

1 cup water
1/2 cup butter or margarine
1 cup flour
4 eggs
2 small boxes of instant
    vanilla pudding
8 ounces cream cheese
1 large container of Cool Whip,
chocolate sauce
chopped pecans

Bring water and margarine to a boil. Add flour all at once stirring rapidly, remove from heat and cool. Beat in 4 eggs, one at a time with spoon or mixer, mixture will be stiff. Mix well. Spread on ungreased 11 x 15 cooking sheet. Do not pack. Leave as is and bake at 400 degrees for 30 minutes, cool. Mix pudding according to package directions. Beat in cream cheese. Blend well, spread on crust. Chill 20 minutes. Top with Cool Whip, drizzle with chocolate sauce and chopped pecans.

Cindy Scott - Indianapolis, Indiana

Pecan Caramel Cheesecake

1/3 cup firm butter or margarine
1 package Betty Crocker
    golden pound cake mix
1/2 cup chopped pecans
3/4 cup sugar
1 teaspoon grated lemon peel
1 teaspoon vanilla
2 eggs
2 8-ounce packages cream cheese,
    softened
caramel ice cream topping
pecan halves

Heat oven to 350 degrees. Cut margarine into dry cake mix until crumbly. Stir in crushed pecans, reserving 1/2 cup of the mixture. Press remaining crumbly mixture into bottom and about 1 inch up the side of a springform pan, 9 x 3 inch, round. Beat remaining ingredients, except caramel topping and pecans, on medium speed until almost smooth. Pour into pan. Sprinkle with reserved crumbly mixture. Arrange pecan halves on cheesecake. Bake about 50 minutes or until center is firm. Cool to room temperature. Refrigerate 3 hours. Drizzle caramel topping over cheesecake. Loosen edge of cheesecake before removing pan.

Robin Brown - Warsaw, Indiana

Turtle Cake

1 (18 1/2-ounce) package
   German chocolate cake mix
1 (14-ounce) bag caramels
1/2 cup evaporated milk
3/4 cup butter
2 cups chopped pecans
1 cup mini chocolate chips

Heat oven to 350 degrees. Prepare cake mix using package directions. Pour 1/2 of the batter into greased 9 x 13-inch pan. Bake 20 minutes. Melt caramels, evaporated milk and butter in a saucepan on low heat; stirring constantly. Pour over the warm cake. Sprinkle 1 cup nuts and mini chips over caramel filling, then pour on remaining batter. Sprinkle with remaining nuts. Bake additional 25 minutes.

Betty LeCount - Warsaw, Indiana

Twinkies

1 box yellow cake mix
1 box instant vanilla pudding
1 cup water
4 eggs
1/2 cup Crisco oil

Filling:
3 egg whites beaten
3 teaspoons vanilla
1 1/2 cups Crisco
3 tablespoons flour
5 tablespoons milk
3 cups powdered sugar

Mix cake mix and other indgredients. Divide into two 13x9 cookie sheets. Bake at 350 degrees for 15-20 minutes.
Filling: Mix ingredients in order given. Beat until creamy. When cakes are baked and cooled put filling between cakes.

Patty (Berkey) Beachey - Warsaw, Indiana

Leila's Mom's Dutch Apple Cream Pie

1 large apple
unbaked pie shell
1 1/2 cup sugar
3 tablespoons flour
dash of salt
milk
cinnamon
butter

Place 1 large thinly sliced apple in 10-inch unbaked pie shell. Top with mixture of sugar, flour and salt. Pour milk over all and top with cinnamon and butter. Bake at 400-425 degrees for 20 minutes and then at 350 degrees until set.

Judy Young - Kendallville, Indiana

Chocolate Mint Pie

1 graham cracker crust
1/2 cup soft butter
3/4 cup sugar
3 ounces unsweetened chocolate
1 teaspoon vanilla
1/2 teaspoon peppermint extract
3 eggs
1/2 cup whipping cream,
    well whipped

Beat butter and sugar until creamy. Add melted chocolate, peppermint extract and vanilla. Add eggs one at a time. Beat 3 minutes after each egg. Fold in whipped cream. Pour into crust. Chill 4 hours or overnite. Serves 6-8.

Ruth Miller - Springfield, Ohio

Black Bottom Pie

20 chocolate wafers, crushed
5 tablespoons butter, melted

Chocolate Layer:
2 cups milk, scalded,
4 large egg yolks, beaten,
1/2 cup sugar
1 1/2 tablespoons corn starch
1 1/2 squares unsweetened
chocolate, softened
1 teaspoon vanilla

Bourbon Layer:
1 tablespoon gelatin
2 tablespoons cold water
2 tablespoons bourbon
4 large egg whites
1/2 teaspoon cream of tarter
1/2 cup sugar
sweetened whipped cream
unsweetened chocolate shavings

Preheat oven to 325 degrees. Prepare crust by combining cookie crumbs with enough melted butter to hold together. All butter may not be needed. Press crumb mixture into 9 inch pie dish. Bake 10 minutes. Cool. For Chocolate Layer, mix small amount of scalded milk into egg yolks. Pour yolks into remaining milk, add sugar and cornstarch. Cook over medium heat, stirring often until custard coats the spoon (20 minutes). Combine 1 cup custard with softened chocolate. Reserve remaining custard. Add 1 teaspoon vanilla. Pour into crust. Chill. Dissolve gelatin in cold water. Add gelatin to reserved custard until dissolved. Cool. Stir in bourbon. Beat egg whites until frothy. Slowly beat in sugar and cream of tarter until stiff. Fold into cooled custard. Carefully spoon mixture over chocolate layer in pie crust. Chill until set. Top with sweetened whipped cream and shavings of chocolate.

Christine Hackl - Indianapolis, Indiana

Fresh Peach Pie

1 cup sugar
1 1/2 cups cold water
2 1/2 tablespoons cornstarch
pinch of salt
1 box peach Jell-o (3 ounce size)
4 cups sliced fresh ripe peaches

Cook the first four ingredients until thickened and clear. Remove from heat and add jello. Cool until lukewarm, and add sliced peaches. Pour into a 9 inch baked pie shell.

Coral Cochran - Terre Haute, Indiana

Hershey Derby Pie

1 unbaked 10-inch pie shell
1 stick butter (melt and cool)
8 ounces chocolate chips
3/4 cup pecans
1 cup sugar
2 tablespoon cornstarch
4 eggs
1 teaspoon vanilla

Melt and cool butter. Sprinkle chocolate chips and pecans on bottom of pie shell. Mix together sugar and cornstarch. Set aside. Beat together eggs and vanilla. Add sugar and cornstarch mixture and beat until blended, slowly adding butter while continuing to beat the mixture. Pour into pie shell and bake at 350 degrees until golden brown and crusty, approximately 30 minutes.

Jim Adams, owner, Adams Rib and Seafood House
Zionsville, Indiana

Macadamia Nut Tart

2 tablespoons butter or margarine
2 jars (3 1/2 ounces each)
   macadamia nuts
   (coarsely chopped)
1 9 inch tart or pie crust
1/3 cup packed light brown sugar
1/4 cup granulated sugar
1/2 cup light corn syrup
3 large eggs
2 tablespoons dark rum
1 teaspoon vanilla extract

In microwave safe baking dish place 2 tablespoons butter. Microwave on high 30 seconds. Stir in nuts and microwave on high 7 minutes or until nuts begin to brown. Stir every 2 minutes. Set aside. In medium bowl, beat sugars, corn syrup, eggs rum and vanilla until blended. Stir in nuts. Pour into prepared crust. Bake in 350 degree oven for 45 minutes. Serves 8.

Karen Rowland - Warsaw, Indiana

Peaches And Cream Cheese Cobbler

3/4 cup flour
1 teaspoon baking powder
1/2 teaspoon salt
1 package vanilla instant pudding
3 tablespoons butter, melted
1/2 cup milk
1 15 ounce can sliced peaches
    or 3 cups fresh peaches

Filling:
1 8 ounce package cream cheese
1 cup sugar
3 tablespoons peach juice
    (may use apple juice or milk)

Topping:
1 tablespoon sugar
1/2 teaspoon cinnamon

Combine first 6 ingredients. Beat 2 minutes at medium speed. Pat into a greased 9 inch pie dish. Add peaches. To make filling combine cream cheese, sugar and juice and mix well. Spoon onto peaches. Combine cinnamon and sugar for topping and sprinkle on top of cream cheese mixture. Bake for 30 minutes at 350 degrees. Serves 6.

Tammy Dalton - Warsaw, Indiana

Pineapple Cheese Chiffon Pie

1 9 inch graham cracker pie shell
1 9 ounce can crushed pineapple,
    drained, reserve syrup
1 3 ounce package lemon gelatin
1 8 ounce package cream cheese,
    softened
3/4 cup sugar
1 cup evaporated milk, chilled
2 tablespoons lemon juice

Chill pie shell. Add enough water to pineapple syrup to make 1 cup liquid. Heat liquid to boiling, remove from heat and stir in gelatin. Let stand. Combine cream cheese, sugar and pineapple in large mixing bowl. Beat at medium speed until creamy. Beat in gelatin at low speed. Chill until thickened. Chill small mixing bowl and beaters. Pour milk into cold bowl and beat at high speed until fluffy. Add lemon juice and beat until stiff. Add to chilled gelatin and mix at low speed. Chill until mixture will mound and spoon into crust. Chill 2-3 hours until firm. Serves 8.

Irene Saylor - Manchester, Kentucky

Pumpkin Dutch Apple Pie

2 medium-size green apples,
    peeled and sliced
1/4 cup sugar
2 teaspoons flour
1 teaspoon lemon juice
1/4 teaspoon cinnamon
1 unbaked pie shell
1 1/2 cups pumpkin
2 eggs
1 cup undiluted evaporated milk
1/2 cup sugar
2 tablespoon margarine (melted)
3/4 teaspoon cinnamon
1/8 teaspoon nutmeg
1/4 teaspoon salt

Crumb Topping:
1/2 cup flour
5 tablespoons sugar
3 tablespoons margarine or butter

Mix first 5 ingredients and put in unbaked pie shell. Mix ingredients 7 through 14 and pour over the apple mixture. Bake at 375 degrees for 30 minutes. Meanwhile mix together the ingredients for crumb topping. Sprinkle crumb topping on pie and bake 20 minutes longer, or until brown.

Bertha Sisk - Warsaw, Indiana

Raspberry Cobbler

5 cups fresh or frozen
    raspberries (or blackberries)
1 1/2 cups sugar
1 cup all-purpose flour
1 1/2 teaspoons baking powder
1/4 teaspoon salt
3/4 cup milk
1/2 cup butter or margarine,
    melted
Vanilla ice cream
    or whipped cream

Toss together the berries and 1/2 cup sugar; set aside. In another bowl, combine remaining 1 cup sugar, flour, baking powder and salt. Add the milk, stirring just till batter is smooth. Melt margarine; pour into a 2-quart baking dish. Spoon the berries over melted margarine; pour batter on top. Bake in a 350 degree oven for 40-45 minutes or until top is golden brown and a toothpick inserted near the center comes out clean. Serve with ice cream or whipped cream. Yield: 8 servings.

Mary Armstrong - Warsaw, Indiana

Raspberry Topped Lemon Pie

1 10-ounce package frozen red
    raspberries in syrup, thawed
1 tablespoon cornstarch
3 egg yolks
1 14-ounce can Eagle Brand
    condensed milk
1/2 cup Real Lemon
Yellow food coloring (optional)
1 6-ounce graham
    or vanilla pie crust
Whipped topping

Preheat oven to 325 degrees. In small saucepan, combine raspberries and cornstarch; cook and stir until thickened and clear. In medium bowl, beat egg yolks with condensed milk, lemon juice, and food coloring (if desired). Pour into crust; bake 30 minutes. Spoon raspberry mixture evenly over top. Chill 4 hours or until set. Spread with whipped cream. Garnish as desired. Refrigerate leftovers.

Samantha Zackrich - Fort Wayne, Indiana

Strawberry Pie

3 ounces semi-sweet chocolate
2 tablespoons butter
3 ounces cream cheese, softened
1/2 cup sour cream
3 tablespoons sugar
1/2 teaspoon vanilla
Strawberry jam or glaze
1 pint strawberries
1 baked pie shell

Melt 2 ounces of chocolate and butter and coat bottom and sides of baked pie shell. Put in refrigerator for chocolate to harden. Mix cream cheese, sour cream, sugar and vanilla. Spread filling in the pie shell and return to refrigerator. After filling firms, place strawberries as you like and glaze with jam or glaze. Melt remaining chocolate and drizzle over top.

Jill Bales - Warsaw, Indiana

Chocolate Chip Cookies

1 cup shortening
1 cup brown sugar
1/2 cup white sugar
2 eggs
2 teaspoons vanilla
2 1/4 cups flour
1/2 teaspoon soda
1 teaspoon salt
12 ounce package chocolate chips

Mix shortening, sugars, eggs and vanilla. Sift together flour, soda, and salt. Add flour mixture to creamed mixture. Add chocolate chips last. Spoon on to greased cookie sheet. Bake at 350 degrees for 10-12 minutes.

Doris Wall - Syracuse, Indiana
and Richard W. Cross, M.D. -
Warsaw, Indiana

Amish-Raisin And Oatmeal Cookies

6 cups flour
2 1/2 cups sugar
1 1/4 cups shortening
1 tablespoon soda
1 tablespoon baking powder
1/2 tablespoon cinnamon
1/4 pound chopped peanuts
3 cups oatmeal
1/2 cup sour milk (or substitute
    2 tablespoons vinegar
    to 1/2 cup milk)
2 eggs
1/4 cup corn syrup
3/4 teaspoon vanilla
1 cup chopped raisins

Mix all ingredients all at once. Roll ball of dough and flatten on greased cookie sheet. Brush top of cookies with beaten whole egg. Bake at 400 degrees for 12-15 minutes.

Doris Wall - Syracuse, Indiana

Banana Bars

1 1/2 cups sugar
1/2 cup margarine, softened
2 eggs
1 cup sour cream
3 large ripe bananas, mashed
2 teaspoons vanilla
1 teaspoon salt
1 teaspoon baking soda
2 cups flour

Frosting:
1/4 cup margarine
2 cups confectioner's sugar
3 tablespoons sour cream

Cream together sugar and shortening. Add eggs and sour cream. Mix well. Add bananas and vanilla. Stir together salt, soda and flour. Add to banana mixture. Mix well. Spread dough on greased and floured jelly roll pan. Bake at 350 degrees for 20-25 minutes. To prepare frosting, melt margarine over low heat until light brown and bubbly. Remove from heat and add confectioner's sugar and sour cream. Beat with a mixer until creamy.

Joyce Hawkins - Indianapolis, Indiana

Brownies

1 cup flour
1 cup sugar
1 stick soft margarine.
1 can Hershey's syrup
4 eggs
1 cup chopped nuts.

Frosting:
1 stick butter or margarine
3 tablespoons cocoa
1/4 cup milk
1 teaspoon vanilla
1 pound powdered sugar

Blend flour, sugar and butter. Add 1 can Hershey's syrup. Add eggs one at a time. Beat well. Add nuts. Pour into jelly roll pan and bake at 350 for 25 to 30 minutes. For frosting mix together milk, vanilla and powdered sugar. Spread on brownies while warm.

Annette Jones - Fort Wayne, Indiana

Chocolate Chip Cookies II

5 cups quick-cooking rolled oats
2 cups butter, softened
2 cups granulated sugar
2 cups packed brown sugar
4 eggs
2 teaspoons vanilla
4 cups all-purpose flour
2 teaspoons baking powder
2 teaspoons baking soda
1 teaspoon salt
2 12-ounce packages
    semi-sweet chocolate chips
8 ounces milk chocolate
    candy bar, finely grated
3 cups chopped nuts

Heat oven to 375 degrees. Blend small amounts of oats in blender until it turns to powder; set aside. In large bowl, cream butter and sugars. Add eggs and vanilla; mix well. In separate bowl, combine flour, oats, baking powder, soda and salt. Stir into butter mixture; mix well. Stir in chocolate chips, candy bar and nuts. Shape into golf-ball size cookies. Place 2 inches apart on ungreased cookie sheets. Bake about 6 minutes or until golden brown. Yield: 9 1/2 dozen.

Lee Collins - Fort Wayne, Indiana

Coconut Classics

1 cup margarine, softened
1 cup sugar
1 teaspoon vanilla
1 egg
2 cups flour
1/2 teaspoon baking soda
2 cups coconut

Cream margarine and sugar. Add vanilla and egg and mix. Add flour, soda and then coconut. Drop by spoonfuls onto greased cookie sheet. Press cookies down with bottom of sugar-coated glass. Bake at 325 degrees for 12 minutes.

Sara Rose - Fort Wayne, Indiana

English Current Cakes

2 cups flour
1/2 teaspoon soda
1/2 teaspoon salt
1/2 cup shortening (Crisco)
1/2 cup sugar
1/2 cup raisins and nuts
3/4 cup sour milk (may use milk
    plus a little vinegar
    to make sour milk)
12 currents

Sift together: flour, soda and salt. Add to this shortening, sugar, raisins, currents and nuts. Add milk (enough to make a soft dough). Pat out on a floured board to about 1/2 inch thickness. Cut into desired shapes with a sharp, floured knife. Sprinkle a little sugar on top and bake in a moderate oven about 8-10 minutes or until light brown around edges.

Dorothy Cross - Rochester, Indiana

Oatmeal Peanut Butter Cookies

1 cup butter
1 1/4 cups white sugar
1 1/4 cups brown sugar
1/2 cup peanut butter
2 eggs
1/4 cup water
1 1/2 teaspoons soda
1 1/2 teaspoons salt
2 1/2 cups flour
3 cups oatmeal

Cream shortening and sugars. Add eggs and peanut butter, beating well after each addition. Sift together dry ingredients. Add alternately with water. Add oatmeal last. Drop by teaspoons on greased cookie sheet Bake at 350 degrees until brown. (may add chocolate chips)

Patty (Berkey) Beachy - Warsaw, Indiana

Grandma's Snickerdoodle Cookies

Mix together:
1 cup soft oleo or butter
1 1/2 cups sugar
2 eggs
2 tablespoons mayonnaise

Sift:
2 3/4 cups flour
2 teaspoons cream of tartar
1 teaspoon soda
1/2 teaspoon salt

Cinnamon-Sugar Mix:
1/2 cup white sugar
2-3 teaspoons cinnamon

Cream sugar, butter and mayonnaise; add eggs; mix well. Add dry ingredients, mix well. Roll by teaspoonfuls in cinnamon-sugar mixture. (Chill dough if too soft to form firm ball) Bake on ungreased cookie sheet. Bake 400 degrees; 8-10 minutes until lightly browned. Makes 6 dozen.

Mrs. E. S. (Barbara) Purrington - Warsaw, Indiana

Kiflis

1 pound flour
1/2 pound butter
6 egg yolks, beaten
1/2 teaspoon vanilla
1/2 of 1/2 pint of sour cream

Filling:
2 pounds walnuts, ground fine
1/2 box powdered sugar
1 teaspoon vanilla
6 egg whites, beaten stiff

Filling: Fold filling ingredients together.

Dough: Cut butter into flour. Add egg, vanilla and sour cream. Pinch dough into balls (walnut size) Refrigerate 6 hours. Roll out thin on floured board. Take 1 teaspoon filling and place on rolled out ball. Roll up and shape in a crescent shape. Bake at 325 degrees about 20 minutes. Roll in powdered sugar. Makes 65 Kiflis.

Karol Pieuch - Warsaw, Indiana

Mystery Bars

40 saltine crackers crushed
1 cup butter
1 cup brown sugar
2 cups chocolate chips
3/4 cup chopped nuts

Line cookie sheet with foil - grease lightly. Place crackers in single layer. Boil butter and sugar for 3 minutes. Pour over crackers. Bake at 350 degrees for 10 minutes. Put chocolate chips on top. Spread after they melt. Add nuts. Cut while warm.

Stephany Mullen - Valparaiso, Indiana

Scandinavian Kringler

1 cup Pillsbury's best all purpose
 or unbleached flour
1/2 cup butter or margarine,
 chilled
2 tablespoons ice water

Puff Topping:
1 cup water
1/2 cup butter
1 cup flour
3 eggs
1/2 teaspoon almond extract

Frosting:
1 cup powdered sugar
1 tablespoon butter or
 margarine (softened)
1/2 teaspoon almond extract
2-3 tablespoons milk or cream
sliced almonds or
 chopped nuts, if desired

Heat oven to 350 degrees. Lightly spoon flour into measuring cup; level off. Measure 1 cup flour into mixing bowl. Using a pastry blender, cut 1/2 cup butter into flour until particles are size of small peas. Sprinkle with water, 1 tablespoon at a time, mixing lightly with a fork until flour mixture is moistened and soft dough forms. Divide dough in half. On ungreased cookie sheet, press each half into a 12x3 inch strip. In medium saucepan, heat water and 1/2 cup butter to boiling. Remove from heat; immediately stir in 1 cup flour until smooth. Add eggs, 1 at a time, beating until smooth after each addition. Stir in 1/2 teaspoon almond extract. Spoon over crust, spreading to 1/4 inch from edges. Bake 50 to 60 minutes until golden brown and puffy. Cool. Blend powdered sugar, butter, almond extract and milk until smooth. Frost cooled kringler. Sprinkle with nuts. Cut each into 8 to 10 slices to serve. Makes 16 to 20 slices.

Linda Stouder - Warsaw, Indiana

Special K Squares

1 12 ounce package
 butterscotch chips
1 12 ounce package
 chocolate chips
6 cups Special K cereal
 (do not substitute with
 Rice Krispies)
1 8 ounce jar creamy
 peanut butter
1 cup white Karo syrup
1 cup white sugar
2 teaspoons vanilla

Butter a 9 x 13 glass dish. In a double boiler start melting chips. Stir well. In a large, heavy saucepan put Karo syrup and sugar. Stir, over high heat, until it comes to a full rolling boil. Remove from heat and quickly add peanut butter and vanilla. Stir well and immediately add the cereal. Stir well again until well mixed. Quickly spread evenly in the greased pan, using the back of the spoon to fill the corners and flatten the mixture. Spread melted chocolate/butterscotch (chip) mixture evenly over top. Cut into squares when cool and chocolate has set. Do not put into refrigerator to cool; chocolate will turn white.

Jane Grossnickle - Warsaw, Indiana

Starlight Sugar Crisps

1 package active dry yeast
1/4 cup warm water
    (105 to 115 degrees)
3 1/2 cups Pillsbury's Best
    All Purpose or
    unbleached Flour
1 1/2 teaspoons salt
1/2 cup butter or margarine
1/2 cup shortening
2 eggs, beaten
1/2 cup dairy sour cream
1 teaspoon vanilla
1 1/2 cups sugar
2 teaspoons vanilla
1/2 teaspoon almond flavoring,
    if desired

In small bowl, dissolve yeast in warm water and set aside. Lightly spoon flour into measuring cup and level off. In large bowl combine flour and salt. Using pastry blender, cut in butter and shortening until particles are size of peas. Add beaten eggs, sour cream, 1 teaspoon vanilla and softened yeast. Mix well. Cover and chill 2 hours. Heat oven to 375 degrees. In small bowl, combine sugar and 2 tablespoons vanilla. Sprinkle about 1/2 cup flavored sugar on pastry cloth or board. Divide chilled dough in half. Roll out half of dough to a 16x8 inch rectangle on sugared cloth. Sprinkle dough with 1 tablespoon flavored sugar. Fold dough to make 3 layers. Sprinkling with sugar after each fold. Roll out to a 16x8 inch rectangle. Cut into 32 4x1 inch stripes. Twist each strip 2 or 3 times and place on ungreased cookie sheet. Repeat with remaining dough and flavored sugar. Bake 15 to 20 minutes until light golden brown. Makes about 5 dozen twists.

Linda Stouder - Warsaw, Indiana

Sugar Cookies

1 cup granulated sugar
1 cup powdered sugar
1 cup crisco
1 cup cooking oil
Beat together until very fluffy
and add the following:
2 eggs, one at a time
1 teaspoon vanilla
1 teaspoon lemon extract
Sift together and add to mixture:
4 cups flour
1 teaspoon baking soda
1 teaspoon cream of tarter
1/2 teaspoon salt

Chill dough. Form into little balls. Flatten lightly with a fork. Decorate with white sugar, chocolate bits, nuts, etc. Bake at 350 degrees 10-12 minutes. Do not overbake; they should still be white on top and light brown on the bottom.

Delores Basey - Fountaintown, Indiana

Sugar Cut-Out Cookies

1/2 cup butter
1/2 cup shortening
1 cup sugar
3 eggs
3 1/2 cups flour
1 teaspoon baking soda
2 teaspoons cream of tartar
1 1/2 teaspoons vanilla

Cream together butter, shortening and sugar. Add eggs. Sift together flour, soda and cream of tartar. Add flour mixture gradually to creamed mixture. Add vanilla. Chill dough. Roll on floured pastry cloth (about 1/4 inch thick) Cut with cookie cutter. Place on ungreased cookie sheet. Bake at 425 degrees for 6-7 minutes. Makes 6-8 dozen.

Doris Wall - Syracuse, Indiana

Sugar-Nut Cookies

1 1/2 cups sugar
3 eggs
1/2 cup shortening
1/2 cup butter
1 cup sour milk (may substitute
   2 tablespoons vinegar to
   1 cup milk)
3 1/2 cups flour
1 1/2 teaspoons soda
2 teaspoons baking powder
2 teaspoons nutmeg
1 1/2 cups chopped pecans

Blend sugar, eggs, shortening, and butter. Add milk. Sift dry ingredients and add to sugar mixture. Add nuts. Spoon onto greased cookie sheet. Bake at 350 degrees for 10-12 minutes. Makes 8-9 dozen.

Doris Wall - Syracuse, Indiana

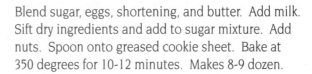

Mayonnaise Cake

1 1/2 cups sugar
1 cup salad dressing
1 cup warm water
3 teaspoons cocoa
2 cups flour
2 teaspoons soda
1 teaspoon vanilla
pinch of salt

Preheat oven to 350 degrees. Mix sugar and salad dressing in large mixing bowl. Mix cocoa with water and add alternately with flour and soda to sugar mixture. Add remaining ingredients and bake in greased and floured 9 x 13 inch pan at 350 degrees for about 30 minutes. Frost with butter icing.

Good Luck! "Dream high and smile wide."
Tiffany Storm, Miss Indiana 1994
Bloomington, Indiana

Triple Layer Brownies

First layer:
4 ounces unsweetened chocolate
1 cup butter (no substitution)
3 eggs
2 cups sugar
1 teaspoon vanilla
1/2 teaspoon almond extract
1 cup flour
1/2 teaspoon salt

Second layer:
6 tablespoons butter
    (no substitutions)
3 cups powdered sugar
4 to 6 tablespoons milk
1 teaspoon vanilla

Third layer:
4 ounces semi-sweet chocolate
6 tablespoons butter
    (no substitutions)
slivered almonds

First Layer: Melt chocolate and butter, stir in sugar. Add beaten eggs and extracts. Add in flour and salt, stir gently. Bake in 9 x 13 pan sprayed lightly with Pam at 350 degrees for 35 minutes or until toothpick comes our clean. Cool, do not chill.

Second Layer: Brown butter very carefully until carmel colored, but do NOT burn. Add in powdered sugar. Stir in milk and vanilla. Should be consistency of peanut butter. After first layer is completely cool, spread this on top.

Third Layer: Over very low heat, melt chocolate and butter. Pour over the top and tilt pan to spread evenly. Sprinkle with almonds. Recipe freezes well.

Cindy Baldauf - Indianapolis, Indiana

Chocolate Chip Brownies

2 1/3 cups shortening or
    margarine (softened)
1 cup white sugar
2 cups brown sugar
2 teaspoons vanilla
4 cups and 4 tablespoons flour
2 teaspoons baking powder
2 teaspoons soda
1 teaspoon salt
4 eggs
2 small packages chocolate chips

Cream together shortening or margarine), sugar, brown sugar and vanilla. Sift together flour, baking powder, baking soda and salt; add to cream mixture. Add 4 eggs and 2 small packages of chocolate chips. Bake at 350-375 degrees for 14 minutes.

Patty (Berkey) Beachy - Warsaw, Indiana

Turtle Cookies (Grandma Hilda's Recipe)

1/2 cup butter or margarine
1/2 cup firmly packed brown sugar
1 egg
1 egg yolk, well beaten
    (reserve white)
1/4 teaspoon vanilla
1/4 teaspoon maple flavoring
1 1/2 cups flour
1/4 teaspoon soda
1/4 teaspoon salt
1 pound pecan halves

Chocolate Frosting:
1/3 cup semi-sweet chocolate
    pieces
1/4 cup milk
1 tablespoon butter or margarine
1 cup powdered sugar

Cream together butter and brown sugar. Add egg and egg yolk. Blend in vanilla and maple flavoring. Add dry ingredients gradually, mix thoroughly. Chill dough. Arrange pecan halves in groups of three on greased baking sheets (one at top for head, 2 at sides for feet). Mold dough into balls; dip bottoms into unbeaten egg white and press lightly on nuts. Use a rounded teaspoon of dough for each so tips of nuts will show when cookie is baked. Bake at 350 degrees for 10-12 minutes. Cool and frost tops.

Frosting: Combine chocolate pieces, milk and butter in top of double boiler until melted. Add 1 cup powdered sugar. Beat until smooth and glassy.

Peggy Sawyer - Warsaw, Indiana

Apricot Balls

1 8-ounce package dried
    apricots, ground fine
2 1/2 cups flaked coconut
3/4 cup Eagle Brand milk
3/4 cup lemon juice or
    Real Lemon
2/3 cup finely chopped pecans

Mix apricots, coconut, milk, lemon juice. Shape into 1-inch balls (will be sticky). Roll in chopped pecans. Let stand several hours to firm-up. Store in airtight container in cool place. Yield: approx. 4 dozen.

Ruth Zurakowski - Elkhart, Indiana

Caramels

1 1-pound box brown sugar
1 1/2-pound butter
    (no substitute)
1 can Eagle Brand milk
1/2 teaspoon cream of tartar
3/4 cup light Karo syrup

Mix all ingredients and boil 12 minutes over medium heat, stirring constantly. Watch carefully— it will scorch if heat is too high. Pour into buttered 8 x 8, or 9 x 9 inch pan. Let set overnight. Cut and wrap in Saran wrap. Store in airtight container in cool place.

Ruth Zurakowski - Elkhart, Indiana

English Toffee

1 pound butter
2 heaping cups sugar
    (granulated)
4 tablespoons water
1 12 ounce package semi sweet
    chocolate bits
1 cup finely chopped nuts

In heavy pan, stir and boil all ingredients, except chocolate bits, to hard crack. Pour onto large cookie sheet with sides (buttered). While still hot, sprinkle chocolate bits over hot candy. When soft, spread with spatula. Sprinkle with finely chopped nuts. Press into chocolate. Let cool. Can be broken into pieces.

Arlene Koors - Warsaw, Indiana

Grandma's Atomic Fudge

1 stick margarine (do not
    substitute butter or crisco)
4 cups sugar
2 large bars Hershey's Chocolate
    Bars (1/2 pound bars)
    break into small pieces
1 12 ounce can Milnot
1 7 1/2 ounce jar marshmallow fluff
1 12 ounce bag semi-sweet
    chocolate morsels
1 teaspoon vanilla
1 cup chopped walnuts or pecans

Thoroughly grease a 9x13 pan or a jelly roll pan of same size. Melt the margarine in microwave or on the stove. Add sugar and can of milnot. Heat until the sugar is dissolved, about 4 minutes on high in microwave. Bring to a rapid boil; this takes another 4-5 minutes in microwave. Cook for 6-7 minutes after it comes to the rapid boil. Take out of microwave/off stove. Stir in chocolate bars, then semi-sweet morsels, and then marshmallow fluff and vanilla. Chopped walnuts or pecans may be added at this time. Then pour into the pan and let cool. Cut into small squares, once totally cooled. Put into an air tight container or cover with clingwrap. Makes a great holiday gift.

Meg Trausch - Chicago, Illinois and
Ruth Zurakowski - Elkhart, Indiana

Milk Chocolate Fudge

12 ounce milk chocolate chips
4 cups sugar
1 stick margarine
1 can lite evaporated milk
1 small jar marshmallow cream

Combine margarine, milk, sugar in large heavy pan. Bring to boil, stirring. Turn down heat and stir while boiling to soft ball stage (234 degrees candy thermometer). Remove and pour over chips and marshmallow. Stir until both are blended. Pour in greased pan and cool. Makes 3 pounds.

Anne Watts - Warsaw, Indiana

Millionaire Turtle Candy

1 package carmels
1 teaspoon vanilla
1/4 cup evaporated milk
pecan halves
6 Hershey bars
1/3 bar parain

Melt carmels, vanilla and milk. Remove from heat. Add pecans until carmel mixture seems "full". Butter a cookie sheet and spoon carmeled pecans on by teaspoon. Refrigerate. Melt hershey bars and parafin. Keep over low heat. Dip carmeled pecans into chocolate. Millionaires will set up within minutes. No need to refrigerate.

Cindy Gillaspy - Indianapolis, Indiana

Reese Cups

4 cups peanut butter
6 cups powdered sugar
1 cup brown sugar
1 tablespoon vanilla
1 cup margarine, melted
2 pound block milk
    chocolate bark

Melt 1 pound of chocolate bark, which has been cut into small pieces, in the top of double boiler over very hot (not boiling) water. Stir until all is melted. Spread evenly over bottom and halfway up sides of 10x15 jelly roll pan. Chill until just set, about 1 minute in freezer. Mix peanut butter, sugars, melted margarine and vanilla together well, starting with a mixer then using a spoon to make sure all is well mixed. Pat on top of chilled chocolate. Melt remaining bark in top of double boiler and spread on top. Let stand until set and then score off pieces on top chocolate layer. Put in refrigerator until set and finish cutting. Freezes well, too.

Shirley Secrist - Warsaw, Indiana

Angel Delite

1/4 cup butter
2 cups powdered sugar
2 teaspoons vanilla
4 egg yolks
1 large angel food cake
    cut in pieces
1 pint whipping cream
1 large Heath bar, crushed
1/2 cup nuts

Cream butter, powdered sugar, vanilla and eggs. Fold whipping cream into butter mixture. Pour over cake pieces. Add candy and nuts. Blend together and chill. Serves 12.

Norma Ferguson - Warsaw, Indiana

Cherry Dessert Surprise

First Layer:
2 cups vanilla wafers, crushed
1/4 cup butter, melted
1 cup chopped nuts
    (pecans are good)

Second Layer:
1 package cream cheese
    (8 ounces)
2 tablespoons milk
1 cup powdered sugar

Third Layer:
2 envelopes of Dream Whip
1 can of "Thank-You" cherries
(large size or 2 small cans)

First Layer: Mix wafers, butter and nuts. Take half of mixture and press firmly into baking dish.

Second Layer: Mix well and spread over first layer. Spread remainder of vanilla vafers on top of cheese mixture.

Third Layer: Whip Dream whip and spread over top. Add cherries on top. Set in refrigerator a few hours or overnight. Serves 8.

Barb Lembke - Rochester, Indiana

Dump Cake Dessert

1 large can crushed pineapple
(20 ounce size) undrained
1 can cherry pie filling
    (21 ounce size)
1 box yellow cake mix
1 cup chopped nuts
1 stick margarine

Spread pineapple on bottom of 9x13 ungreased baking dish. Spread pie filling on top. Do not mix layers. Sprinkle cake mix evenly over top. Sprinkle nuts on last. Cut margarine into 12 patties or more and place over top. Bake at 350 degrees for 1 hour. Serve warm with whipped topping or ice cream.

Lora Kipker - Warsaw, Indiana

Chocolate Mousse

4 eggs
1 6-ounce package semisweet
    chocolate pieces
5 tablespoons butter
2 tablespoons cognac or brandy
whipped cream
candied violets

One day before serving, separate eggs, turning whites into a medium bowl. Let whites warm to room temperature. In top of double boiler, over hot, not boiling water, melt chocolate and butter; stir to blend. Remove from hot water. Using a wooden spoon, beat in egg yolks, one at a time, beating well after each addition. Set aside to cool. Stir in cognac. When the chocolate mixture has cooled, beat egg whites with rotary beater just until stiff peaks form when beater is slowly raised. With rubber scraper or wire whisk, gently fold chocolate mixture into egg whites, using an under-and-over motion. Fold only enough to combine--there should be no white streaks. Turn into an attractive 1-pint serving dish or 8 individual sherbet dishes. Refrigerate overnight. To serve, decorate with whipped cream and candied violets or wafers of your choice. Yield: 8 servings. Note: this is very easy. Do the day before and makes a very gourmet-ending for a special dinner!

Jackie Rucka - Warsaw, Indiana

Hot Fruit in Sherry Sauce

1 medium can pineapple chunks
1 medium can peach halves
1 jar apple rings
1 medium can pear halves

Sauce:
2 tablespoons flour
1/2 cup brown sugar
1 stick butter
1 cup sherry

Drain all fruit and arrange in ovenproof dish (9 x 13). Combine butter, flour, sugar and sherry. Cook over double boiler until thick, stirring constantly. Pour over fruit in dish. Let stand overnight. Bake at 350 degrees for 20 minutes or until hot and bubbly. Yield: 12 servings. Good with pork or chicken.

Carol Rogers - Newburgh, Indiana

Chocolate Truffle Torte

1 1/2 pounds semisweet
   chocolate (recommend
   Ghirardelli semisweet bars)
2 cups heavy cream
2 tablespoons unsalted butter
unsweetened cocoa powder
   for dusting

Raspberry Sauce (optional):
2 10 ounce package frozen
   raspberries in syrup, thawed
1/4 cup sugar
2-3 tablespoons Grand Marnier
   liqueur

Combine the chocolate, cream and butter in the top pan of a double boiler over simmering water. Do not allow the chocolate to become too hot. When the chocolate mixture is melted, remove from the heat and whisk until all the ingredients are well incorporated. Line the bottom of a 9 inch spring-form pan with waxed paper and pour the chocolate mixture into the pan. Let cool, cover, and chill for at least 6 hours or for up to 48 hours before serving. Unclasp and remove the ring from the pan. Run a long, flat icing spatula between the torte and spring-form pan bottom to detach the torte. Invert a serving plate over the torte and turn over. Using a fine-holed shaker, dust the top with cocoa powder.

Raspberry Sauce: Drain 1 package of raspberries and discard juice. Retain juice from other package. Puree fruit, juice, sugar and liqueur in food processor or blender. Chill until ready to use. Makes 1 1/2 cups.

Nancy Drake - Plano, Texas and Warsaw, Indiana

Grandma's Banana Pudding

2 cups milk
1 tablespoon butter
2 eggs
2 heaping tablespoons flour
1 cup sugar
1 teaspoon vanilla
5-6 sliced bananas
1 cup chopped peanuts

Cook first five ingredients in double boiler until thick. Add vanilla, bananas, and peanuts. Chill before serving.

Janet Arnett, R.T.(R)(M), R.D.M.S. - Warsaw, Indiana

Creme Brulee

6 extra large egg yolks
1 1/4 cups sugar
3 cups heavy cream
1 vanilla bean, split
1 cup raspberries
8 puff pastry shells (Follow directions for baking shells).

Raspberry Sauce
2 cups fresh raspberries
1/2 cup simple syrup

Combine egg yolks and 1/2 cup sugar in top half of double boiler over very hot water. Whisk (or beat with hand mixer) until lemon-colored and the consistency of mousse. Remove from heat and set aside. Place cream and vanilla bean in a heavy saucepan over medium heat. Bring to a boil and immediately remove from heat. Strain through a fine sieve. Slowly pour into egg yolks, whisking rapidly as you pour. Return double boiler to heat and cook, stirring constantly, for about 10 minutes or until mixture is quite thick. Remove top half of double boiler and place in a bowl of ice. Stir occasionally while mixture cools until it reaches the consistency of a very thick custard. Spread a single layer of fresh raspberries over the bottom of six baked pastry shells. Pour cooled creme over raspberries to top of shells. Refrigerate for at least 3 hours (or up to 8 hours) When chilled, sprinkle 2 tablespoons sugar over each filled shell and place about 6 inches away from broiler flame for about 3 minutes or until sugar caramelizes. Do not overcook or cream will melt! Immediately remove from heat. Pour raspberry sauce over the bottom of each of six dessert plates. Place a Creme Brulee in the center and serve immediately. Serves 8. Creme may be made up to 3 hours in advance. Pastry shells may be baked up to 3 hours in advance, but do not let them get damp or place them where they can absorb moisture.

Puree raspberries in a blender or food processor. When smooth, strain through an extra-fine sieve to remove all seeds. Stir simple syrup into raspberry puree until well blended. May be made up to 24 hours in advance.

Nancy Drake - Plano, Texas and Warsaw, Indiana

Ice Cream Dessert

2 sticks butter
1/2 cup brown sugar
1/2 cup rolled oats
2 cups flour
1 cup nuts chopped
1/2 gallon vanilla ice cream
    softened
1 small jar ice cream topping

Melt butter. Add brown sugar, rolled oats, flour, and nuts. spread on cookie sheet. Bake for 15 minutes at 350 degrees until slightly brown. Crumble immediately. Grease 9 x 13 pan. Spread 1/2 of the crumbs on bottom, add ice cream. Dribble topping of choice, Add remaining crumbs, and freeze.

Mary Louise Miller - Winona Lake, Indiana

Oreo Dessert

2 boxes French vanilla instant
    pudding (small packages)
2 envelopes Dream Whip
8 ounces cream cheese
3 1/2 cups milk
1 package oreo cookies
1/4 cup melted butter

Crush cookies (reserve 1 cup for top). Mix with butter and place on bottom of 9 x 13 pan. Mix remaining ingredients and pour on top of crust. Top with remaining crushed cookies. Chill.

Tena Huffer - Warsaw, Indiana

Pavlova

3 egg whites
3 tablespoons cold water
1 cup sugar
1 teaspoon vinegar
1 teaspoon vanilla essence
3 teaspoons cornstarch

Beat eggs until stiff. Add cold water and beat again. Add sugar gradually, while still beating. Slow mixer and add vinegar, vanilla and cornstarch. Place on greased paper (wax paper) on greased tray. Bake at 300 degrees for 45 minutes, then leave to cool in the oven. Serve decorated with cream and fresh strawberries or other fresh fruit.

Tamara Basey-Wilson - Westotago, New Zeland

Ruby Berries and Cream

2- 10 ounce packages frozen
    raspberries, thawed
1 cup sifted powdered sugar
2 tablespoons Cointreau
1 tablespoon orange juice
6 cups fresh strawberries, hulled

Press raspberries through a sieve to remove seeds. Discard seeds. Combine raspberry puree and 1/2 cup powdered sugar, Cointreau, and orange juice. Stir well. Combine strawberries and 1/2 cup powdered sugar. Toss. Pour raspberry sauce over strawberries. Cover. Chill 3 hours. Divide into 6 dessert dishes.

Mary Louise Miller - Winona Lake, Indiana

Sherried Bread Pudding with Citron and Currants

day-old challah or other egg
    bread, crusts removed, cut
    into 1/2 inch cubes to equal
    4 cups, about 5 ounces
    with crusts
3 tablespoons currants
1/4 cup dry sherry
4 large eggs
1/2 cup superfine sugar
1 teaspoon vanilla extract
1/4 teaspoon salt
1/4 teaspoon grated nutmeg
1 1/4 cups heavy or
    whipping cream
1/2 cup milk
grated zest of 1 orange
1/3 cup plus 2 tablespoons
    candied citron,
    finely chopped
1/3 cup slivered almonds
Confectioners' sugar,
    enough to dust pudding

Lightly butter 9 inch deep sided ceramic pie dish. Soak currants in sherry for at least 30 minutes. In a large bowl and with an electric mixer set on medium speed, beat together eggs, sugar, vanilla, salt, and nutmeg. Reduce mixer speed to low and add cream and milk; continue beating until well mixed. Place bread cubes in a separate large bowl. With a fine mesh sieve, strain custard mixture over bread. Add currants and sherry, zest, and citron; with a spoon, toss to combine. Let stand for 30 minutes so that the bread absorbs the liquid. Preheat oven to 350 degrees. Pour pudding mixture into prepared dish, distributing currants evenly. Sprinkle top with almonds. Bake for 50 to 55 minutes, or until custard is set (knife inserted 1 inch from center comes our clean), pudding is puffed, and top is golden brown. Remove from oven onto a wire rack and cool for at least 20 minutes. Dust pudding generously with confectioners' sugar. Cut into wedges. Serve warm, at room temperature, or chilled.

Barbara Hayford and Linda Hegeman
Indianapolis, Indiana

Easy Peach Jam (Frozen)

2 1/4 cups chopped peaches
   (peeled and pitted; may use
   potatoe masher or
   food processor)
5 cups sugar
2 tablespoons fresh lemon juice
3/4 cup water
1 box fruit pectin (1 3/4 ounce)

Mix peaches, lemon juice and sugar thoroughly. Set aside for 10 minutes. Stir pectin with water in saucepan. Bring to a boil, stirring constantly. Boil 1 minute. Remove from heat. Stir mixtures together until sugar is completely dissolved and no longer grainy; about 3 minutes. Pour into plastic containers and cover. Let stand at room temperature 24 hours. Jam is now ready to use. Store in refrigerator (3 weeks) or in freezer (1 year) Thaw in refrigerator. Makes about 6 cups. Important Notes: Measure all ingredients exactly; do not change amounts or jam will not set properly. Glass jars may also be used successfully; be sure to leave room at the top for expansion and put the lids on after the jam is frozen.

Debbie Willis - Indianapolis, Indiana

Rouladen

1 slice round steak—
   1/4 inch thick
bacon
onion
salt and pepper
mustard
flour

Trim out the bone of the round steak and trim off all the fat. Fry fat in skillet. Cut meat along veins—a few will be large, cut these in half. Spread each with mustard, then a strip of bacon and some chopped onion. Roll into bundles and secure with two round toothpicks. Dredge in flour and brown in fat already prepared in skillet. Usually it will be necessary to add some additional shortening. A good brown crust adds to the flavor of this dish, so do not hurry this process. When all are brown, add water and cover pan. Simmer or bake for 1 1/2 or 2 hours adding water as necessary.

Dr. and Mrs. Otis R. Bowen - Bremen, Indiana

Recipe Index

Z

Notes

_____

_____

_____

_____

_____

_____

_____

_____

_____

_____

_____

Diseases desperate grown
By desperate appliances are relieved,
Or not at all.

Hamlet,
ACT IV SCENE 5

Order Blanks

Send me _____ copies of your cookbook at $15.00 *per copy* plus $4.50 per copy for postage, handling and taxes where applicable.

Enclosed is my check or money order in the amount of $_____.

Name: _____

Address: _____

City _____ State _____ Zip _____

Make checks payable to: JUST PEACHEY, P.O. Box 1823, Warsaw, IN 46581-1823.
To order by phone (Visa or Mastercard) call: 219•268•9015.

- -

Send me _____ copies of your cookbook at $15.00 *per copy* plus $4.50 per copy for postage, handling and taxes where applicable.

Enclosed is my check or money order in the amount of $_____.

Name: _____

Address: _____

City _____ State _____ Zip _____

Make checks payable to: JUST PEACHEY, P.O. Box 1823, Warsaw, IN 46581-1823.
To order by phone (Visa or Mastercard) call: 219•268•9015.

- -

Send me _____ copies of your cookbook at $15.00 *per copy* plus $4.50 per copy for postage, handling and taxes where applicable.

Enclosed is my check or money order in the amount of $_____.

Name: _____

Address: _____

City _____ State _____ Zip _____

Make checks payable to: JUST PEACHEY, P.O. Box 1823, Warsaw, IN 46581-1823.
To order by phone (Visa or Mastercard) call: 219•268•9015.